RESISTING SPIRITS

CHINA UNDERSTANDINGS TODAY

Series Editors: Mary Gallagher and Xiaobing Tang

China Understandings Today is dedicated to the study of contemporary China and seeks to present the latest and most innovative scholarship in social sciences and the humanities to the academic community as well as the general public. The series is sponsored by the Lieberthal-Rogel Center for Chinese Studies at the University of Michigan.

Resisting Spirits: Drama Reform and Cultural Transformation in the People's Republic of China
  Maggie Greene

RESISTING SPIRITS

Drama Reform and Cultural Transformation in the People's Republic of China

Maggie Greene

UNIVERSITY OF MICHIGAN PRESS

Ann Arbor

Published in the United States of America by
the University of Michigan Press

First published August 2019

A CIP catalog record for this book is available from the British Library.

ISBN 978-0-472-07430-3 (hardcover)
ISBN 978-0-472-05430-5 (paper)
ISBN 978-0-472-12610-1 (ebook)

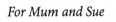

For Mum and Sue

Others may forget you, but not I.
I am haunted by your beautiful ghost.
    —The Empress Yamatohime

Contents

Digital materials related to this title can be found on the Fulcrum platform via the following citable URL: https://doi.org/10.3998/mpub.9969070

Acknowledgments

Since I was a teenager, poetry has calmed me in stressful times. Few things in life have been more stressful than seeing this book to completion; accordingly, since I began work on the project in 2009, I've read a lot of poetry. Lyric snippets often take on talismanic qualities for me, and my poetic talisman for almost the entirety of this project, from its inception as a research seminar paper a decade ago, has been the opening of "Burnt Norton," from T. S. Eliot's *Four Quartets*. It reads in part:

> Footfalls echo in the memory
> Down the passage which we did not take
> Towards the door we never opened
> Into the rose-garden. My words echo
> Thus, in your mind.
>   But to what purpose
> Disturbing the dust on a bowl of rose-leaves
> I do not know.
>   Other echoes
> Inhabit the garden. Shall we follow?

An old term for the Chinese theatre world is "the Pear Garden" (*liyuan*), and so these lines have always seemed especially appropriate. This work is ultimately about the echoes in and of the garden; but more importantly, Eliot's words remind me that "we" are exploring it, for a book does not come to fruition through the efforts of a single person, even if only one person (in this case, me) is responsible for any errors in it. I am supremely grateful for everyone who has guided and aided my exploration of this particular garden and helped me chase lingering echoes.

I arrived in the fall of 2007 to the University of California, San Diego, nervous, excited, and terrified. I still have no idea what glimmer of promise my advisors, Paul Pickowicz and Joseph Esherick, saw in my application—I was a fresh BA with precious little experience, here to get a PhD in modern Chinese history. I am grateful that they took a chance on me and hope that I have validated their gamble. Joe, with his keen and masterful eye, always challenged me to be a better historian: we all knew I could write and write well, but, of course, a historian needs to be more than a wordsmith. Much of my graduate career was spent trying to become worthy of his time and detailed commentary. Paul was, and is, an incredibly supportive, attentive mentor and teacher—I carry his lessons not only into my approach to scholarship but also into the classroom. His example continues to inspire me on a daily basis to be a better scholar and a better teacher. I have benefited from their care, mentoring, and uncompromising rigor in so many ways, and I wish all graduate students could experience what it is to be so nurtured by giants of their fields.

UCSD was a transformative and magical experience for many reasons beyond our program, and I benefitted immensely from teachers and friends across fields and disciplines. Ye Wa alerted me to the mere existence of *Li Huiniang*, and I still have the paper she scribbled notes on one February morning of 2009 in the East Asian reading room of the Geisel Library. That sheet of paper, too, is a talisman for me. I wish I could carry her knowledge, insights, and wisdom with me into every new project. My committee members—Ari Heinrich, Nancy Guy, and Suzanne Cahill—pressed me to be better, always. A project such as this one is necessarily interdisciplinary, and I benefitted greatly from their varied insights into what my research could mean beyond my claimed field. I spent many, many hours in Stefan Tanaka's office—time that he didn't have or need to spare for an often-hysterical PhD student who wasn't even one of his own. Nevertheless, his door was always open to me. He was an important intellectual anchor for me throughout my graduate career, and I sometimes find myself longing to make the walk up to his old fourth-floor office in the Humanities and Social Sciences building just once more.

I learned not only from my professors, but from my fellow students at UCSD—and I continue to learn from and lean on them to this day. David Chang Cheng, Jenny Huangfu Day, Judd Kinzley, Jomo Smith, Brent Haas, Stephen "Rui" Mandiberg, and Jeremy Murray all provided—and continue to provide—insights, opportunities, and support throughout our various adventures in and outside of academia. William Huber and I spent many a lunch hour at Las Cuatro Milpas, talking about scholarship and life while eating insanely good and cheap food, and I am glad we are still finding things to collaborate on. Amy O'Keefe and her wonderful family gave me a home away from home (and pancakes) while I was visiting San Diego for my qualifying exams and dissertation defense. Emily Baum and Justin Jacobs have patiently tolerated years of my novella-length e-mails, and both have been exceptionally generous in reading large portions of my work over and over again. I hope in all cases that our intellectual exchanges have been as fruitful for my friends as they have been for me, and I look forward to many more in the future.

California was a wonderful state in which to be a Chinese historian-in-training, and my life continues to benefit from the many relationships I made there. In particular, Amanda Shuman has been one of my best friends since we were in coursework, and she has always made life in the archives and in general livelier and more bearable. I treasure memories of sweltering midsummer evenings in Shanghai's French Concession, pleasant late summer walks in Berlin's Tiergarten, and a lot of time spent on Skype. Alan Christy has provided a kind ear and lots of advice over the years. Menghsin Horng and I met before we were both PhD students in the UC system, but she has made so much of this journey, from moving to Taiwan for language training to life as a grad student, less terrifying and filled with more good food and curly-tailed dogs than one person should be lucky enough to experience in a lifetime. I miss lazy, chatty evenings at the "House of the Two Bows."

In China, Jiang Jin at East China Normal University entirely changed my thinking on the early outlines of this project with one simple question. Gao Jun of the Shanghai Academy of Social Sciences has been a wonderful friend and has gone to great lengths to help me track down even minor pieces of this project. At Montana State University, many of my senior colleagues—including Brett Walker, Mary Murphy, Kristen Intemann, and Peter Tillack—have provided advice and support along the way. Michael Reidy has frequently opened his home and backyard to me and Wumbum for dog time, mountaineering history chat, career advice, and beer. Jim Meyer wisely counseled me, at a critical juncture, to embrace my great affection for "my dudes" and let it shine through, a piece of advice I will remain eternally grateful for. Amanda Hendrix-Komoto has been an excellent listener, sage advice giver, and a true friend as we have navigated the sometimes terrifying trenches of junior faculty life and book publishing together.

My colleagues at the University of Montana provided Asia-centric intellectual stimulation in a state that is not exactly overflowing with

Asianists. Rob Tuck—title inventor extraordinaire, now at Arizona State—noted back in 2016, at the inaugural gathering of the "Montana East Asia Workshop" (affectionately known as MEAW, which must be pronounced with something approaching a donkey's bray), that *Resisting Spirits* would be a great book title. I cheerfully stole it, for it is more perfect a title than I ever could have hoped for. I appreciate his and Brian Dowdle's literary insights into my work. Eric Schluessel is a dear friend and tireless advocate for getting more East Asian-focused initiatives going here in Montana. Our MEAW gatherings, organized by Eric with the financial support of the University of Montana's Mansfield Center and the Association for Asian Studies China and Inner Asia Council, were real bright spots on the yearly calendar. As an editor, he also whipped me and the manuscript into shape with an amazing amount of patience and wisdom, often on insane deadlines I threw at him. His trenchant, kind, and funny marginalia made the revision process much more bearable.

Also in Montana, "Reed-kun" Knappe gave me and Chumbawumbum many happy memories of traipsing through the beautiful landscape we live in. He also drew out my latent ability in hawk spotting, the only outdoor skill I've acquired and mastered since moving to the state. Natalie Scheidler has been an absolute rock in my life, from the highest of highs to the lowest of lows. Were I ever to acquire a nom de plume along the lines of Tang Xianzu's "Jade Tea Leaf Studio," I would borrow the name of the "Porch of Love, Truth, and Happiness" where we have spent so many hours. I look forward to many more years of intellectual and personal exchange, champers, and good food together as we continue to achieve personal and professional milestones.

The denizens of the online community of NPS have proven, over and over again, what a kind, generous, and talented group of people they are. It is hard to believe we have been together nearly two decades! I am thankful for their constant support and friendship, even when it's come in the form of tough love. My fellow Eorzeans, the other players I have had the good fortune to befriend while in the world of *Final Fantasy XIV*, have also made the past two years, and the extremely lonely and isolating process of working on a book, much more tolerable. From poetry-reading nights with my Mai to exuberant dungeon runs with Cy, Irene, and sweet Wendel (Zalera server's best sleeping tank), I have been blessed to count so many wonderful people as friends. And thanks to them, I've learned some salient, if weird, lessons. First, the process of "questing for pants" (upgrading your gear) in a massively-multiplayer online game bears a startling resemblance to life as a junior academic—every time you reach one eagerly anticipated goal, there's another obstacle thrown in your path. Second, sometimes you just have to admit that there are mechanics you don't know how to deal with even as you throw yourself headlong into them. Ultimately, the important thing, as Wendel likes to remind me, is that you've surmounted a challenge, no matter how messy and fraught the process was ("The boss is dead" is his usual response to my fretting over a stressful, but successfully completed, battle—that is, we achieved our goal, even if it didn't play out as smoothly as we would've liked). The Lotus Skies crew has generously allowed me to play "Mingmom" to veteran and new players alike, and our weekend events and Discord chats were real treats as I worked through revisions.

Many parts of this work have benefitted from being discussed by talented colleagues at conferences and workshops over the years. I especially thank Liang Luo for bringing together a fantastic ACLA panel in 2016, where I met Tarryn Li-Min Chun—without whose advice I would probably still be trying to find an appropriate press for this book. Tarryn's efforts in organizing a workshop for an edited volume on Chinese socialist performance practice gave me critical feedback from wonderful scholars on my use of archival sources.

At the University of Michigan, Xiaobing Tang has been a model of professionalism and efficiency from my very first correspondence with him in May 2017, and I also appreciate his insights into the project. The University of Michigan Press and the Lieberthal-Rogel Center for Chinese Studies provided support for a book workshop, where Judith Zeitlin, Emily Wilcox, and S. E. Kile provided sharp and insightful commentary that later drafts have benefitted from enormously. Christopher Dryer has been a kind shepherd, guiding this book from manuscript to launch under challenging deadlines. Research and writing of *Resisting Spirits*—dating back to its origins as a dissertation—has further been supported by a Fulbright-Hays Doctoral Dissertation Research Abroad grant, a UCSD dissertation writing fellowship, Montana State University Faculty Excellence Grants, and an MSU Scholarship and Creativity grant.

This book is dedicated to the two historians who have had the most profound impact on my life and career. Susan Fernsebner serendipitously arrived at Mary Washington in the fall of 2004, right as I was trying to figure out what my future as a historian would look like. I was the undergraduate equivalent of a big, exuberant puppy in that first class I took with her. Nevertheless, Sue nurtured my interest, gracefully put up with my incessant questions, helped me figure out moving to Taiwan for language study, navigating grad school applications, and everything else since then. I am very proud to tell people I was Sue's student, and I hope I have made her proud in turn.

My mum, Renee Hylton, is one of the finest historians I've ever met, and I would put her head-to-head with any of the greats in my field (though perhaps not on the subject of Chinese history) purely on the basis of her steel trap of a mind and exhaustive knowledge of varied topics I can't even keep up with, though I try. I occasionally comment to students and colleagues that my youthful, naïve declaration at the age of twenty-four that I was *not* going to do cultural history was simply a misguided attempt to outrun destiny, because she raised me, intentionally or not, to be a cultural historian. She has supported me in all ways, and nothing to this point would have been possible without her. We still drive each other crazy, as we have for most of my life, but even so, I wouldn't trade her for the world.

Finally, it has been a privilege to research and write about these brilliant writers and artists for so many years. I hope, above everything else, that I have done them and their stories a modicum of justice, which so many of them sorely deserve. I will miss them.

Introduction

Resurrecting Ghosts

In 1981, a Chinese ghost character with a history stretching back centuries stepped once more into cultural prominence with the premiere of the opera film *Li Huiniang*. The film begins on a darkened, foggy set, as the actress Hu Zhifeng glides across the stage, playing the titular concubine whom the cruel and rapacious Song dynasty (960–1279) prime minister Jia Sidao has unjustly murdered. Her long white robe with trailing sleeves amplifies her elegant, swirling movements. As she moves across the set, three more close-ups of the actress—in varying degrees of translucency—are overlaid on the scene, drawing attention to the glittering silver fringe of her robe's mantle and her sparkling headdress. Her ghost, however, is not silent: with her entrance onto the screen, she gives a simple, haunting cry. "*Yuanwang!*"—the injustice! And just as the multiple, half-translucent visions of Li Huiniang add to the ghostly, foreboding atmosphere, for a few seconds multiple cries of "*yuanwang!*" gradually overlap, twisting together to create a mournful song.[1] It is a rather striking introduction to the film that follows, just the latest in a long line of reimaginings of this tragic concubine.

A year prior, in 1980, a woman named Meng Jian set pen to paper and recalled the last words of her father Meng Chao. "His last words, '*Yuan na!*' [the injustice] stay behind in my ears," she wrote. She was speaking of the May 1976 death of her father, a veteran writer who, like many writers and artists, had suffered mightily during the Cultural Revolution.[2] In a letter to an old friend of her father's, she remembered his words slightly differently: "On May 1st, 2nd, he stayed at my house. He was very sad, and said: '. . . *Yuanwang a* [the injustice]! My state of mind is very bad, I can't bear the pain. . . . *Yuanwang a!*'"[3] It is a curious echo of Hu Zhifeng's cries in her cinematic portrayal, for one reason for Meng Chao's suffering—and by extension, that of his whole family—was having imagined his own version of Li Huiniang. In 1961, his Kun opera version of the tragic concubine's story, also titled *Li Huiniang*, had premiered to great acclaim in the People's Republic of China (PRC). Four years later, it would be the target of cultural radicals in the drive toward the Cultural Revolution, decried as a "poisonous weed," its author an "anti-Party, anti-socialist thought" enemy of the Chinese Communist Party (CCP). Meng Jian tells of standing in front of her father's urn and silently cursing his literary creation: "It's all because of wanting to write *you*, having written you that it's come to such an end! You are an ancient, immortal ghost—you can become a celestial immortal, but my father is a new ghost, and that fact is extremely hard to swallow, it is an extraordinary injustice [*yuan de hen na*]!"[4] Meng Jian's essay was, in fact, written for the republication of *Li Huiniang*, which was by then her father's most famous literary product. "Injustice" echoed across the book, from the preface, through the script, and back in time to Meng Chao's last days.

Li Huiniang was, true to Meng Jian's words, something of an "ancient" ghost, and certainly the character had lived innumerable lives on stages across China. She made her first literary appearance in *New Tales Told by Lamplight (Jiandeng xinhua)*, Qu You's late fourteenth-century collection of classical stories. In her debut, she was nameless, simply called "the woman in green" (*lüyiren*), a beautiful, mysterious woman involved in a supernatural love affair.[5] In the late sixteenth century, Zhou Chaojun penned *The Story of Red Plums (Hongmei ji)*.[6] This thirty-four-act play set entirely in the Southern Song (1127–1279) built upon Qu You's story but made significant changes. "The woman in green" became Li Huiniang, a concubine in the household of Jia Sidao, while her love interest transformed into Pei Yu, a young scholar who opposed Jia Sidao's callous rule. Instead of being put to death for an actual love affair, as in Qu You's original story, Li Huiniang was murdered for murmuring an admiring comment— "What a handsome youth!"—after seeing Pei Yu at Hangzhou's West Lake. She returned as a ghost seeking to protect the young man from the prime minister's wrath. The script proved popular in numerous derivative forms, many performed under the name *Red Plum Pavilion (Hongmei ge)*. From the nameless woman in green, Li Huiniang developed into a ghost that captured the imaginations of audiences for centuries. She was quite a compelling character, and she received not one, but two, important adaptations in the high socialist period. Later, as traditional dramas returned to stages in the wake of the Cultural Revolution, Meng Chao's *Li Huiniang* found favor with new audiences.

"Stories of the strange," anomaly accounts, and all manner of ghosts, gods, and spirits have long been important parts of the Chinese literary canon.[7] From folk stories to highly literary compendia, from plays to novels to film, they appear in many forms and in many periods.[8] One of the most important forms of strange tales is the ghost opera (*guixi*), which constitutes a number of important works in many operatic forms and was a beloved genre for literati and popular audiences alike.[9] In using the term "ghost opera," I hew to how the phrase was deployed throughout much of the high socialist period, defined as "the time between agricultural collectivization and nationalization of industry in the mid-1950s through the end of the 1970s," although my study begins in the early 1950s.[10] Between 1949 and 1966, the general idea of what a *guixi* was remained relatively static. While not all plays involving ghosts were labeled as "ghost plays," all ghost plays shared some common features. Most notably, they were always discussed in the context of "traditional Chinese opera" (*chuantong xiju*) and nearly always associated closely with historical (pre-twentieth century) settings. In 1961, the writer Liao Mosha remarked that "people say, 'Without coincidences there would be no stories' [*wuqiao bucheng shu*], as it happens . . . 'without ghosts there would be no plays' [*wugui bucheng xi*]."[11] Liao's rhetorical overstatement notwithstanding, his point that ghosts formed a very important part of the canon is key. Ghost stories litter the Chinese literary landscape, and even in the Maoist era, they were still important—and still potentially dangerous, particularly in a period that emphasized overcoming China's "backwardness" through scientific, rational thinking. Audiences, artists, and writers were able to connect to a literary tradition stretching back centuries by viewing, performing, and writing such dramas, but there were serious questions about their suitability for a new, socialist China.

Concern over China's potentially "backwards" culture, which included popular literature, and the impact such culture had on the masses, was a key component of intellectual and political discussion from the late nineteenth century onwards. In 1902, the reformer Liang Qichao fretted about the negative effects of Chinese literary traditions, claiming that a whole range of "superstitious practices," ranging from geomancy to "praying to spirits," all found their roots in fiction.[12] Chen Duxiu, cofounder of the CCP, insisted fifteen years later that political reform could only come with the reform of literature, which in his view consisted of little more than "kings and officials, ghosts and spirits, or the fortunes and misfortunes of a single individual."[13] That is, in his telling, the literary canon was made up of individualistic, superstitious, or elitist tales, and precious little that spoke to the common person. More practical antisuperstition campaigns aimed at religious institutions were a feature from the Republican era (1911–49) onwards.[14] As Rebecca Nedostup has explored, reformulating ideas about "religion," including the creation of the category "superstition" (*mixin*), was an important part of the "construction of Nationalist modernity and political power" during the Nanjing Decade (1927–37).[15] By the socialist period, supernatural tales presented a particularly difficult conundrum for cultural and political leaders. These works were not just popular among the masses, but celebrated by the artistic and intellectual elite. The "strange tales" of Pu Songling and *The Peony Pavilion* (*Mudan ting*) of Tang Xianzu, among a host of other works, were considered by many to represent some of the very finest achievements of pre-twentieth-century literary production. The question of what to do with this heritage—great cultural treasures on the one hand, but perhaps propagating "superstition" and "backwardness" on the other—would be of utmost importance to writers and artists even after 1949.

In 1963, theatrical ghosts would be banned entirely from Chinese stages for "spreading feudal and superstitious thought among the masses," one of the earliest indications of the increasing radicalization of the cultural world.[16] Between 1949 and 1963, theatrical ghosts had been bound up in larger questions regarding theatre reform and the scope of socialist culture. Naturally, cultural workers pondered how to incorporate beloved popular stories whose pasts were often questionable from a strictly socialist viewpoint. Ghosts could be read in many ways: as teaching tools, as representations of feudal superstitions, as encouraging fatalism. But until the total ban on ghost opera on 1963, a balance was maintained between two opposing viewpoints. Many cultural workers argued for the inclusion of even potentially problematic forms, such as ghost opera, on their didactic merits: theatrical ghosts were presented in ways that underscored their bravery and righteousness, and their ability to teach people how to resist great evil. However, an opposite line lumped ghostly literature in with other "superstitious" practices that the CCP was dedicated to stamping out. In this view, ghosts represented real-world forces that were frightening, and thus needed to *be* resisted. When this tension came to the fore in 1963, the critique of ghostly literature became the harbinger of increasingly vitriolic attacks on veteran cultural workers such as Meng Chao, which ultimately culminated in the launch of the Great Proletarian Cultural Revolution (1966–76).

According to policy and theory that emphasized "modern" artistic forms and themes, scientific and rational thinking, and the stamping out of superstition among the masses, the hostility displayed toward writers of ghost drama and their defenders in the mid-1960s seems unsurprising. But many artists, writers, and critics proved resistant to pruning the classical canon, particularly supernatural subjects. The CCP assigned the task of rectifying Chinese culture to "cultural workers" (*wenyi gongzuozhe*), a term for all artists involved in producing art and literature for the state, precisely in those fields that Mao asserted to be key components of revolutionary struggle. Who was—and was not—considered a cultural worker varied throughout time, and one person's status could shift over the course of a lifetime. Cultural workers were bound to the state through institutions such as writers' unions intended to focus the creative energies of their generation on the project of continuing revolution. Yet cultural workers, critics, and bureaucrats hotly debated traditional subjects in ongoing discussions that far predated 1949. Were such subjects suitable for a socialist society? What did they offer audiences and artists? Could the cultural world be remade without destroying treasures of the imperial past, even the problematic ones? What constituted the important parts of the literary canon? To what extent could a play with hundreds of years of history be changed to suit contemporary needs?

Despite the seeming paradox of imperial concubines and spirits on socialist stages, many cultural and political elites enthusiastically supported these popular parts of the literary canon for both their artistic and didactic qualities. Ghost characters, for instance, were often described as imparting a "resisting spirit" (*fankang de jingshen*) to audiences, while the special techniques, such as the "ghost step" (*guibu*) that actors deploy to make it appear as though they are gliding, were praised for their artistic value. Yet such support did not go uncontested, and anxiety often underpins many of the discussions on both sides. By the Cultural Revolution, many cultural workers, including Meng Chao, would be branded *niuguisheshen*, or "ox ghost–snake spirits," an old Buddhist phrase that came to mean bad elements par excellence. Far from being a minor artistic or ideological row, many of the cultural and political tensions of the first decade and a half of Communist rule can be seen in the debates, products, and fates of artists, writers, and supernatural literature itself.

Resisting Spirits argues that the creation, discussion, and reception of these potentially troublesome plays underscores the experimental nature of cultural production in the high socialist period, as writers and artists attempted to figure out what parts of the canon were key and how art could be redeployed to resonate with contemporary concerns—all while dealing with unsettled and often contradictory policies. Such discussions also underscore the cultural and bureaucratic challenges of moving from a "revolutionary" to "postrevolutionary" context.[17] In arguing this, I trace the uneasy and sometimes hostile relationship the CCP had with traditional, particularly supernatural, subject matter on stages, but I also explore how many cultural workers navigated complicated bureaucratic waters. *Resisting Spirits* probes how many senior writers, who had imbibed deeply from the twin cups of Marxist thought and modern literary forms in the Republican period, became the vanguard in protecting celebrated works of the imperial Chinese past from a more radical present. Yet I also examine how many sought to protect culture, not by ossifying it, but through change and adaptation. I consider how authors, in attempts to keep abreast of changing regulations and dramatic shifts in policy and ideology, took experimentation with content to daring levels. Such modifications to form and content within shifting cultural and social contexts was nothing unique to the socialist period, as Joshua Goldstein's examination of Peking opera (*jingju*)[18] in the late nineteenth and early twentieth centuries has shown.[19] Nevertheless, the political context of the time marks these experiments as "new," at least in regard to the ideological and bureaucratic pressures that created them.

The history of these discussions over Chinese ghosts underscores the flexible ways in which cultural workers and cadres understood and applied rhetoric and policy. Studies of the political organization of the PRC have long noted that, even though internal and mass communications tend to deploy terminology with a rhetorical precision, that appearance of clarity was not matched by consistent definitions.[20] This meant that important concepts were constantly undergoing negotiation, examination, and discussion in both the highest *and* lowest levels of the bureaucracy, and in society more broadly. The debates on theatre, particularly traditional opera, elucidate the impact of this kind of policy across many sectors. Moreover, while these pressures certainly encouraged censorship and self-censorship, particularly in the early 1950s, they also produced a paradox: sometimes, quickly changing and often stifling regulations wound up encouraging experimentation. Indeed, what is often most startling, particularly when examining the debates and literary products produced in the early 1950s, is the extreme lengths to which writers went in attempting to bring cherished parts of the Chinese literary canon into compliance, or, in some cases, how little they attempted to tamper with the essence of imperial-era literary culture. It is true that this creativity often produced products of dubious literary quality. Nevertheless, by considering these works through the lens of experimentation, I open new ways of considering the process by which bureaucratic interference and artistic production interact.[21]

The past fifteen years have seen a number of studies on modern Chinese drama by scholars from many disciplines. Many of these tackle the question of theatre reform and regulation, at least in part, and most are interested in exploring the political, social, and cultural position of Chinese opera (*xiqu*) in the late nineteenth and twentieth centuries, rather than focusing on literary analysis. Joshua Goldstein's *Drama Kings: Players and Publics in the Re-Creation of Peking Opera*, Jiang Jin's *Women Playing Men: Yue Opera and Social Change in Twentieth Century China*, and Andrea Goldman's *Opera and the City: The Politics of Culture in Beijing, 1770–1900* all consider the political, cultural, and social context of traditional Chinese opera in the late imperial and Republican periods. I have sought to add to these discussions by considering the contexts traditional opera found itself in during the high socialist period.[22] Catherine Swatek's *Peony Pavilion Onstage: Four Centuries in the Career of a Chinese Drama* masterfully illustrates how to approach one drama, over a long period of time, through several different lenses.[23] Although my study does not concern itself with issues of "performance," Swatek nevertheless pointed the way to how to treat continuities and fissures across time and space. Many Chinese scholars, in particular Fu Jin, have also explored issues of reform and regulation during the twentieth century in extraordinary depth—Fu's latest work covers the twentieth century in two volumes.[24] I have found a wealth of inspiration in these works in fleshing out both the period before 1949, as well as (in many cases) traversing the 1949 "divide." Anne Rebull's recent dissertation, "Theatres of Reform and Remediation," also takes up the issue of the 1949 divide, and was particularly useful in understanding continuities and breaks *throughout* the twentieth century, especially as many scholars, including myself, tend to fall on one side or the other.[25] On the subject of the transformation of other Chinese performance traditions, Emily Wilcox's challenge to "the common assumption that post-1970s economic liberalization produced more artistic innovation than was present in the early socialist decades" in her study of Chinese dance over the course of the twentieth century proved useful while ruminating on the reform of traditional Chinese theatre.[26]

Other recent studies are particularly concerned with opera at the grassroots in the Republican and high socialist periods. Brian DeMare's *Mao's Cultural Army: Drama Troupes in China's Rural Revolution* (spanning the decades between the 1920s and early 1950s) and Wilt L. Idema's *The Metamorphosis of Tian Xian Pei: Local Opera under the Revolution (1949–1956)* are two recent examples.[27] Both studies elucidate conditions on the ground, for "grassroots" producers and consumers of drama. Although my focus here is on relatively elite echelons of cultural production and critique, for the most part, both have provided valuable insight into the workings of theatre reform at many levels. Max Bohnenkamp's dissertation "Turning Ghosts into People"[28] was illuminating reading on the creation of the famous revolutionary drama *The White-Haired Girl* (*Baimao nü*), which has obvious ghostly overtones. Bohnenkamp's thorough study of the origins and promotions of the drama was useful in considering other deployments of ghost (or ghost-like) characters in a socialist context, as well as the invention of cultural products in general. *Resisting Spirits* also connects to studies of supernatural literature and ghost opera in particular. There are a number of excellent works on ghost opera in the imperial period, most notably Judith Zeitlin's *Phantom Heroine*, Catherine Swatek's *Peony Pavilion Onstage*, and several important Chinese works, chief among them Yang Qiuhong's *Research on China's Pre-Modern Ghost Plays* and Xu Xianglin's *Chinese Ghost Plays*, both primarily focused on the imperial period.[29] Zeitlin's work, in particular, is especially important in analyzing issues of gender at play in these literary products, particularly as many stories centered on women were written by men. This dynamic continues throughout the socialist period, and I have tried to be attentive to the possible meanings and political ramifications of men writing women, particularly in regard to the connection between plays of the mid-1950s and the promulgation of the New Marriage Law. Further, the imperial-era groundwork laid by scholars such as Zeitlin has helped me connect socialist cultural production to a much longer past.

The problematic aspects of supernatural literature and updating potentially troublesome forms are, of course, not an exclusively Chinese problem. I see *Resisting Spirits* as a work in concert with a host of others from elsewhere around the globe, and the story of ghostly literature in the high socialist period has much to offer similar stories elsewhere, and vice versa. For instance, I found much familiar about Christina Ezrahi's *Swans of the*

Kremlin, on ballet in the Soviet Union: How does a system update potentially problematic, yet culturally important, forms for a new political context?[30] Yet Chinese opera is different from ballet: whereas ballet was the domain of elite Russians in the imperial period, the numerous genres of Chinese opera meant that it was an art form open to everyone. Thus, in many respects, the challenges and potential rewards were even greater. The tension between "modernity" and supernatural tales is well represented in scholarly literature dealing with other countries. Monographs such as Michael Dylan Foster's *Pandemonium and Parade: Japanese Monsters and the Culture of Yōkai* and Gerald Figal's *Civilization and Monsters: Spirits of Modernity in Meiji Japan* underscore some of the universal tensions between "modernity" and "superstitions," but also highlight why studies of the fantastical can be extremely useful in looking at modern history.[31]

Resisting Spirits contributes to these interdisciplinary, global conversations by focusing primarily on the period between 1953 and 1966 in the PRC, thirteen years of often intense discussion regarding reform, reuse, and reimagining of literary products whose histories, in some cases, dated back centuries. Tracing the production, reception, and discussion of revised dramas over this period offers insights into the tumultuous high socialist period at key moments. But it is also a way to bridge temporal divides. Just as a number of scholars have questioned the 1949 divide, in tracing the history of reform and reuse of ghost opera, I bridge the pre- and post–Great Leap Forward divide by illustrating the intimate connections between 1950s discussion and production and the early 1960s cultural milieu. The premiere of *Li Huiniang* did not lead "to a spurt of interest in ghost plays"; rather, it was seen in the early 1960s as a crowning achievement following over ten years of debate.[32] Furthermore, using these debates has allowed me to get beyond what Gail Hershatter describes as "campaign time," the tendency to locate historical phenomena within the various mass political campaigns of the 1950s and 1960s.[33] The discussions on opera were of course influenced by their specific historical moments, but usually stretch far beyond them. The Hundred Flowers campaign, for instance, may have had an ameliorating effect on the discussions I examine in this narrative, but it by no means created them. Likewise, the flourishing of so-called new historical plays—and the enthusiastic reception of *Li Huiniang* in particular—should be understood as part of a much longer temporal arc of critique, reuse, and re-creation, not simply confined to the relatively more relaxed period of the early 1960s, and by no means solely concerned with "remonstrance" and criticism of party policy.

Cultural workers deployed a variety of "sophisticated and time-honored forms of remonstrance" in order to discuss the present, among them historical scholarship, theatre, and *zawen* (short, satirical, subtle essays, usually on historical subjects).[34] Scholarship has typically analyzed plays such as *Li Huiniang* within this context of "indirect" remonstrance. Of course, the "new historical plays" were created amid the political and social crisis of the Great Leap Forward, Mao's ill-fated attempt to vault China into an ambitious new era that saw tens of millions starve to death in the Great Famine. It is thus natural to read them as their authors' attempts to offer critiques of their present.[35] Merle Goldman, for instance, used an aria of *Li Huiniang* and Meng Chao's postscript as evidence that "the Leap had produced the chill and that [Meng Chao], like his traditional forebears, sought to alleviate the distress of the peasants."[36] I am sympathetic to such readings of these plays—it is in fact within this context that my first study of Meng Chao and *Li Huiniang* was conducted.[37] However, to focus on what an author might have been implying, as opposed to what the text overtly states, is to gloss over an important part of the discourses and practices of literary production.

This book also seeks to add to the growing body of literature examining the interplay of official and grassroots culture. As defined in Jeremy Brown and Matthew Johnson's *Maoism at the Grassroots*, the grassroots encompasses the "complex interplay between provincial, county, commune, and village officials, and among people who had no official titles whatsoever."[38] This volume, and many others, has complicated the picture of state control of various facets of life. It is important to recognize that the problems of imposing such control ranged from elite intellectuals to local society.[39] As Matthew D. Johnson has noted, "unrealistic economic planning . . . fostered limitations to state cultural reach" at the local level.[40] But this limited reach applied to the cultural world more broadly, even so-called official culture, as is exceptionally evident in the theatre world: throughout much of this narrative, cultural workers—even those that were relatively elite "cadres of the country"—show themselves unwilling to submit entirely to state demands. And indeed, those state demands were often less homogenous than they might appear at first blush. As I show, the relationship of elite debates to practical changes at the grassroots level was an important and mutually constitutive one. I further argue that just as cultural practices were contested at the grassroots, they were extremely contentious subjects at the highest echelons of the political and cultural realms. Although this is a study largely centered on elite cultural workers and their published texts, it would be a mistake to view these discussions as entirely removed from the day-to-day reality of repertoire reform and dramatic performance. Many of the essays and opinions found on the pages of major papers and journals like *Guangming Daily* (*Guangming ribao*) or *Theatre Report* (*Xiju bao*) are reflected in—and themselves reflect—the archival record of municipal- and provincial-level cultural bureaucracies.

These discussions were not limited to the world of drama, and debates on theatre extended to those on art and cultural production more broadly. Reading the 1950s debates on superstition and mythology in ghost plays against the popular antisuperstition campaigns, for example, reveals both interpenetration between these discourses and subtle differences. Doing so underscores the relative flexibility of terms and policies that seemed well defined, as the debate over a policy's meaning encouraged experimentation and adaptation, including across media. Highlighting the history of supernatural literature in the PRC, and the cultural workers who produced and consumed it, allows us to consider the culture of regulation, the relationship between mass campaigns and popular culture, and the ways in which cultural workers navigated complicated political contexts.

People and Plays

I arrived at the subject of ghost opera in the high socialist period in a roundabout way. Having developed an affection for Tang Xianzu's *Peony Pavilion* over the years, I was curious as to why it needed several "revivals," some more radical than others, in the late 1990s and 2000s.[41] After sitting down with a decade's worth of officially compiled theatre yearbooks from the 1980s, it seemed clear that *Peony* had indeed been in need of a revival, with relatively few performances recorded, just a scant decade after Mao's death. It was equally apparent to me that the reasons for that need would be hard to uncover from my position as a graduate student on the shores of La Jolla, California. Hoping to salvage a research project, I made a spreadsheet consisting of every play performed by the Kun opera troupes listed in the yearbooks between 1979 and 1988. In the end, I had a long list of (to me) completely incomprehensible—if potentially interesting—data, at the time not being terribly familiar with the vast number of plays and scenes that make up the repertoires of Kun opera troupes, to say nothing of Chinese opera as a whole.

I asked Dr. Wa Ye if she could shed light on any of my findings. Her eyes immediately hit upon one line from the Jiangsu Kun Opera Troupe, *Li Huiniang*. "What is this doing here?" she queried. I responded that, according to the official figures, out of 223 performances the troupe had put on in 1982, ninety had been *Li Huiniang*, roughly 40 percent.[42] "Do you know anything about this play?" she asked. I, of course, had never heard of it. She told me she remembered seeing, as a teenager in Beijing in the mid-1960s, big character posters criticizing the play and its author. "It's like *Hai Rui Dismissed from Office* [*Hai Rui baguan*]," she explained. "But it's a ghost opera. Why don't you go see what you can find?"

As I quickly discovered, *Li Huiniang* and its author Meng Chao had been almost entirely eclipsed by their more famous counterparts: Wu Han and his *Hai Rui*, Tian Han and *Xie Yaohuan*. All had been important in the early Cultural Revolution and the period immediately before, and Wu Han and Tian Han were recognizable cultural and political figures, with many articles and books devoted to them. But who was Meng Chao? This dramatist and his ghost were lucky to get a sentence or two in most English-language publications covering the period. As Rudolf Wagner pointed out in his landmark work, *The Contemporary Chinese Historical Drama*, Meng Chao and *Li Huiniang* have received precious little attention in Western language scholarship, and this fact still holds more or less true over a quarter century later; Tian Han and his *Xie Yaohuan* received somewhat more, and Wu Han and *Hai Rui*, the lion's share.[43] For my part, I was fascinated to discover that a *ghost play* had played a crucial role in 1960s politics. It seemed counterintuitive to someone still learning their way around the high socialist period. Despite reading about the political and cultural role and importance of, say, calligraphy and traditional painting in the years after 1949, theatrical ghosts seemed so much more at odds with what the CCP was attempting to accomplish in the years after "liberation."[44]

I began with newspapers and journals from the 1950s and 1960s. The more I read, the more I found that not just *Li Huiniang* in particular, but ghost opera in general, had occupied an important role in cultural and political discussions between 1949 and 1963. I moved on to the Shanghai Municipal Archives. Startlingly, when I appraised the evidence that emerged from archival fieldwork, it really *did* appear that such potentially troublesome content, at least in the form of ghost opera, was better represented in the Maoist 1950s and early 1960s than it was in the "Reform and Opening Up" of the 1980s. I was fascinated, so I worked backwards from

Meng Chao and *Li Huiniang*: many of the discussions of the early 1960s, which celebrated the Kun opera, referenced the possibility of the "ghost-less ghost play." It was only after more digging that I realized such a contradiction had actually existed in the form of Ma Jianling's 1953 *Wandering West Lake* (*You xihu*). What political and cultural conditions allowed for such a play to be written and performed in the high socialist era?

In *Resisting Spirits*, I am primarily concerned with how cultural workers have recycled, reinterpreted, and redeployed culture through time, and what those various reuses signal about their particular political, social, and cultural contexts. Most importantly, I wish to explore how those people navigated the troubled cultural and political waters of the day. This book's primary concern is not ghost opera; neither is it ghosts, nor opera, though I am of course interested in all of these things. Meng Chao was the focus of my initial research, and his figure still looms large in the work. And still, the center of this study is not Meng Chao. But ghost opera, and his ghost opera in particular, has provided a fascinating lens through which to view the high socialist period; it often gives glimpses of something unexpected, and not just because of the ghosts. Rich discussions over art and culture that spanned more than a decade allowed me to connect the creations of the early 1960s to their 1950s forebears, as well as link high socialist cultural production to pre-1949 (even imperial-era) and post-Mao cultural milieus. In tracing how ghost opera has been presented, discussed, and used over the span of three decades, I shed light on how cultural workers made the transition from "revolutionary" to "postrevolutionary" society, as well as how they transitioned from the high socialist period to the period of reform and opening.

Further, an examination of the cultural workers and critics who debated and produced drama on supernatural themes provides unique opportunities to elucidate the connection between the vaunted pre-twentieth-century literary canon and the post-1949 socialist world. The debates on ghosts, as well as the production of newly written ghost plays, underscore the relative richness of the period, and the varied production writers and artists engaged in. To read Meng Chao's *Li Huiniang*, for instance, is to see classical Chinese idiom and form unfurling quite naturally from the mind of a writer who displays mastery over those traditions. When he wrote in the poetic prologue to the play that his "intentions and energy link to a long rainbow," he was not tying himself to the youthful literature of the socialist world, but to celebrated Chinese works stretching back centuries.[45] When fellow authors wrote of the duty to preserve China's "literary inheritance," they were not speaking of the Henrik Ibsens and Nikolai Gogols that had entered the Chinese intellectual scene in translation decades before, or of the patriotic anti-Japanese plays of the Yan'an period (1936–48), but of Tang Xianzu, Li Bai, and all the great literature of the "feudal" past. Many of these revolutionaries, baptized in the radical discourse of the 1920s and 1930s that sought to tear down "tradition," found themselves in a wildly different position after 1949: no longer scrappy revolutionaries, but cadres and artists tasked with administering, shaping, and reimagining the cultural world.

The heart of my narrative is an examination of three versions of the tale of Li Huiniang, two of which opened the introduction. All three fall in the general category of "Chinese opera" or theatre (*xiqu*), as opposed to spoken-language drama (*huaju*) or Western-style opera (*geju*). There is no *one* Chinese opera—there are or were hundreds of regional styles, each with their own specialties, tunes, and dialects—but all Chinese opera combines "music, singing, speech, dance, and postures in order to narrate a story."[46] I borrow from those critics and artists working and writing in the 1950s and 1960s, who often referred to the objects of their interest, at least generally, as "traditional" (*chuantong*) (Chinese) theatre. However, "traditional" should not be taken to mean "static"; as this study, like many others, underscores, the world of "traditional" Chinese opera was (and is) quite dynamic.

The first play I consider in depth is an adaptation of the Li Huiniang story called *Wandering West Lake*, which premiered in 1953. The veteran dramatist Ma Jianling adapted the plot to *qinqiang*, a Shaanxi style of opera and a regional variant of clapper (*bangzi*) operas. Historically, it had been considered "plain, popular, crude" (*su*), in contrast to other forms of drama seen as more suitable for refined audiences.[47] Of course, *qinqiang*'s proletarian roots made it a perfect vehicle for party cultural engineering. Ma, who had made a name for himself during the Yan'an period creating dramas on contemporary and revolutionary themes, put forth a rather novel attempt to maintain the high points of traditional theatre while excising the problematic parts—in this case, the ghost. His "ghostless ghost play" gave rise to a heated discussion of the suitability of ghosts to socialist stages; critics were, in many cases, horrified by what they viewed as a desecration of China's "literary inheritance," yet the play proved popular among audiences and troupes. Ma would go on to revise his revision, and a new version—complete with ghost—premiered in 1958. Years later, many remembered his daring, if problematic, attempt to rectify the "suitability" of a ghost opera for the socialist stage.

The second version is an adaptation written by Meng Chao, who originally gained some measure of prominence for his activities in the radical, cosmopolitan, left-wing literary scene of 1920s and 1930s Shanghai. His *Li Huiniang* is a Kun opera (*kunqu*), one of the oldest and most elite styles of traditional theatre; in contrast to *qinqiang*, Kun opera alone held "the privileged designation *ya* [elegant, refined]" during the Qing dynasty (1644–1911).[48] Originally a southern form, it is notable for its "softness, smoothness and delicacy," most appropriate for the literati homes it flourished in from the Ming dynasty onwards.[49] This Kun version premiered in 1961, in an environment very different from that which had received Ma Jianling's *Wandering West Lake* in the early 1950s. By 1961, the PRC was emerging from the manmade disaster of the Great Leap Forward and its terrible consequences. But *Li Huiniang*'s ultimate import is perhaps not the glowing reception it received in 1961, but the role it and its author were to play in the high political drama of the 1960s. In 1963, ghost operas were banned entirely from Chinese stages, and by 1965 the play and its author faced severe criticism from cultural radicals led by Jiang Qing. These criticisms presaged the attacks on Wu Han, Tian Han, and their respective plays *Hai Rui Dismissed from Office* and *Xie Yaohuan* in late 1965 and early 1966, attacks that are often described as the "prelude" to the Cultural Revolution.

Li Huiniang is generally grouped with what were and are termed "new historical plays" (*xinbian lishiju*). These twentieth-century dramas written on imperial-era, rather than "contemporary" (*xiandai*) or "revolutionary" (*geming*), themes rose to particular prominence in the late 1950s and early 1960s. These plays were not simple revisions, but brand-new creations, although many were produced under heavy political supervision, and often tied to the contemporary political situation. These plays never constituted large parts of the repertoire: in Shanghai, for instance, they represented between 0.5 percent and 1.7 percent of scripts performed between 1955 and 1963.[50] Despite this, they dominated discussion in political and artistic spheres between the Great Leap Forward and the Cultural Revolution, and indeed have also dominated the historiography to the present—this book is no exception.[51] Historians and literary scholars have frequently focused on what the content of these plays reveals about the discontent of writers and cultural workers with the state; Wagner's study is an illuminating model in this regard.[52] This is particularly true in the case of a small group of plays written in the wake of the disastrous Great Leap Forward, the most famous among them Wu Han's *Hai Rui* and Tian Han's *Xie Yaohuan*. However, the focus on the plays' connection to high politics, as well as the emphasis on reading between the lines and focusing on their role as vehicles for "indirect remonstrance," can divorce such plays from a much broader cultural and literary context. This is particularly obvious in the case of Meng Chao's *Li Huiniang*, which, unlike *Hai Rui* or *Xie Yaohuan*, was not simply historical in setting, but centered on the return of a slain concubine in the form of a ghost. The character of Li Huiniang thus was not only associated with debates on drama reform and the work of revising traditional productions, but to questions about mythology, superstition, and the suitability of supernatural subjects in the high socialist period. In other words, I propose to read these plays outside of "campaign time" and instead in a longer "literary time" that connected the Mao era to the deeper cultural past.

While these two versions comprise the center of my narrative, I also explore what the post-Mao landscape looked like, and what Li Huiniang's reemergence might signal about the period. By 1979, traditional dramas could safely reappear on stages, and for many, they were probably reminders that other, more recent specters of the past were dead or at least in jail. Meng Chao's *Li Huiniang*, for instance, reappeared in 1979 to great acclaim. But it was not simply old versions that artists presented; new generations found inspiration in traditional tales. Hu Zhifeng's Peking opera version of *Li Huiniang*, which premiered on stages in 1979, resembles in some ways the versions Ma Jianling and Meng Chao had written decades before, but is also a product of its time. Could Meng Chao ever have imagined his ghost on screen, featuring a host of special effects alongside the singing and acting? Furthermore, Hu's Li Huiniang moved through spaces, such as representations of the underworld and a meeting with Yama, the King of Hell, which had been deliberately excluded from high socialist revisions, even those that hewed strongly to the original plot of Zhou Chaojun's play. Even the way critics discussed the Peking opera version of *Li Huiniang* was substantively different than the discussions centered on Ma Jianling and Meng Chao's respective versions: questions that had been of prime importance in the 1950s and 1960s, such as the didacticism of the operas, were firmly subordinated to artistic matters for this post-Mao creation.

In selecting these three plays, I explore what each meant in their specific context, the ways in which they were repurposed *and* reproduced, the links—but also the fissures—across time. The social, cultural, and political context of 1953's *Wandering West Lake* was radically different than in 1979, when Hu Zhifeng's version of *Li Huiniang* premiered and Meng Chao's own version returned to stages after a sixteen-year absence. And how different was the post–Cultural Revolution milieu that Meng Chao's ghost found herself in from the attitudes and expectations of 1961, the year the Northern Kun Opera Troupe premiered the drama. But in addition to how the plays themselves reflect on and are reflective of specific historical moments and trends, *Resisting Spirits* is concerned with how the cultural workers—the authors of these plays, Ma Jianling and Meng Chao in particular, and also theatre artists—navigated shifting cultural and political contexts.

It is true that this literary and political nexus often placed frightening strains on creativity and autonomy, and often had negative repercussions for workers within the system. Yet, even within a constrained literary system, writers and artists found creative ways to maneuver. I highlight the continuing output of artists and writers, their success in linking themselves to pre-1949 cultural forms, and their passionate defense of what they saw as China's literary treasury—even when this defense could occasionally appear as desecration. Certainly, many of these writers produced a great deal of work that was dull, pedantic, and hewed closely to what we might think of as "typical," highly politicized socialist literature and intellectual discourse. But in contrast to their rote justifications of classical culture on socialist merits, which do often seem to confirm our worst ideas about the impact of Maoist thought and policy on cultural production, their plays and vibrant literary debates underscore the broad talents of these writers. They often seem to come alive once they have dispensed with the expected language of class consciousness, Marxist-Leninist theory, and Maoism. It is impossible to know exactly what Meng Chao thought while writing his revised ghost opera, but one imagines it must have been something of a pleasure: an escape from those often-dull essays, a chance to plunge into the full capabilities of the Chinese language. Indeed, Meng Chao's language is often positively luxurious in comparison to his writings in intellectual journals and newspapers; how could it have not conveyed some delight in its creation?[53]

Sources and Approaches

In this book, I focus primarily on the published output of authors and critics, particularly in the form of articles found in journals and newspapers, as well as published scripts. This is naturally only one part of the creation of theatre, and the connection between the preoccupations of elite cultural workers on the pages of journals like *Theatre Report* and what theatre artists were actually practicing can sometimes be tenuous at best. However, while I recognize the limitations of such sources, they prove valuable and interesting on their own merits; I have not tried to divine aspects of actors' or audiences' lived experience from them. However, in one avenue for exploring this relationship between writers and theatre artists, I have also made use of a number of primary documents purchased in China, such as "practice editions" (*pailianben*) used by troupes. Comparing the May 1961 practice edition of Meng Chao's *Li Huiniang*, created and used by the Northern Kun Opera Theatre, to the late summer publication of the play in *Play Monthly* and the 1962 publication in book form (discussed in chapter 3) yields rather interesting insights regarding one of the most contentious lines of the play, and also complicates the relationship between published text and performance. The profusion of 1979 and 1980 versions of *Li Huiniang* from troupes all over the country also speaks to the post-Mao cultural world and what theatre troupes were working with. Of course, this is hardly an exhaustive collection, its acquisition being shaped heavily by the vagaries of time and the secondhand book market, but the deployment of such sources is complementary to the use of other types of print sources.

My approach to these sources has also been shaped by the fact that many analyses of cultural debates in the high socialist period have often focused on what such discussions reveal about ideological splits among cultural elites.[54] These writers and critics were certainly using traditional theatrical subjects as a conduit for debates on Marxism, historical materialism, and other ideological issues. Likewise, it would be unwise to imply that the content of the plays themselves carried no coded political criticism. But in *Resisting Spirits*, I utilize what Sharon Marcus has termed "just reading" or "surface reading."[55] This is an approach complementary to "symptomatic reading," wherein one looks for what is *not* said, "reads between the lines," and considers what absences and silences reveal about a work's meaning. Certainly, as Marcus points out, symptomatic reading is "an excellent method for excavating what societies refuse to acknowledge," and there was much in the high socialist period that could often neither be acknowledged nor spoken of openly.[56] In paying attention to the "surface" of discussions—that is, what critics and artists openly and plainly said, particularly in the 1950s and early 1960s—I aim to add another layer to the growing body of scholarship on twentieth-century Chinese drama and offer a fresh perspective on these literary products and the discussions surrounding them. This is not to deny the utility of a symptomatic approach; rather, surface reading allows me to tap into other areas of interest, and in particular allows me to focus on linkages across time. It is exceptionally useful in the case of the reception of *Li Huiniang* in the early 1960s: by placing it in the context of discussions dating to the earliest days of the PRC, I connect the "liberal moment" of the post-Leap period to the longer temporal arc of cultural critique and debate.[57] I argue that between 1949 and 1963, ghost plays and new historical plays were important sites of discussion for writers and artists not simply because they offered a chance to offer coded commentary on contemporary policies of the CCP or further theoretical debates, but because they were themselves a subject of interest and highly contentious. They raised further questions of importance beyond the world of theatre: What *is* the role of traditional culture in socialist China? To what extent does classical culture need to be expunged or preserved? Should art comment on and critique the present? And how?

In writing of the lives of many of the authors I discuss, I utilize memoirs and reminiscences written in the post-Mao period. These sources often prove illuminating about the personal lives and motivations of cultural workers; however, they, too, are not without their problems. The explosion of discontent in the wake of Mao's death and the fall of the Gang of Four certainly had the effect of coloring memories, and thus these types of sources are not necessarily the most reliable. However, they are still exceptionally useful in fleshing out the lived experiences of authors who—as in the case of Meng Chao and Ma Jianling—did not outlive the high socialist period. An example of the problematic, but enlightening, nature of memoirs may be found in the example of Mu Xin, a deputy editor for the *Guangming Daily* from the mid-1950s onwards. Much of the information regarding Meng Chao's personal story and details of the internal workings of the paper are passed down through Mu Xin's autobiographical writings. His reminiscences are a treasure trove for examination of the ghost play problem, albeit a somewhat problematic one: on the one hand, he circulated in top intellectual circles and was active during several critical periods, and had personal relationships with many of the people he discusses, including Meng Chao. At the same time, he was without a doubt a "radical" and a member of the Central Cultural Revolution Group established in 1966, though he was purged in 1967.[58] Mu Xin's post–Cultural Revolution writings, particularly those published outside of the PRC, show a rather stunning reversal, and he clearly has an axe to grind regarding several major political figures. However, while he may not be the most unbiased observer, he certainly has intimate knowledge of the events he discusses; his insights would be impossible to replicate using only sources published in the 1950s and 1960s.

In combination with a variety of print materials, I also deploy a number of archival documents from the Shanghai Municipal Archives (SMA). The SMA, historically one of the most open archives, if not *the* most open archive, in the PRC, houses a treasure trove of records relating to the city's theatre world between 1949 and 1965, which has allowed me to consider the relationship between elite debates and productions to the theatre world at the grassroots. I primarily utilize repertoire records that were kept between those years. Often, the long lists of dramas being staged each year would later be used and reused in documents tallying numbers and types of performances in the city. These documents give insight into what active repertoires looked like, how they changed over time, and how cadres in the Shanghai Culture Bureau were conceiving of categorization and overall trends in the drama world, often expressed quantitatively in percentages. Except where noted, I have taken the percentages I use directly from the documents themselves. It may seem strange that a newly written drama comprising several acts and presented in toto would be treated, for the purposes of these statistics, in the same way as an excerpt from a traditional play, several of which would be staged during one performance. However, it appears to be the case, which in and of itself is a comment on how cadres were conceiving of the opera world: it is obvious, looking at the statistics, that those in charge of recording the numbers saw traditional drama as the overwhelming presence in repertoires. In chapter four, on the critical year of 1963 when ghosts were banned entirely, I let the words of theatre artists take center stage with a fascinating document: records of troupe meetings held in the autumn of that year to discuss problems in the theatre world, in particular the "ghost play problem," based on a series of articles published in the *Guangming Daily* newspaper. The records are revealing on many levels, particularly for how they lay bare the impact fifteen years of changing regulations, pressures from upper echelons of bureaucracy, and general confusion over what constituted "appropriate" art had on cultural workers responsible for carrying out these dictates day after day.

Overview of the Chapters

Chapter 1 serves as an introduction to the cultural and political significance of traditional theatre to the CCP, particularly in the early years of the regime between 1949 and 1952. The tone for the next decade of discussion was set in these early debates; intellectuals and cadres discussed the appropriate classification of plays, the problems with refashioning classical tales to resonate with the present, and what drama reform ought to look like. Chapter 2 considers the early debates over reform from a different angle. One of the omnipresent themes is the appropriate definition of "mythology" (*shenhua*) and "superstition" (*mixin*). As early as 1950, high-ranking cultural cadres argued that great care needed to be taken when defining these two types of cultural products. I demonstrate that popular campaigns aimed at stamping out "superstition" among the people were quite separate from the intellectual debates over "superstitious" and "mythological" literary products. The centerpiece is a case study of one of the most important and contentious reformed dramas, which has received little attention from scholars, Ma Jianling's *Wandering West Lake*. In a creative attempt to "fix" a popular ghost play, he removed the ghost character through a complicated plot twist. This change, far from being welcomed by the cultural establishment, was thoroughly savaged in the press, leading to Ma's decision to put the ghost back in the ghost play in 1958.

Chapter 3 further connects to the themes and plots introduced in the first two chapters by looking at 1961, a critical year for the production of supernatural literature in a socialist context. In particular, I focus on *Li Huiniang*, which was both the zenith and nadir of the political and cultural debate over ghost literature in the PRC. *Li Huiniang* is one of the three plays that helped launch the Cultural Revolution—and Meng Chao, one of the three intellectuals. Whereas scholars generally read it in the context of intellectuals' dissatisfaction with the Great Leap Forward, I argue that it must be seen in its broader context of reformed drama and the discussions about superstition and mythology in literature. I further examine the production and reception of *Stories about Not Being Afraid of Ghosts*, a state-sponsored collection of stories drawn from classical compendia. I contextualize these literary products in several ways. I pay particular attention to the diverging discourses on ghosts: ghosts-as-heroes on the one hand, and ghosts-as-enemies on the other. The latter paradigm, wherein ghosts could represent a limitless number of enemies of the CCP, is one that would render many cultural workers ghosts themselves during the Cultural Revolution, in the form of *niugui-sheshen* "ox ghost–snake spirits," enemies of the Party and not even worthy of being called human.

Chapter 4 centers on what I see as a pivotal year in both the cultural and political realms. In March 1963, the Ministry of Culture entirely banned ghosts from Chinese stages in a stunning reversal of general policy between 1949 and 1962. While the late 1965 attack on Wu Han and his *Hai Rui Dismissed from Office* is often described as the "prelude" to the Cultural Revolution, I argue that the debates over theatre in 1963 illustrate the actual turning point in the increasing radicalization of culture and politics. Using an important series of essays and letters in the *Guangming Daily*, as well as other published sources, I show how the discourse surrounding supernatural subjects shows a marked shift from those discussions examined in the first three chapters, yet is distinct from the pre–Cultural Revolution attacks launched on intellectuals between 1964 and early 1966. Further, by tying analysis of the *Guangming Daily* debates to specific meetings in Shanghai, I illuminate the connection between published discussion and the experience on the ground.

Chapter 5 argues that ghost plays and other supernatural subjects are key to understanding both the cultural and political environment of the PRC prior to the Cultural Revolution. The chapter shows how debates on ghosts and subsequent policy decisions were the first indicators of a more radical cultural and political environment, as tensions increased steadily between 1964 and 1966. Using discussions of two important theatre festivals, as well as published attacks on Meng Chao, Liao Mosha, and other intellectual luminaries, I illustrate the sharp shift in discourse after 1963. Whereas only the plays themselves had been under attack in that important year, by 1964 there was a specific assault on the writers and artists who were presented by critics as being "antiparty, antisocialist thought." Using archival records of theatre repertoire, I also illustrate the relative "ease" in which the theatre world was remade between 1964 and 1965, but also emphasize the resistance that emerged at the grassroots to these top-down changes that were enacted seemingly overnight. Chapter 6 traces the post-Mao history of Li Huiniang in her many versions, with a particular focus on Hu Zhifeng's Peking opera version. While tied to the same tradition that bound Meng Chao and Ma Jianling's revisions, Hu Zhifeng's ghostly concubine found herself in a wildly different context, one in which daring and experimentation with form was celebrated, and in which political and ideological matters took a backseat to artistic innovation. Finally, in the coda, I consider what lessons may be taken from the story of theatrical ghosts, their authors, and their critics in the high socialist period.

CHAPTER 1

Demons and Marvels

Early Drama Reform in the PRC

By 1951, Chinese artists brought forth a wide variety of characters on stages: from valiant revolutionaries to evil prime ministers, imperial concubines to ghostly peasant women. New-style revolutionary dramas on contemporary themes had been a staple of cultural production since the Yan'an period, but audiences had not lost their taste for traditional opera featuring a wide array of mythological and imperial-era subjects. With mandates to create art for the people, cultural workers struggled to balance audience desire with pedagogical goals: Was it possible to make beloved tales, some centuries old, comment on thoroughly modern concerns? Could White Snake reflect on marriage law reforms? Could *The Cowherd and the Weaving Maid* speak to the Korean War? Audiences were thus presented with a theatrical tradition in the midst of an identity crisis: stubbornly old-style plays shared space with new takes on classical tales and their contemporary-themed brethren. While some playwrights insisted on sticking close to traditional stories, no matter how "feudal" or "bourgeois" they might appear to a new socialist literary system, others took a radically different tack. Harry Truman appeared in the guise of Yama, King of the Underworld; the Weaving Maid became a model worker, forsaking love in order to labor harder; ancient myths were deployed to exhort audiences to "Resist America and Aid Korea." The chaotic mix reflected the challenges facing artists and writers in their attempt to balance socialist dictates on art with a justifiable pride in China's artistic achievements of decades and centuries past. Reforming the repertoire—never mind audiences and artists—would be no easy task.

Theatre had been recognized by intellectuals, officials, and artists long before the establishment of the PRC as a crucial tool in reaching the masses. That it remained a key component of cultural policy in the PRC is clear when considering the effort expended on the pages of newspapers, in work meetings and conferences, and in the establishment of committees dedicated to shepherding the appropriate development of repertoires and troupes across all of China. But because of its prominent place in the CCP's cultural toolbox, theatre was heavily contested at all levels of the bureaucracy and among intellectuals and artists. While gesturing toward the need for ideologically correct art, as well as the didactic functions of drama, many writers and cadres argued against subordinating artistic concerns to political ones. Others, however, believed that only by wholesale change would the cultural world be satisfactorily remade. These discussions of the early 1950s set the tone for policy for over a decade, but also underscored tensions and anxieties that would never be fully resolved.

This chapter introduces the prerevolutionary history of drama reform in China and some of the major preoccupations of dramatists, artists, and critics in the early years of the PRC. In particular, I focus on the discussion surrounding adaptations of the folktale "The Cowherd and the Weaving Maid" (*Niulang zhinü*), which exemplified an important sticking point in the high socialist period, the differentiation between "mythology" and "superstition." I underscore the malleability of the socialist vocabulary, particularly regarding this division that would remain important up to and beyond the Cultural Revolution and that provides a foundation for the chapters that follow. At the same time, however, I highlight the anxieties and tensions even among the highest levels of producers and critics of "state-sponsored culture." Although those who argued for the inclusion of traditional culture helped set policy until 1963, their position was never fully secure, and this often produced a chilling effect on repertoires as artists and cultural workers struggled to make sense of competing, and often conflicting, demands.

Theatre Reform: Continuity and Change

"Full-fledged" Chinese theatre has occupied an important social and cultural place since the Yuan dynasty, deriving from a host of even older performance traditions.[1] Traditional opera encompassed a wide variety of forms that could reach different dialects, had large local audiences who eagerly anticipated performances at fairs and festivals, required little more than actors and musicians, and required no literacy to be understood. A powerful didactic tool, drama could impart "moral and social values," teach history—or perhaps introduce or reinforce undesirable beliefs and behaviors.[2] Even the act of reading drama could potentially be fatal, as in the case of women of the Ming-Qing period enchanted with the *Peony Pavilion*.[3] These dual possibilities of drama—didactic or dangerous—continued into the high socialist period. As such, CCP concern over what was being staged and what lessons plays imparted to audiences was in many respects nothing new. From many vantage points, the post-1949 obsession with reform, revision, and redeployment of theatre was simply the latest effort in controlling these arts. From regulation of troupes, spaces, actors, to the content of the plays themselves, successive regimes tried to harness the popular power of theatre for political ends.

As Andrea Goldman and others have noted, by the end of the Qing dynasty, "new-style intellectuals looked to opera as a medium for fomenting 'enlightenment' among the lower classes."[4] Theatre held the tantalizing possibility of bringing together disparate groups of people, from cosmopolitan elites to illiterate rural masses, as well as effecting real political change. In 1904, the first journal "dedicated to dramatic reform" was founded, only to be shut down a year later by the Qing government for "subversion," but the use of theatre reform for cultural and political purposes continued to grow.[5] It is unsurprising, then, that fledgling Communists would also turn to theatre as a form of critique and a tool for teaching the masses, particularly after the move to Yan'an. Ma Jianling, discussed in chapter 2, rose to prominence as a playwright with his influential Shaan-Gan-Ning People's Troupe, utilizing local Shaanxi forms and a generalized North China dialect to produce dramas on contemporary themes. Other cultural workers, such as Meng Chao, used newer forms such as spoken language drama to comment on political events of the day (indeed, Meng Chao's own take on the May Thirtieth Massacre, in the form of a play, was the earliest appearance of the events in fictionalized form).

Theatre reform in the Republican era joined a host of other measures intended to "modernize" popular thought and belief. The Guomindang (GMD) and CCP both concerned themselves with eliminating what they judged to be harmful "superstition" while promoting "mythology" that they believed would be beneficial to mass mobilization in pursuit of social, economic, and political reform. Rebecca Nedostup details the program of "psychological construction" that the GMD undertook in parallel with the "construction" of the Republic during the Nanjing Decade.[6] Seizure of temple lands supported the statist project of economic development, while control over these institutions was meant to strip ceremony—including ritual theatrical performances—of its religious content, turning it into civic ritual. Labeling one thing "superstition" and another "mythology" was a means to specify ideological enemies of the state, but not a means to advance a coherent definition of either. Indeed, the vagueness of either term gave it its power.

At Yan'an, the CCP fleshed out the ideological lines that would shape approaches to cultural production for decades. Mao Zedong's words at the 1942 Yan'an Forum on Literature and Art retained their power for years to come, and references to them persisted in the literary discussions of the high socialist period. Mao's message encapsulated the duality of cultural production in the high socialist years—what might be termed a destructive impulse on the one hand, and one dedicated to preserving the artistic heritage of the people on the other. He stridently noted that "creative moods that are feudal, bourgeois . . . liberalistic, individualist, nihilist, art-for-art's sake, aristocratic, decadent or pessimistic, and every other creative mood that is alien to the proletariat . . . . Should be utterly destroyed. And while they are being destroyed, something new can be constructed." But this was not the end of the matter.[7] "[W]e must take over all the fine things in our literary and artistic heritage," he also said at the forum, "critically assimilate whatever is beneficial, and use them as examples. . . . [W]e must on no account reject the legacies of the ancients . . . or refuse to learn from them."[8] This highlights tensions that were never fully resolved by cultural workers and cadres, even into the 1980s. While Mao's list of "things to be destroyed" seems clear enough, most anything belonging to the "legacies of the ancients" could be argued to belong to any number of those negative categories.[9]

Owing to its importance in people's lives, reform of the cultural world on a national scale was a priority for the CCP from its early years. As Siyuan Liu has described, pre-1949 directives were generally local or regional in nature, though the People's Liberation Army tended to publish lists of censored and banned plays as they advanced throughout the country.[10] Thus, reform was often chaotically managed, leading to attendant confusion and anxiety among cultural workers. These regional policies tended to be far harsher than the later national directives, and in some cases, opera repertoires were gutted thanks to vague directives ordering "elimination of poisonous elements in old plays."[11] There is no doubt that overzealous application of socialist dictates on art and literature did have many negative consequences for theatre troupes and the traditional repertoire. Lists of banned plays numbered into the hundreds in some areas, with the most deleterious effects in Peking and Ping opera repertoires, both popular in the north and northeast.[12] The impulse from upper leadership, at least in the Ministry of Culture, was to rein in overzealous lower-level officials who were eager to refashion repertoires in their local areas, often to disastrous consequences. The top echelon of the cultural bureaucracy wanted to prevent extreme, wide-ranging bans that negatively impacted the ability of opera troupes to make a living. This was a battle that would continue for years, although the story was usually not as simple as a conflict between the central ministry and lower-level cadres.[13] At the same time Ministry of Culture directives criticized overzealous application of policy and directives, the policies themselves encouraged a cautious attitude toward repertoires, and this would spell disaster for many troupes across China in the early 1950s. Hesitant of running afoul of vague policies, cadres would often restrict the performances of plays that were not on the banned list, believing the banned plays to gesture toward even more plays that should not be performed.[14] In a pattern that would be repeated over and over, policy thus veered from one extreme to another, as directives piled up attempting to correct the excesses of previous statements, with the eventual net effect of producing exhausted, confused artists who struggled to make sense of changes.

Theatre reform was never going to be an easy task, and the legacies both of pre-1949 attempts at reform and of the confusing early days of the PRC would continue to have ramifications for years. A large part of the problem was the sheer amount of work required to manage the entirety of the expansive, diverse Chinese theatre world, with hundreds of genres and thousands of plays. Upper-level leadership quickly realized that this scattershot regional approach was clearly not going to work, and so established the Opera Improvement Bureau under the Ministry of Culture in October 1949.[15] But even with ostensible direction from the top, the experiences of cultural workers varied widely from area to area. In most respects, repertoires and troupes across China were simply too varied and diverse to be comfortably served by Ministry of Culture one-size-fits-all policies. Aware that the myriad of national and local policies were confusing at best, several early statements from the Ministry of Culture and associated senior cultural workers attempted to sort through the issues. In 1949, the ministry's Opera Improvement Bureau had ordered that plays falling into three categories be excised from the repertoire, including those that propagated "feudal slave morality and superstition."[16] The vice minister of culture, Zhou Yang, who like many senior cadres had been active in left-wing literary circles in the 1930s, went so far as to ask eminent cultural figure Tian Han to compile a list of plays to be banned; Tian argued strenuously against this approach, advocating for a thorough examination of the traditional repertoire.[17] Such effort would avoid sloughing good plays into a list of banned and censored plays, and would allow the inclusion of even "bad" plays with some revisions; this was a much more flexible approach than blanket bans, such as those undertaken in 1963. However, this ambitious project never went beyond the planning stages—the amount of effort required would have been extreme. But the idea of placing the onus for reform on the lower levels would turn out to be just as damaging as heavy bans. In essence, by generally refusing to enact "hard" censorship in the form of bans, the Ministry of Culture instead subjected artists and lower-level bureaucrats to years of anxiety and uncertainty. This would continue to have a negative effect on troupes and repertoires for years, as troupes struggled to draw in audiences through ever-popular plays, while still hewing to directives that emphasized the need for new types of productions and a lessening emphasis on traditional repertoires.

The limited national-level ban instituted by the Ministry of Culture was intended, at least on the surface, to prevent lower-level authorities from being overzealous. Between 1950 and 1952, a total of twenty-six plays were banned, the vast majority being Peking opera (fifteen), with Ping opera (*pingju*, seven), Sichuan opera (*chuanju*, two), and plays not to be staged in minority areas (two) making up the rest.[18] After an initial wave of twelve plays banned in 1950, others were added piecemeal over the next two years.[19] But this solution did not fix the problem of officials taking matters into their own hands. As Fu Jin has described, there was simply too much variation from area to area, and the net effect was that on local and provincial levels, members of the cultural bureaucracy were still deciding what could or could not be staged.[20] Fearing trouble from above for staging "inappropriate" works, local officials instead suspended performances, then told superiors that troupes had declined to perform the suspect works.[21] This pattern would continue, particularly in periods of frequent changes of policy: whoever was responsible for the decision to remove potentially problematic plays from the active repertoire, it would be attributed to artists' refusal to perform such plays. This was likely due in no small part to the implication—intended or not—that the twenty-six plays represented only a subset of "bad" plays, and the bans (limited as they were) encouraged a more cautious attitude toward many scripts that were not explicitly included.[22] Often over the next decade, when the consequences of policy decisions were made clear, the Ministry of Culture fell back on a position that blamed the lower ranks of the artistic bureaucracy, rather than its own policies that encouraged a wary attitude toward large swaths of repertoires all over China.

Shortly after the founding of the PRC, the scale of the challenge facing the fledgling government and still-unsettled cultural world was made clear at the November 1950 All-China Theatre Work Conference, hosted by the Ministry of Culture in Beijing. At stake were questions about the future of Chinese theatre, particularly insofar as creating new works while preserving older treasures was concerned—especially because, as a *People's Daily* roundup of the meeting succinctly noted, "opera is the most important tool with which to connect to the masses."[23] And what a tool it was, or could possibly be. Statistics trotted out at the conference illustrated both the enormous potential and pitfalls facing the party in attempting to remake the theatre world. Surveys put the number of opera forms in active performance somewhere around one hundred; storytelling techniques (such as Shanghainese *pingtan*) numbered more than 200. Even when only considering six major cities—Beijing, Tianjin, Shanghai, Wuhan, Xuzhou, and Shenyang—the numbers still illustrated the vastness of the theatre landscape in terms of the people involved. The survey estimated there were nearly 80,000 performers, most of whom worked in the nearly 1,400 theatres or 400-odd teahouses that hosted performances. In Shanghai alone, which had the largest, most diverse number of troupes and performers, there were more than 8,000 actors.[24] Considering the sheer numbers involved, it should be little surprise that even minor decisions could lead to deleterious economic and cultural effects from overzealous interpretation of Ministry of Culture dictates. Even so, there was an ostensible commitment to creating new plays for repertoires. The success and reach of the contemporary repertoire tended to be overreported through 1965. Certainly, the various national-level committees and local offices were dedicated to the work of reform and adaptation; we should question, however, what that (re)creation looked like. The *People's Daily* piece pointed to the strong efforts aimed at theatre reform since 1944, and claimed that more than 190 new scripts had been created in the year since liberation.

Despite all the data collected, authorities still seemed resistant to admitting what audiences actually watched, and generally *wanted* to watch. Insights into how theatre was experienced on the ground can be gleaned even from the general statistics collected by municipal culture bureaus. In

Shanghai, meticulous repertoire records were kept between 1949 and 1958. These documents do not detail the number of performances or audience sizes, but do list—by genre, including Peking, Kun, Yue, spoken language, and several other local operatic styles—what troupes were active in the city and what plays or excerpts comprised their repertoire each year. These records were likely the basis for later documents that give a "bird's eye view" of the theatre world in terms of generic *types* of plays performed (e.g., "contemporary themes," "traditional opera," and so on) (see figure 1).The latter documents show a relatively stable number of troupes and ratio of traditional to contemporary plays performed. Total numbers of contemporary-themed plays generally hovered around 15 percent of the active repertory, with most popular types of drama (including Peking opera and Yue opera[25]) never performing more than a handful of these new scripts until 1958.[26] Traditional opera, in contrast, never made up less than 79 percent of the total repertoire (see table 1). Typically, the object of discussion on elite levels belies the carefully noted statistics of at least one major cultural center: just because elite cultural workers and cadres were discussing plays on contemporary themes and brand-new reworkings of classic dramas did not necessarily mean people were *watching* them.

Just as in previous regimes, the CCP cultural apparatus attempted to harness theatre as a form of mass cultural reform. But the sheer size of the theatre world meant this was a daunting task, as sorting through the repertoires of every troupe in China was clearly an impossibility. Yet vague directives encouraged cadres to view more than just the handful of banned plays with deep suspicion, forcing them off stages.

Table 1. Shanghai Performance Statistics, 1950–1958

	1950	1951	1952	1953	1954	1955	1956	1957	1958
Troupes	125	109	97	70	87	117	109	99	125
Plays (Total)	1706	1525	1281	998	1019	1767	1562	1501	1975
Contemporary themes	230	232	164	158	169	260	188	223	390
Traditional plays	1474	1292	1110	839	848	1503	1371	1243	1578
Foreign plays	2	1	7	1	2	4	3	35	7
% Traditional plays	86.4	84.7	86.7	84.1	83.2	85.1	87.8	82.8	79.9

Source: SMA B172-1-326

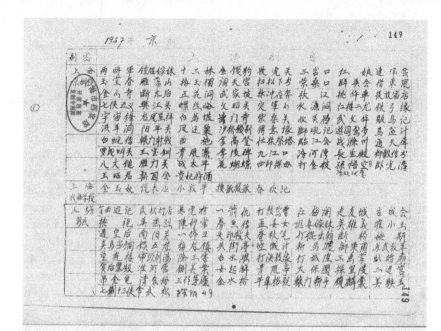

Fig. 1. The top document shows the style of repertoire records kept between 1949 and 1958; the top notes the year and genres (in this case, a mix of Peking and Kun opera troupe repertoires from 1957), while the left sidebar notes the troupes. The bottom document is a "bird's eye view" of the repertoire. While the categories and precision of those categories change over time, the format remains relatively consistent. From left to right, the columns denote genre, number of troupes active, overall number of scripts, number of plays on contemporary themes, number of traditional plays, foreign plays, and then the percentage of the repertoire made up of plays on contemporary themes. *Source*: SMA B172-4-917 & SMA B172-1-326.

Parsing Categories: "Mythology," "Superstition," and the Fluidity of Labels

One of the most consistently troublesome aspects of drama reform was defining what, exactly, was and was not permissible. Although the approach to assessing drama advocated by Tian Han and others—a careful, play-by-play analysis of good points and bad, primarily done on a local level—seemed to be relatively permissive, it wound up having a constricting effect on repertoires across China. Local cadres continued to make their own decisions regarding repertoires, banning plays on their own interpretations of whether or not they were appropriate to be staged, with little attention to the dictates of the Ministry of Culture.[27] One of the fundamental problems underlying reform efforts was the sheer broadness and fluidity of labels. The categorization of dramas would continue to be an issue of prime importance throughout the high socialist period, and the shifting definitions in play between 1950 and 1963 give insight into cultural and political trends that reached far beyond Chinese stages. The early debates on proper categorization, particularly in the case of defining plays as "mythological" or "superstitious" in content and character, would provide a foundation for nearly fifteen more years of discussions. In fact, echoes of the earliest debates, examined below, are often found well into the 1980s.

One of the earliest explications of official attitudes, at least in terms of important cultural workers and cadres, toward the differentiation between "superstition" and "mythology" came in 1950, when the dramatist, critic, and party secretary of the Opera Improvement Bureau Ma Shaobo delivered a speech on the promises and pitfalls of theatre reform. Ma himself had experience updating traditional tales for contemporary audiences, in addition to being a noted historian of Chinese theatre.[28] Ma was not the first to pay attention to the problems posed by conflating the two categories. The Ministry of Culture's Opera Improvement Bureau had earlier noted the critical nature of appropriately defining superstition and myths, declaring that the difference primarily came down to whether or not something was frightening for the audience. In what would become a standard defense for "good" ghost opera and other fantastical literature, Ma followed in the footsteps of the committee and claimed that plots involving cosmic judgment and scenes of Hell were most certainly bad. Meanwhile, mythological tales were simply the "naïve fantasies of ancient people," and these could be put to good use.[29]

Ma's attempt to parse the differences between mythology and superstition underscored the difficulties encountered by bureaucrats and artists in reforming repertoires. While pointing out that many "fearsome" plays had been incorrectly classed as benign, he seems much more concerned with the opposite phenomenon: "good" plays that had been mislabeled as dangerous. "Superstitious dramas," such as *Visiting Yin Mountain* (*Tan yinshan*) (a play in which the character of Judge Bao visits Hell, eventually one of twenty-six plays banned by the Ministry of Culture), were sometimes called benign "myths," and "mythology plays" such as the *Legend of White Snake* (*Baishe zhuan*) or *Journey to the West* (*Xiyou ji*) derivatives were labeled as dangerous superstitions.[30] The trend of excising anything with the merest whiff of unsuitability was, to Ma's mind, an alarming development. As his speech makes clear, even plays with superstitious scenes could be performed with minor deletions and alterations. It was this point of view that was the dominant paradigm for dealing with traditional theatre until 1963. The point was not to suppress traditional subjects entirely, particularly since many such plays were the core of active opera repertoire, and exactly what audiences wanted to see on stages.

A further problem that Ma attempted to deal with, one that would continue to be a conundrum for critics and artists, was the connection between popular belief and what was seen on stages, or indeed, whether there was such a connection. Theatre had long held important ritual functions for promulgating orthodoxy and religious precepts, so it is no wonder CCP cadres pondered the relationship between plays and belief.[31] As opera was recognized as a powerful didactic tool, it stood to reason—for some people, at least—that exposure to the fantastical in the form of theatre could have an impact on audience ideas about the world around them. In contrast to many writers in the late 1940s, who emphasized that theatre brought superstitions to life, so to speak, Ma noted that enjoying "mythology" did not necessarily mean *believing* in it. He related an anecdote about an acquaintance concerned for his wife's interest in the Double Seven Festival (*Qixi*). The lore surrounding the festival involves the story of the Cowherd and the Weaving Girl, a very popular subject for dramas. This pair of lovers—represented celestially by the star Vega and part of the Aquila constellation—was kept separate by a deity angry that the two neglected their duties in favor of lovemaking. Only on the seventh day of the seventh lunar month were they allowed to come together for their single night together each year. In the imperial period, during Double Seven women competed in a variety of contests designed to show off their domestic skills, such as threading needles by moonlight, in what was known as "begging for skill" (*qiqiao*).[32] Ma's acquaintance was concerned that his wife, having seen a play focused on the story of the Cowherd and the Weaving Maid, wanted to go stargazing on the Double Seven Festival and "beg for skill." Ma responded with two arguments. The first was that myths had positive didactic qualities; he also added that not everyone engaged in so-called superstitious behavior actually believed in it. Ma argued that stargazing "should not necessarily be seen as superstitious behavior. Chinese people are a brave, hard-working, mighty race, and also ought to be a race rich in humor. Women comrades going to look at stars, admiring [the idea that] men plow and women weave, the idea of eternal love, this especially is '*qiqiao*'—it's hoping for exemplary labor, achievements in work—how is this not good?"[33] Thus, he suggested that this woman's *qiqiao* was quite possibly a bit tongue in cheek, and the principles underlying it, particularly the celebration of productive labor, were positive.

His note that one could engage in "superstitious" behavior without *being* "superstitious" usually remained unsaid or was deemphasized. This would be underscored during the proscience, antisuperstition campaigns of the 1950s: "superstitions" on theatrical parade were generally not a target when the CCP attempted to stamp out popular superstition among the people. The arguments of Ma and others, including the Ministry of Culture committee, gave wide latitude for writers and artists to defend traditional drama. The only themes, at least insofar as potentially "superstitious" plots were concerned, that were explicitly off limits were those that could be construed as "frightening." In this case, it meant plot points that could be interpreted as ways for the elite to control commoners. Many other subjects that at first glance appeared to fall into the "fearsome" category, vengeful ghosts among them, were read as expressions of resistance against feudal forms of oppression, as later chapters will show. Still, Ma and others like him were only one side of the discussion; just as vociferously as they argued for the preservation of traditional drama (mostly) as it was, others would insist that theatrical fantasy had the potential to actively harm audiences.

Radiant Achievements? Cultural Experiments of the Early 1950s

Despite early efforts at mapping an appropriate course for the reform of theatre, many questions remained. What was the ultimate goal of reform?

To what extent could—or should—traditional dramas be changed? This tension between new creations and contemporary reworkings on the one hand, and a much more hands-off approach on the other, would continue to dog writers throughout the 1950s. Developments on the international stage made the basic questions of theatre reform even more pressing. Regardless of the actual popularity of theatre on contemporary themes among audiences, many dramatists were concerned with making the past (or mythology, as the case might be) resonate with present concerns. That troupes needed to perform dramas with a modern twist was underscored by the constant references in essays on the state of theatre to the campaign to "resist America and aid Korea," and the centrality of drama to supporting patriotic endeavors. The combination of contemporary political events, in the form of the Korean War, with early attempts at theatre reform produced page upon page of heated debate.

Certainly, there was an explicit acknowledgment of the importance of maintaining and developing traditional theatre. Zhou Weizhi, who had been influential in left-wing music groups of the 1930s and continued to be a force for revolutionary song composition in the Yan'an period and after, expounded on the central role of traditional plays in a *People's Daily* essay.[34] Despite emphasizing the importance of work on contemporary themes, he spent some time discussing the role of traditional drama in China. "Every type of old drama derives from the people, was created by the people," Zhou said, and traditional drama "has turned into the art form that the people love. They have a deep basis among the masses, they are the riches of the people, riches of the country, and are a rich legacy among old art and literature." He continued that even in a socialist society, "we have the right and *the duty* to develop the outstanding traditional [dramas], this theatrical inheritance" (emphasis mine).[35]

If sorting through the myriad repertoires of local and national forms and scores of traditional plays was no easy task, the attempts at creating something new from old themes proved even more difficult and contentious. Despite those urging caution, some members of the theatre world were still advocating for drastic changes to the existing repertoire. Considering the calls for drama and art on contemporary themes, it is hardly surprising that people would regard the re-creation of traditional drama with a more modern image as one wave of the future. After all, if reinterpretations of traditional mythology plays could be made to speak to the Korean War or land reform, who could accuse them of being feudal relics? On the other hand, many cultural workers were aghast at these attempts to make "the past speak to the present." These tensions came to a head in 1951, over dramatists' attempts to remake *The Cowherd and the Weaving Maid* into a product that could speak to contemporary events. The debate illustrates the sometimes extreme lengths dramatists went to in an attempt to balance competing demands creatively, but also the deep support a relatively hands-off approach to drama reform enjoyed. It also elucidates the problems facing cultural workers on both sides of the spectrum: whatever one's personal opinion, there were many political and cultural forces at work, often with competing messages and conflicting visions for cultural reform. Although this exchange has been read as a debate on historical materialism, I am interested here in the surface of the discussion.[36] Theoretical issues may also have been at stake, but the state of traditional drama was not merely a smokescreen for lobbing ideological grenades. The debate between three highly regarded cultural figures illuminates two positions regarding theatre reform. The first, represented by the poet Ai Qing and critic Ma Shaobo, held that while theatre needed *some* reform, utmost caution needed to be taken in handling these literary treasures. In Ai's view, forcing beloved mythological tales to resonate with contemporary concerns often had the effect of ruining them; for him, art should not be entirely subsumed to politics. The opposite view, represented by the dramatist Yang Shaoxuan, argued that "art for art's sake" was an inappropriate use for drama. In his telling, to *not* do everything to make mythological tales resonate with present concerns was simply playing into the hands of imperialists and "enemies of the country."

In August 1951, Ai Qing wrote an essay on the many stagings of *The Cowherd and the Weaving Maid* that had appeared after 1949, and he was critical of what he viewed as unrestrained adaptations. Ai, one of the most prominent poets of the twentieth century, had enjoyed a particularly cosmopolitan youth, spending three years in France as a young adult, and participating in Shanghainese left-wing literary circles upon his return.[37] Although he joined the CCP in 1941 and spent time in Yan'an, Ai Qing had historically opposed "political control over literature,"[38] writing in March 1942 that a writer was "not a singer who sings solely to please others."[39] Despite ongoing issues with the leadership of the CCP, he was still a major literary figure who served on committees and edited major literary publications; thus, his critiques carried weight.

Ai criticized several approaches to dealing with drama, neatly outlining a position that would be held by many others in the succeeding decade. The first type of play was one that had been changed in minor

ways, or perhaps not at all, and pandered to "the urban petty bourgeoi-
sie's backwards tastes," which often verged on the obscene or farcical.[40]
On the opposite end of the spectrum were heavily edited or rewritten versions that integrated domestic and international politics: "land reform,
the struggle against local despots, suppression of counterrevolutionaries,
resisting America and supporting Korea, safeguarding world peace . . ." As
Ai pointed out, such versions relied almost exclusively on the talent of the
writer to make a reasonable end product; in his view, most of these new
versions were not handled terribly adeptly.[41] What he did not acknowledge
were the political and ideological pressures that made such experiments—
risky ones, to be sure—seem an appealing, or necessary, option.

Ai's irritation is palpable as he lists several new scripts, which range
from a plot where the celestial lovers have a happy ending to plays ending in peasant uprisings. He points to a version by Yang Shaoxuan where,
among other shocking things, the "old willing ox" sings a line of Lu Xun's
poetry: "With a scowl, I ignore a thousand pointing fingers; with head
bowed, I serve the children like a willing ox."[42] This was, in his view, a
"most devastating" trend, culminating in a Shanghainese version where
a variety of supernatural beings were forced into one-to-one correlations
with contemporary things. Spirits under the command of the Demon
King lost their original associations, and the Demon King himself became
an embodiment of Harry S. Truman. *Tange*, a bug, became *Tanke* (tank);
Feizhi, an owl, became *Feiji* (airplane), and so on.

While criticizing plays that seemed *too* bourgeois or proletarian in
their leanings, Ai did reserve praise for those versions that paid homage to
the original tale. He argued that sensitive handling of such stories was, in
fact, patriotism writ large in and of itself. His portrayal of the celestial tale
as the "people's inheritance" would be repeated in many other contexts
over the next thirteen years, including stiff defenses of ghost opera. Ai
passionately argued that when revising the play, authors should "take folk
tales seriously, preserving the original beauty of the plot as far as possible."
Writers and artists ought to "cherish myths that have spread widely over
a long period among the people—they are an expression of our patriotic
spirit."[43] Patriotism, that is, could reside in the celebration of one of "the
best literary works of the Chinese people," and it need not resonate with
land reform or the Korean War to do so.[44] Ai Qing emphasized the healthy
and national characteristics of China's literary heritage; unfortunately, this
was often not reflected in the overarching demands placed on artists and
cultural workers.

Ai Qing's essay provoked a harsh response from Yang Shaoxuan, who wrote the *People's Daily* and criticized the editors for publishing Ai's essay.[45] And while the paper published his response in November, the damning editor's note made it clear that the paper came down firmly on the side of the poet's call for restraint: "Although [Ai Qing's] essay could be said to have incomplete parts, nevertheless, its general point of view is correct." The note continued that the editors "believe Comrade Yang Shaoxuan's basic point of view and attitude both have errors."[46] In his response, Yang positioned himself in opposition to men like Ai Qing, and relied, reasonably enough, on well-trod political rhetoric to portray his actions in a positive light. His work was not "art for art's sake," or "mythology for mythology's sake"; it was work designed to serve the masses, just as Mao had called for in the Yan'an Forum. The new movements in art and literature were, no doubt, at the beginning stages of development. Yang acknowledged that such works might look "very coarse, quite ridiculous" to elite cultural workers. But he hotly contended that this was because this bourgeoning movement had to follow a natural course of development. If there were no simple works in the beginning, there would be no foundation to build upon for better, more sophisticated pieces.[47] Yang was making an entirely reasonable point: without experimentation, regardless of its success, there could be no development. Without development, how would art be able to live up to the demands placed on it in the socialist system?

Yang further criticized Ai for what he saw as the latter's misunderstandings of his revisions. In his script, an owl was caught; "according to Ai Qing's logic, this was part of [my] 'savage behavior'—why? Because he believed that 'owl' was 'referring to' the 'Truman' in his article; in truth, Mr. Ai Qing is neurotic. I wrote that 'owl' to embody a general idea of a saboteur, [something] destroying . . . a happy marriage . . . a helpmate of feudalism." While Truman could *perhaps* be read into his description of production-destroying, feudalism-supporting owl-saboteur, what was so wrong with that?[48] In a supporting letter, he explicitly points to Mao's words to justify his revisions, as well as to attack what he saw as the poet's incorrect political position. Relying on Mao's comments that "we must move two great mountains"—imperialism and feudalism—he stated that Ai Qing was simply attempting to impede the efforts to get out from under those twin yokes of oppression.[49] Yang eventually claimed that advocating for a more tempered approach to the classics was, in effect, "supporting the enemy" and staunchly defended the rights of authors to "make" mythology refer to anything, a tit-for-tat argument that probably could have continued indefinitely. And yet, despite the aspersions he cast on Ai's ideological position as well as his literary knowledge, the editor's note makes clear that it is *Yang's* point of view that was out of favor.

It is difficult not to feel a pang of sympathy for Yang Shaoxuan; he surely did not anticipate the negative spin that *People's Daily* would put on his letters. Yang was hardly a minor figure in the theatre world, and he had been a director of the Peking opera troupe in Yan'an in the 1940s.[50] The year before the debate, in 1950, the inaugural issue of *People's Theatre* reproduced a 1944 letter written by Mao praising a play, *Driven to Join the Liangshan Rebels (Bishang Liangshan)*, that Yang and Qi Yanming had revised.[51] Considering the accolades from no less than Mao himself, was it a surprise that many writers and artists believed "it was indeed possible to rewrite the traditional repertoire of various kinds of regional theater?"[52] Not only that, at the time of the letter was written, Yang was Tian Han's "second in command" in the Opera Improvement Bureau.[53] Regardless of the artistic quality of his revisions, he was taking chances in order to further develop theatre; he no doubt believed he was executing acceptable modifications in order to bring a great tradition in line with contemporary dictates on art and theatre.

Unfortunately for Yang, his response, at least as presented on the pages of the *People's Daily*, appeared to be a spectacular overreaction. It does, however, give some indication of exactly what serious business drama reform was, and would remain, throughout the high socialist period. It also underscores the playwright's attitude toward drama reform and its political significance. Yang sent three additional missives, which were appended to the *People's Daily* main essay, objecting to Ai's original essay on political and artistic grounds. On September 1, he wrote: "Does [Ai's essay] not expose a resentfulness towards the resist America, aid Korea [movement]?" He pondered further on September 7: "I think [Ai's] essay is a typical example of 'mythology for mythology's sake,' it doesn't have any thinking, and it cannot solve any problems. . . . It is the muzzle of a gun pointed [at the country], it is helping the enemy; it is attacking the playwrights [who are] resisting America and supporting Korea, it is help-ing the American imperialist Truman." Finally, on September 21: "Speak-ing of the problems of this essay, the words 'feeble minded and ignorant' will suffice; at its base, it violates the rules set down for literary workers."[54] From Yang's position, performing unrevised or lightly revised originals was tantamount to subversive action taken against the regime. The poten-tial political stakes of the Ai/Yang debate were high: Yang was not simply questioning Ai Qing's artistic points of view, but his very commitment to the socialist project, as seen through his opinions on reforming literature.

The day after the publication of Yang Shaoxuan's rebuttal to Ai Qing, Ma Shaobo—who had written of the mythology and superstition problem the year prior—waded into the fray, responding specifically to the Yang/Ai fracas, as well as the problems of revising the repertoire more broadly. In his November *People's Daily* piece, he covered much the same ground as he had the year before: making distinctions between "mythology" and "superstition" was critical. He complained that people were confused "to the point that some people incorrectly believe that 'if it has a speaking spirit' [*you shen shuohua*] then it is 'mythology' [*shenhua*]."[55] He noted two specific problems with the trend of revising traditional scripts, largely echoing Ai Qing's complaints. The first was forcing mythological subjects to speak to obviously contemporary problems and political situations. Giving several examples, he pointed to one Shanghainese version that enhanced the Cowherd and Weaving Girl's devotion to work so that it resembled "the patriotic pledge." In this version, the lovers met only once yearly of their "own volition"—a very different situation than the two being kept apart forcibly, as in the original, which was often read as a critique of the "feudal" marriage system. Ostensibly designed to "intensify" audience member's patriotism and desire to aid in the "Resist America and Support Korea" campaign, Ma suggested that such changes instead both damaged a treasured Chinese mythological tradition and distorted "the reality of struggles"—that is, the issue of free love in feudal society.[56]

However, just like Ai, he criticized those scripts that seemed mostly unaltered. Using the example of a revised version called *Lovers on the Milky Way* (*Tianhe pei*), written by Wu Zuguang, he complained the play left in "the vulgar bits," and also managed to weaken the plot—having the overall effect of forgetting the "resisting spirit" of the original. Just as overly politicized versions could be damaging, so too could these types of uncritical revisions be dangerous for ideologically solid plays.[57] His general recommendations remained the same as those he and others had given the year before: delete the superstitious bits that "encouraged fatalism," and let the sections that encouraged resistance to oppression remain intact. He gives the example of *Liang Shanbo and Zhu Yingtai*, where the two young lovers, their passion and devotion for each other thwarted by an arranged marriage, turn into butterflies upon their untimely deaths.[58] "This is mythology, not superstition," Ma declared. Liang and Zhu represented resistance to the norms of the old society, and such plays were a "radiant achievement of national art, and should not be looked upon as superstition."[59] He flatly stated that Yang Shaoxuan's tack of attempting to use such literary treasures to reflect contemporary events was improper.

What seems to go largely unacknowledged in these discussions is the tremendous difficulty of finding the perfect middle ground: cultural workers were struggling with competing demands that would be nearly impossible to execute perfectly. Moreover, they did so in a political climate and framework that placed certain kinds of artistic production at the pinnacle. Ma Shaobo and Ai Qing may have advocated for a gentle touch on the classics, but could anyone actually forget some of Mao's more strident calls at the Yan'an Forum? Of course, in print, Ma and many others expressed the point of view that, after "liberation," artists enjoyed more freedom than ever before. In contrast to the Republican period, wherein writers like Lu Xun and Guo Moruo were forced to use historical themes to speak to the present in order to avoid censorship and oppression, there was "ample freedom of speech" in 1951. Artists, that is, did not have to resort to such methods to express their opinions—or so Ma claimed.[60]

For poor Yang Shaoxuan, the dressing down on the pages of *People's Daily* did not end with Ma's critique. Ai Qing offered a cutting reply on November 12, nine days after Yang's letters had been published.[61] Criticizing not only Yang's changes, but his literary talent and ability to string a plot together, Ai—with Ma Shaobo and *People's Daily* on his side—thoroughly trounced Yang in this particular literary game. Ai insisted the issue had nothing to do with literary works of the masses. The problem was the attitude of one man toward his responsibilities of safeguarding China's national dramatic heritage, his methods of creation, and his attitudes regarding literary criticism. Ai minced no words about his target—Yang Shaoxuan—and the stakes of theatre reform more broadly: "We are by no means expressing an opinion on the agenda of a certain primary school's parent-teacher association meeting, nor on a workers' amateur theatre troupe production—we are putting forth a point of view on the type of specialists' work like [that of] Comrade Yang Shaoxuan."[62] He airily dismissed Yang's accusations, stating that he (and others like him) were simply advocating for a sensible approach to sorting through China's literary treasures. Ai pointed to the artistic deficiencies of Yang's work, such as the internal inconsistencies of the script, particularly those related to "superstitions," roundly deriding Yang for preposterous leaps in logic and confusing plot developments. The reasons for this, at least in Ai's view, were clear: "Because this work was knocked together, it of course is full of contradictions." That is, Yang tried so hard to avoid "superstitious" elements that he wound up creating a plot that made little sense. Trying to do too much, or avoid too many things, the work ultimately failed for Ai because it wound up doing nothing at all.[63] And just as bad, if not worse, than Yang's literary failings was his inability to take criticism with grace. Criticisms and self-criticisms were necessary parts of revolution, Ai opined. Thus, what had started as a discussion on the appropriateness of plot revisions ended with a warning about proper behavior for revolutionaries:

> If one resembles Comrade Yang Shaoxuan, who on account of some people pointing out the flaws and deficiencies of his work, immediately stamps his feet in a rage—to the point of developing an uncontrollable appearance—and stands out for his unparalleled confusion, agitation, and indignation; in point of fact, [one has] already started to lose the most basic quality of a revolutionary. I do hope Comrade Yang Shaoxuan will promptly forbear against this.

Wisely, Yang did not engage in any more repartee on the subject. Still, despite the (perhaps unwarranted) vitriol directed at Yang Shaoxuan, one can almost hear the other questions that underpin the somewhat anxious discussion about mishandling and misinterpreting folk tales. If such stories were forced off popular stages (or changed to be nearly unrecognizable, and in less than artistically sound manners), what about more elite literary products, such as the great dramas of Tang Xianzu? The stories of Pu Songling? What of all of the great Chinese literary achievements that had occurred before 1911 or 1949: Li Bai and Du Fu, Li Qingzhao and Xin Qiji? From the earliest days of the PRC, it seems the danger of a "slippery slope" was, at the very least, in the minds of many cultural workers. But for many others, questions of how to appropriately remake traditional culture in order to resonate with the masses and the present—just as they had been asked to do, in many cases—were clearly just as serious, and potentially anxiety-inducing.

Challenges of Managing the Theatre World: The Shanghainese Example

It was not simply dramatists and critics who displayed concern over the unsettled cultural realm of the early years of the PRC. Artists—who bore

the brunt of the changes—saw, in many cases, a radical shift in their livelihood, from both reorganization and dictates on what should be put on
stages alike. There is no doubt that the confusion and vague statements of
the early 1950s had a severe impact on troupes and the traditional repertoire. As evidenced by the rush to ban plays en masse, simply announcing
three types of plots that were inappropriate, such as those that promulgated superstition, left the door open for wildly different interpretations.
The attempt at giving regional and local governments a certain amount
of latitude resulted in repertoires stripped of their plays and troupes
unable to make a living. Documents from Shanghai illustrate the very real
impact upper-level decisions and, in some cases, indecision had on grassroots troupes and artists. Although the debates between cultural workers
like Ai Qing and Yang Shaoxuan on the pages of *People's Daily* might, at
first blush, appear to be far removed from the day-to-day reality of theatre troupes attempting to make a living, the debates themselves reveal
the fissures even among those members of the "state-supported cultural
apparatus"—fissures that were reflected in the response of theatre artists
attempting to navigate often contradictory regulations.

Despite the emphasis from some quarters on developing drama on
contemporary themes, traditional subjects remained by far the most popular fare for most theatre troupes in Shanghai. Table 1 lists the total plays
performed—and tallied by the state—in Shanghai between 1950 and 1953.
As evidenced by the numbers, traditional subjects or new plays on historical themes made up the lion's share of performed plays throughout
the period. The statistics make clear that there was a sharp drop in the
number of plays performed in 1953, most likely due to the same confusion
and anxiety about "proper" repertoire that swept the rest of the country,
as well as a contraction in the number of troupes as the theatre world was
reorganized.[64] Even so, the general percentage of repertory that was made
up of traditional plays remained consistent.

The confusing climate of the early 1950s—particularly the Ministry of
Culture–promulgated bans—obviously had a chilling effect on the number of plays performed even in Shanghai, which seems not to have been
subject to the extensive bans or capricious cultural policy of other areas
(Xia Yan commented in 1950 that in a year's worth of work, Shanghai had
not banned even one play).[65] At the same time, the maxim that "There's no
need to read [the ads] when you open a newspaper, for there is nothing
but *Liang Shanbo and Zhu Yingtai*, *The West Chamber* [*Xixiang ji*], or *The*

Legend of White Snake" is clearly a vast overstatement, particularly outside the nadir of plays performed in 1952, 1953, and 1954.[66] The rebound of 1955 more or less continued until 1963. Even accounting for the multiple versions of plays across various styles, there was still a relatively diverse body of plays being performed.[67]

With that said, the drop in plays performed after 1951 is quite striking. Table 2 tallies the number of plays performed by two of the major Peking opera troupes in Shanghai in the first five years of the PRC, a pattern replicated with other troupes and other styles, as well.[68] Although some of the shifts could be explained by the instability of the artistic world after 1949—the Shanghai Culture Bureau statistics show new troupes being created, existing troupes merging or being renamed, and troupes disappearing from the record—the extreme drop in plays performed in 1952 is likely due to the same reasons seen in other areas, namely anxiety produced by vague and conflicting policy.

However, this alarming drop shows the relationship between elite and grassroots culture on two levels: obviously, those responsible for actually managing and performing repertoires were impacted by directives and discussions happening at the highest echelon of the cultural apparatus. But this was not simply a one-way street, and the stifling effect of regulations was noted with alarm by critics, cultural workers, and the bureaucracy alike. What followed the early years of drama reform in the PRC—the debates, discussions, and policies that emerged in the period after 1952—was in large part a reaction to this early blunder. Senior cultural workers found the trend of lower-level officials laying waste to the theatre landscape distressing, and one can imagine what artists felt as they watched their livelihood slip away. The next few years would see attempts to mitigate this early damage; and yet, in a pattern to be repeated over and over, swiftly changing regulations would leave artists and cultural workers struggling to find footing on shifting ideological and artistic ground.

Table 2. Number of Plays Performed by Major Shanghai Peking Opera Troupes

	1949	1950	1951	1952	1953
Zhongguo daxiyuan	103	115	110	17	30
Tianchan	96	139	109	64	30

Source: SMA B172-4-917

Conclusion

In many respects, the tone for the next decade and a half was set by 1951. The separation between what the Ministry of Culture and senior cultural workers ostensibly wished to see, and what was actually imposed on troupes by regional or local authorities, continued. At the same time, the surface of the elite discussions is important and revealing: participants were not simply lobbing ideological grenades at one another, but had a genuine interest in hashing out the future of traditional scripts and literary culture in socialist China, particularly in regard to how far reform could be pushed. Policies were often vague and open to interpretation, which allowed room both for those who wished to see radical changes to the repertoire and those who wanted to see traditional drama "preserved"—albeit with some modifications. This vagueness also created more problems, perhaps, than it solved, for both artists and dramatists alike. Yang Shaoxuan, for instance, seems to have been approaching his revisions to *The Cowherd and the Weaving Maid* in good faith and as an attempt to live up to the dictates on art and literature that dated back to the Yan'an days, yet was thoroughly dressed down by fellow veteran cultural workers *and* the editors of the *People's Daily* alike. Ultimately, this tension was never resolved satisfactorily; in some respects, it's astonishing that writers and artists continued to stretch themselves as much as they did over the next decade.

The early discussion on mythology versus superstition trickled down to debates over the suitability of ghosts and other potentially unsuitable subject matter. Here again, the sheer vagueness of policies left room for cultural workers to maneuver. The initial mishandling of repertoire questions gave officials, artists, and critics a glimpse of what was to come if these issues were not handled promptly and carefully, and it was likely one cause for the lively defense of traditional subjects over the next ten years. The next chapter will explore the continuing efforts to fix the problems created by the early attempts at reforming the repertoire, as well as the beginning of the debate over ghosts, a continuation of the superstition/mythology discussion that came to the fore in the first years of the PRC. It was a debate that, by its zenith, would have serious consequences not only for the theatre world, but for China as a whole.

CHAPTER 2

Wandering West Lake

*Ma Jianling, Ghost Opera, and Discourses of
Mythology and Superstition*

Although the story of Ma Jianling's 1953 foray into ghost opera has gar-
nered little attention, it was this adaptation of the Ming drama *Story of
Red Plums* that attracted notice from cultural critics throughout the 1950s
and early 1960s. For some, it was a positive revision of a dusty, old, and
inappropriate script so that it could be staged without hesitation, even in a
new, communist China. For many, however, it was a shocking example of
what could happen when socialist ideals for literature and art were applied
wholesale to beloved old dramas. Ma's *qinqiang* adaptation, called *Wandering West Lake*, is perhaps the most important adapted ghost play of the
1950s; it certainly attracted the most attention. The play would be trotted
out for years as the example par excellence of how not to revise imperial-
era dramas for a new age. Even so, the discussion about Ma's ghostless
ghost play, and the issue of supernatural themes more broadly, reveals
much about the tensions inherent in the cultural and political world of
the 1950s PRC. It also reflects on the ways in which cultural workers tried
to forge a new path in socialist China. Ma Jianling's attempt to reform
ghost opera speaks to the challenges faced by veteran writers, but also
the creative and experimental ways in which they approached the Chinese literary canon—particularly in a period of changing and often vague
directives.

Had Ma's play premiered a few years earlier, it might have found more
favor in a heady climate that saw the first attempts at strongly regulating drama—although, considering the debate over *The Cowherd and the
Weaving Maid*, perhaps not. But by 1954, the point at which Ma's play
received attention from drama critics writing in influential journals like
Literature and Art News (*Wenyi bao*) and *Play Monthly* (*Juben*), the politi-

cal and cultural milieus had seemingly become ever more receptive to traditional drama just as it was, likely in response to the deleterious outcomes of earlier attempts at reform of repertoires and troupes all over China. By 1956, even the Ministry of Culture would be putting an explicit stamp of approval on ghost plays and many of the plays banned between 1950 and 1952. Yet the furor over *Wandering West Lake* also reveals that while major political campaigns, such as the Hundred Flowers Movement, may have helped continue discussion, open and critical debate on the issue of traditional drama was by no means sparked by it. Furthermore, the discussions over *West Lake* reveal the continuing attempts to determine what constituted key parts of the Chinese literary canon. Did a ghost play *need* a ghost? How far could literature based on imperial-era originals be pushed in pursuit of modern ideals?

Furthermore, in the face of campaigns intended to eradicate "superstition" and encourage "scientific thinking" among the masses in the mid-1950s, cultural workers concerned with China's literary heritage had a vested interest in quickly creating a safe space for ghosts, gods, and other fantastical imaginings to exist. Ma's ghostless ghost play, then, provided the perfect opportunity for comparison and extended discussion. Just as Ma tried getting rid of things that "propagated superstition"—in this case, the ghost Li Huiniang—many other writers were bent on proving that ghosts were not only *not* superstitious, but useful teaching tools for reaching the masses. Many key cultural workers argued that the "resisting spirit" of literary ghosts and the lessons about feudal society contained in old plays were valuable, and valid. Building on the debates of the first years of the PRC, which saw Ma Shaobo and others defending the difference between "superstition" and "mythology," many argued for the continued inclusion of Chinese ghosts as they were.

Superstition in Theatre and Grassroots Culture

The criticisms of Ma's revision hint at the emotions that were aroused when culture, tradition, science, and socialism met. Sigrid Schmalzer has described the popularization of scientific thought in the socialist period, particularly highlighting the tensions between encouraging "mass science" and the view that painted the masses as essentially backwards and "superstitious" as a rule.[1] As she notes, "science dissemination in China was premised on the notion that the people were hampered by superstition," which allowed for attacks on popular culture that existed outside of the state apparatus.[2] But what to do with popular culture that was very much enmeshed in the bureaucracy? The obvious tension between "backwards peasants" and stamping out popular beliefs is not so neatly replicated in the theatre world of the 1950s.[3] But the defense of ghost plays seems to be very much bound up within these larger discussions, with many cultural workers preemptively fending off any potential criticisms of these ghosts as "superstitious" things. Performing theatrical ghosts for the masses was not at all like burning paper offerings, or so many believed.

It was not simply the literati who denied significant connections between theatre and superstition, and even writing aimed at rendering superstitious customs understandable in modern, scientific ways paid little attention to the literary world. Take the 1956 pamphlet *Are There Ghosts or Not?*, which is fairly representative of the type of tract aimed at educating the masses about the true (scientific) nature of many "mysterious" occurrences, and discouraging belief in old, superstitious customs.[4] The story is a dialogue between an educated teacher and the head of a pleasant, but backwards, peasant household, on the subject of ghosts. The peasant had heretofore kept two rooms of the house closed off due to the presence of a ghost of a former occupant who had committed suicide. That occupant also happened to be the second wife of a wealthy man, the current peasant having been given the house during land reform; thus, we have not only a discussion of the problems of superstition, but a further illustration of the ills of the old society and the glories of socialism, particularly insofar as the status of women was concerned. Upon hearing this, the teacher and the peasant have a lengthy chat about the origins of ghosts, the futility of burning paper offerings to ancestors, and the oppressive nature of superstitious customs.

The peasant is a miraculously quick study, and in the course of a ten-minute conversation, becomes a new convert to modern modes of thinking, ready to go preach the wonders of this scientific gospel. The teacher exhorts him to pay particular attention to mothers who use stories of ghosts and monsters to frighten their children into behaving, "because many superstitious thoughts are thus disseminated to children."[5] Discouraging the use of supernatural subjects to frighten people is equivalent to playwrights deleting "fearsome" scenes of the underworld in dramas, a typical method (one critics and cultural workers generally agreed upon) of dealing with potential "superstitions" in drama. However, the overwhelming emphasis of the tract is on the practices that Schmalzer defines as "popular culture," particularly those with a religious dimension, such as burning paper offerings. Many books of this type were published in the mid-1950s, and they focus on this kind of culture. Literature is simply not a bone of contention; the "superstition" that scientists concerned themselves with was found in homes and among the masses, not in literary works or on stages (see figure 2).

"Superstitious" *practices* were the primary concern throughout much of the high socialist period, particularly as they were often seen by officials to be subversive acts against the state. For instance, in exploring the phenomenon of pilgrimages in search of "holy water" in the 1950s and 1960s, Steven Smith notes that while the CCP had practical issues with the unsanctioned movement of people, the "obsessive concern" was that these miraculous events were "manufactured by enemies of the regime . . . in order to sow confusion and undermine public order."[6] The enemies in question were "redemptive societies" (*huidaomen*), a term describing secret sects with "occult and sometimes millenarian beliefs" that the CCP believed had collaborated with the Japanese and strongly backed the GMD during the civil war.[7] Between 1950 and 1954, "withdrawal from the sects" campaigns were carried out, with punishments of life in prison or execution for people who used such societies for "counterrevolutionary" purposes.[8] Whatever faults supernatural literary subjects were seen to have, between 1949 and 1963, "undermining public order," being "counterrevolutionary," and actively subverting the state were not among them. Furthermore, critics and cultural workers argued that theatrical ghosts actively *supported* state goals by teaching audiences how to be brave in the face of great evil. When combined with the broad popularity of traditional drama, ghosts and other supernatural subjects had the potential to reach and teach the masses, quite unlike popular superstitious practices.

And yet the mere existence of so many essays concerned with marking ghost opera as safe indicates that cultural workers did worry about the status of these works. These plays existed both inside and outside of popular culture, and this perhaps explains the sometimes contradictory and confused way in which writers discussed them. Belief in ghosts could be symbols of the superstitious, unscientific backwardness of the Chinese masses; but literary ghosts could also be important contributors to the "realism" of a literary product, as critics would argue in the case of Ma Jianling's *Wandering West Lake*. And even among those entrenched in the "state-supported cultural apparatus," there was not one simple unified front: Ma Jianling could hardly be more different in approach from those who argued against his revisions.

Fig. 2. Four popular science pamphlets from the mid-1950s debunking superstition. Clockwise from upper left: *Daodi youmeiyou guishen* [Are there supernatural beings or not] (Beijing: Jiefangjun bao chubanshe, 1959); Jilin sheng kexuezhishu puji, ed., *Zhen you shengui ma?* [Are there really gods and ghosts?] (Changchun: Jilin renmin chubanshe, 1956); Chen Cisheng, *You meiyou gui?* [Are there ghosts or not?] (Nanjing: Jiangsu renmin chubanshe, 1956); Guangdong sheng kexuezhishu puji xiehui, ed., *Tan "shen" jiang "gui"* [Talking of "spirits" and speaking of "ghosts"] (Guangdong: Guandong renmin chubanshe, 1958).

Ma Jianling and the Uses of Qinqiang

Ma Jianling was born in 1907, into what seems to have been an educated, if unremarkable and nonelite, family, from Mizhi County, north Shaanxi.[9] From a young age, he displayed an interest in theatre and music, picking up proficiency in several instruments. It is this love of music and theatre, not any sort of elite intellectual pursuits, that pervades his biographies. Despite following his older brother to Peking University in 1930, his own writing activities do not appear to have ever been part of the elite literary milieu.[10] However, he was certainly steeped in revolutionary culture from a relatively young age. His older brother, Ma Yuncheng, joined the CCP in 1925 (Ma would join three years later, in 1928), becoming the party secretary of Yulin, Shaanxi, and later taking up teaching posts in Shanxi and Shaanxi Provinces. In 1935, while working within the party's military commission for Beijing, Yuncheng was reported to GMD authorities and executed.[11] One imagines this must have had something of an impact on the twenty-six-year-old Jianling, who by that time had gone to Hebei to teach and run a theatre troupe.

In 1936, he—like many other cultural workers—moved to Yan'an. This was the start of his theatrical prominence: he threw himself into the life of teaching, directing, and writing for the "Native Place troupe" (Xiangtu jutuan) at the Yan'an Normal School. From here, he joined forces with the poet Ke Zhongping in 1938, and established the influential Shaan-Gan-Ning Masses Troupe (Minzhong jutuan) in Yan'an.[12] The troupe became famous for its new productions of dramas on contemporary themes.[13] This combination of veteran cultural worker and playwright passionate about local forms proved fruitful and long-lived. The Ke-Ma collaboration was, in the words of Ellen Judd, "virtually alone in its deep involvement in the local rural culture."[14] Although Ke hailed from Yunnan, Ma's upbringing and early interest in Shaanxi culture shined through. But he did not simply attempt to bring new revolutionary themes to native Shaanxi forms, in Shaanxi dialects. Instead, in one of his earliest plays, *Inspecting Road Passes (Cha lutiao)*, he wrote in a "generalized" dialect suitable for many areas in north China.[15] In contrast to many writers streaming to Yan'an from the cities, bearing their own preferred forms and language—namely, the sort of things current in elite literary circles—Ma and Ke worked hard to create plays that would have broad appeal.

In applying revolutionary themes to popular drama, Ma's lack of literary credentials, at least where leftist societies were concerned, probably stood him in good stead. The disconnect between the cultural elite who flocked to Yan'an and the masses they tried to serve was illustrated by their late 1930s emphasis on poetry as a vehicle.[16] In contrast to writers starry-eyed over foreign imports, Ma's attraction to and talent for reworking local forms immediately gave him better tools to work with. He could apply revolutionary themes to popular, familiar theatre. Consider his 1938 spoken language drama *National Spirit* (*Guohun*). Like most of his plays of this period, it took up a very real subject: the war with Japan. Mao saw a performance at the Military and Political University of Resistance Against the Japanese, and said to Ma after the performance, "You have quite an achievement in the writing of this play, and if you change it to *qinqiang*, its utility will be even greater."[17] Ma duly followed Mao's urgings, and the reset play was called *The Spirit of China* (*Zhongguo hun*).

Ma and Ke's work constituted one of the most important pre-1949 efforts at harnessing popular drama for party goals, and Ma was a respected playwright, particularly talented with local Shaanxi forms. However, following the CCP's ascension to power in 1949, his focus shifted from the revolutionary- and contemporary-themed dramas that had been a hallmark of his pre-1949 works to adapted traditional dramas. Although later historians have generally viewed his activities in reforming drama positively, Ma's attempt at reforming the Ming *Story of Red Plums* did not have such a response from literary critics of his own time.[18] However, his turn toward traditional theatre was well in line with his earlier literary activities, and the same spirit of making works appropriate to the masses, respecting local theatrical traditions, and producing works aligned with socialist literary goals pervades his post-1949 work.

As illustrated in the previous chapter, the reform of drama was a concern of the CCP from the days of Yan'an and beyond, particularly in the creation of new, revolutionary-themed works using older forms. Indeed, Ma's own history highlights the importance attached to producing new drama for the masses. Ma displayed a devotion to making art that could serve the people. He agreed that old dramatic forms were not ideal. But he also argued that old forms had many fine qualities that reflected the lives of average people, and asked "Are our Chinese masses all simpletons that they would all foolishly love this old theatre? To reject the bad, adapt the good, then refine and give it substance, in order to express a new progressive content, is both completely possible and absolutely necessary."[19]

Of course, ostensibly *all* reformed drama of the PRC was aimed at transforming musty forms into healthy, progressive works. But in many respects, the debates that played out on the pages of top literary journals and the scripts that appeared in the same places were written by literary elites for literary elites. In language, references, and historical descriptions, the elite playwrights (or academics-turned-playwrights) were often writing plays aimed at one another. Ma Jianling, on the other hand, maintained his commitment to creating accessible, politically appropriate drama for the masses.

A Ghost Play sans Ghost: Wandering West Lake

Ma's *Wandering West Lake* marked an important point in the debate on reforming traditional theatre—particularly plays with potentially troublesome subject matter—for socialist stages. The play, first published in 1953, proved a lasting example of the limits of drama reform, for while troupes and crowds apparently seized upon it with some enthusiasm, many critics and other cultural elites reacted with horror to Ma's revisions. The old divides first seen in Yan'an, between literary elites who were not entirely convinced they wanted to give up their own preferences and traditions and cultural workers like Ma who embraced both forms and content designed to promulgate socialism to the masses, came to the fore yet again. However, *Wandering West Lake* speaks to the period of its creation, as well as the experimentation cultural workers undertook in an attempt to navigate a cultural climate that was anything but stable.

Ma's play contained many of the important elements and characters of the traditional *Red Plum* derivatives: there was Jia Sidao, the cruel prime minister of the southern Song dynasty, and his concubine Li Huiniang. The setting was West Lake in Hangzhou, where Jia presided over pleasurable diversions while the country was in the midst of crisis. Pei Yu appeared yet again as an upstanding young scholar, bristling at Jia's cruelty and incompetence. The playwright also made a number of revisions that were expected: removing representations of hell, for example, was a typical measure used to reduce the "superstitious" elements of drama. This was precisely the sort of change to traditional plays that Ma Shaobo and others had noted as necessary a few years before. Indeed, the majority of Ma's changes were quite typical. For instance, he excised the subplot that involved Lu Zhaorong, a (living) love interest of Pei Yu's in the original. This was not at all radical, as the story of Li Huiniang has generally proved more compelling for authors and audiences.

However, Ma put several major twists on the original play: first, by giving Li Huiniang and Pei Yu a backstory, and then by excising Li Huiniang's death at the hands of Jia Sidao. The former is immediately clear from the opening lines of the play. Fingering a jade belt ornament, Pei Yu sings not of cruelty and injustice perpetrated on the people by Jia and his henchmen, but of his childhood love: "Huiniang, Li Huiniang!" The twenty-year-old student reminisces on how he "implored" his parents to allow a betrothal between the childhood friends, who had already pledged their love with a painted fan and the aforementioned piece of jade. But before the betrothal could be made official, the evil Jia Sidao used his power as prime minister to make Huiniang his concubine. In this case, the Pei-Jia vendetta is much more personal than in the original. Pei Yu's anger is not aroused by the prime minister's callous, incompetent handling of the common people, as in Zhou Chaojun's version, but by Li Huiniang being "stolen" by Jia Sidao. Ma Jianling's invention of a childhood history and marriage-to-be was a radical revision that fundamentally altered the very heart of the play.[20] However, he went even beyond trimming unsuitable parts and inventing backstories for the main characters. Key to the original *Red Plum* was the unjust slaying of Li Huiniang and her subsequent return as a ghost. Indeed, out of the thirty-four acts of Zhou's play, Li Huiniang spends thirty of them dead.[21] But Ma took the point of view that theatrical ghosts were manifestations of superstition, and ought to be removed. And so, Ma Jianling created a rather unusual product: a ghostless ghost play.

As it turned out, removing the apparition from the play could not be accomplished neatly. Ma's revision required the insertion of new characters—the most important of which was a sympathetic concubine of Jia Sidao's named Sun Ruiniang—who helped this complicated plot twist along.[22] Ruiniang offers to Jia Sidao that *she* will be responsible for poisoning Li Huiniang, who has enraged Jia by holding on to her love for Pei Yu (symbolized by the white fan she carries):

RUINIANG: If you want Huiniang dead, why must you resort to violence? . . . I am thinking that tonight I will ask her to my room, having prepared wine to entertain, my mouth will offer advice with fine words, and to the wine I will add poison, secretly she will die, is this not good? . . .

JIA: Supposing the slut isn't willing to drink the wine, how will you deal with it?

RUINIANG: If she is unwilling to drink, I shall notify the prime minis-

ter . . . [*her tone is disgusted*] and [they] will strangle her while she's
still alive! (27)

But instead of actually murdering the forlorn concubine, Ruiniang explains
to Huiniang that she, too, is a "pitiful person," brought to the prime minister's household under duress, and thus is in much the same situation as
Huiniang. She helps Huiniang play dead, showing off the "corpse" to the
retainers. But just as in the original, Pei Yu is also threatened by Jia Sidao;
without supernatural ghostly powers, how could Huiniang come to his
rescue? In Ma's telling, this required the help of a kindly peasant gardener,
a change of clothes, and Li Huiniang—still alive and well!—play-acting a
ghost to thoroughly frighten Jia and his underlings:

> RUINIANG: Sister! You can't go about dressed like that.
> HUINIANG: How should I dress?
> RUINIANG: You must put on white, wear white—during the day, do not
> dare make an appearance; in case of trouble, go out at night, avoid-
> ing people walking about—very few people will catch sight of you,
> they will think you not a real person, but will act just as they've seen
> a ghost!
>
> If sister will dress as a ghost today,
> Only then will bystanders not harbor suspicions;
> But we must quickly go to the back [of the compound],
> And dress her all in white. (42–43)

While cases of mistaken identities and costumes to fool bystanders
were important features in some imperial-era plays,[23] the change to a
fundamental—and familiar—part of *Red Plum Pavilion* nevertheless represented a major alteration to how the play had traditionally been presented. Li Huiniang's unjust murder and return as a ghost were key plot
points. The play still ended with a devastating fire in Jia Sidao's compound,
but the two living lovers were in this version able to escape, presumably to
live happily ever after.

Ma's revisions were clearly aimed at a much broader cross-section of
society than Meng Chao's later Kun version. *Qinqiang* was a popular style,
quite unlike Kun opera, which was generally popular only among elites.
In both form and content, it was well in line with socialist dictates on
art. Unlike many elite cultural workers, who professed a desire to pro-

mulgate literature for the masses, while at the same time writing exceedingly erudite and complicated essays, poems, and plays, Ma's script was an attempted execution of Mao's dictates on literature and art: serving the masses with ideologically healthy, progressive culture. Certainly, the Xibei People's Press, which published *Wandering West Lake* in book form, seemed to anticipate relatively broad appeal: the initial printing including 14,000 copies, 11,000 more than Meng Chao's script would receive nearly a decade later.

What drove Ma's revisions? In the introduction to the script in book form, the playwright unsurprisingly criticized the traditional tale for including fatalism and superstition. He further complained that many of the characters (including the hero Pei Yu) are frivolous loafers, and the masses were not represented. Ma's neat removal of Li Huiniang's death and ghost-self removed most of the superstitious elements in one move, and his additions fixed the myriad problems he saw with the original. But Ma, whether overtly or not, was also massaging this traditional tale to speak more strongly to concerns of the early 1950s. If the figures of ghostly women had often been an appealing one for a variety of reasons, there was now a new impetus for deploying these characters on stages: support for a showpiece of early legislation, the New Marriage Law.

One of the most important laws put into place in the first few years of the PRC was the New Marriage Law, promulgated in 1950.[24] Work on the law began in 1948, and between 1950 and 1953, a series of campaigns promoted the law; some estimates state that 70 percent of the Mainland was reached by some form of propaganda regarding it.[25] Neil J. Diamant has described it as "one of the most dramatic and far-reaching attempts by a state to reshape 'traditional' marriage and family structures," and it had enormous, though often unintended, consequences.[26] The New Marriage Law was a showpiece of the early years of the PRC, demonstrating the CCP's commitment to shedding China's oppressive past. It was the legal manifestation of decades of discussion surrounding the question of women, marriage, and the evils of "feudal society" in China. While many men, in Gail Hershatter's words, "resisted and blunted the effect" of the law, it did—at least on paper—ban some of the more troubling marriage customs, such as child betrothals, the selling of brides, and concubinage, as well as setting legal minimum ages for marriage and adding new processes for divorce.[27] As with many things in those early years, including the regulation of drama, implementation of the law was not particularly smooth. The potential ramifications of the New Marriage Law had serious implications for familial relations and social standing, and many male rural cadres reacted with "ambivalence or outright hostility."[28] The wide-ranging transformations the central leadership of the CCP imagined for all of Chinese society were not always welcomed warmly.[29]

The "woman question"—how to "liberate" Chinese women, ensuring economic, social, and gender equality—had been one of great importance to reformers throughout the late nineteenth and early twentieth centuries. As Antonia Finnane has noted, progressive May Fourth intellectuals "found in the person of the woman the most dramatic symbol of their own powerlessness."[30] So while many progressive and radical male intellectuals and cultural workers spoke often about the need to reform the family system and propagate gender equality, this was a project located in a strong patriarchal framework, with the body of "woman" acquiring strong metaphorical and symbolic power.[31]

Thus, the image of the downtrodden Chinese woman was a loaded image deployed to validate social policy by many people, including the CCP cultural apparatus. One famous example is the revolutionary drama *The White-Haired Girl* (*Baimao nü*), which tells the story of a rural girl forced into concubinage. Though she manages to escape to live in the mountains, her wretched existence turns her hair entirely white, and she is mistaken in the village for a ghost. (However, like many strange tales, the story has a happy ending.) While *The White-Haired Girl* is traditionally presented as inspired by an "authentic" folktale "discovered" during the Yan'an period, Max Bohnenkamp has argued that it was instead a carefully crafted, modern production designed to link the Communist revolution to women's liberation.[32] Still, *actual* Chinese women were often empowered by the use of cultural forms, such as singing, to provide "personal connection to state initiatives" such as the New Marriage Law, and to "help explain to [women] the significance of what they were doing," in Hershatter's words.[33] Likewise, many old plays and performance practices gained new readings with the introduction of the New Marriage Law, as Ma Jianling's revisions to the old story of *Red Plums* illustrates.

Much as the playwrights discussed in the previous chapter had attempted to make tales of the Cowherd and the Weaving Maid speak to the Korean War, Ma wanted to make *Red Plums* resonate even more strongly with the present. Though he does not mention the New Marriage Law by name, he emphasizes qualities that would have resonated with changes the law was to usher in. The original *Red Plums* was, of course, not entirely bad. He placed particular emphasis on the play's virtues of revealing "the evils of the feudal ruling class" and opposing the "feudal" marriage system.[34] He couched his explanation of some rather unorthodox plot changes, particularly the backstory of Li Huiniang and Pei Yu, as a way to strengthen the positive virtues of the play. In the original, the two have no prior connection; her admiring comment about the handsome young scholar rested entirely on a brief impression of him from a distance. In Ma's revisions, he invented a history for the two: Li Huiniang and Pei Yu were neighbors, and contracted to be married (this is symbolized by the gifts they give each other, and carry throughout the play: his jade belt ornament, her silk fan). The tragedy of Li Huiniang's situation was thus compounded, at least in the playwright's view. Not only was she forced into concubinage, but she was forced to give up her true love, a man she has known since childhood.

Thus, it appears that in addition to axing superstition from the play, Ma intended to make this story of a Song dynasty concubine serve contemporary social reform. Against the backdrop of legal changes related to marriage and gender relations, Ma's determination to "enhance the foundation of the love between Pei Yu and Li Huiniang," so as to better educate audiences on the wisdom of opposing the feudal marriage system, makes perfect sense.[35] His discussion of the play's creation also illustrates the system of drama reform, which was one of working groups, cultural departments, and a fair bit of bureaucratic management. This project was not a solitary one: the Northwest department of culture had convened a group of drama workers to select popular plays—including Wandering West Lake—to revise. After he had revised the script, performers from the Xibei theatre research unit helped prepare it for the stage. Such management should be little surprise: Ma was one of the most prominent authors working with native Shaanxi forms, truly skilled in using qinqiang to express contemporary political lessons. His dramas may have been entertaining, but they were also highly didactic. The medium could not have been better: public performances by opera troupes and other kinds of song and dance groups had long been a staple of political education, and one method many participants found enjoyable. It is not difficult to imagine Ma's Li Huiniang alongside The Legend of White Snake and other favored classics, all of which could be read as supporting new marriage customs.[36]

Ma Jianling seems to have set out with earnest aims, and no doubt believed strongly that removing ghosts from stages was an important component in combating superstitious beliefs among the masses. But his revisions raised important questions for many critics: Could a ghost play really be made "ghostless?" To what extent could—or should—traditional forms be remade? The original, and most of its derivations, hinge on Li Huiniang's death: it is a central plot point, key to the play across centuries and across styles. It could not simply be removed without impacting the rest of the play, and this is where Ma ran afoul of critics and artists.

"While It Has Its Good Points": The Critical Response to Wandering West Lake

Wandering West Lake's 1953 premiere straddles an unsettled period in Chinese drama, sandwiched between the first few years that saw the national bans of twenty-six plays and the 1956 Ministry of Culture pronouncements that they would "relax the limitations" on traditional drama, including ghost plays.[37] But even prior to the official government pronouncements that put a stamp of approval (or at least, not outright disapproval) on ghost opera, some drama critics and artists made known their displeasure with revised versions like Ma's play. The argument over ghost plays was built upon the foundation laid by Ma Shaobo and others, which argued for a clear separation between "superstition" and "mythology" in the earliest days of the PRC. Just as Ma Shaobo had been alarmed by the rampant bans, the fact that a ghostless ghost play was apparently making inroads among many troupes over a reasonably wide area did not sit well with those who wanted to see traditional drama maintained. Probably owing to Ma Jianling's high profile, critics took notice of the revisions. The famous line from White Haired Girl that "old society turned people into ghosts, and the new society turns ghosts into people" took on alarming connotations when it came to the classical canon. In the hands of someone like Ma Jianling, who had impeccable revolutionary and dramatic credentials, it meant making serious changes that many writers found completely unacceptable.

The discontent many critics expressed over Ma's revisions was not quickly forgotten, as journals like Theatre Report, Play Monthly, and Literature and Art News continued to run articles discussing the play's failings years after its premier. While it is difficult to ascertain exactly how popular or widely performed the play was, the discussion indicates that it was more than a simple flash in the pan. According to one 1955 essay, Ma's revised version was performed widely not only by qinqiang troupes but also by Shanxi opera, Puzhou opera (a southern Shanxi form), Peking opera, and Hebei opera troupes, among others.[38] The criticism of *Wandering West Lake* reveals a divide between elite cultural workers, such as those associated with high-level publications, and those operating primarily in a local or provincial context. This is a divide that is mirrored by the political situation, with the divide between the Ministry of Culture and lower-level culture bureaus becoming ever clearer throughout 1954 and 1955.

Early in 1954, the editors of *Literature and Art News* wrote a general overview of responses to *Wandering West Lake*. Characterizing the split opinions of Xi'an audiences as those who thought the revision was "getting rid of the dregs of feudalism" on one hand, and people who "opposed [Ma's] method of adaptation" on the other, it fell generally on the side of the latter.[39] This was not simply a discussion about a single play, but a referendum on an entire theatrical legacy. The fundamental problem underpinning the debate was differentiating between mythology and superstition; despite the early 1950s pleas of intellectuals like Ma Shaobo, the matter had hardly been settled. While noting several positive reviews in Shaanxi papers—which praised Ma for "conforming with the wishes of today's people"—there is little doubt that the *Literature and Art News* writers sympathized with the viewers and performers who believed ghost plays did *not* necessarily constitute superstition. There were "incorrect" parts, which Ma rightly revised, but the ghost in the ghost play was an integral plot point, and the reason for the power of the story.[40]

The editors selected as representative of the anti–*Wandering West Lake* viewpoints two cadres, Li Guang of the Shaanxi Broadcasting Network and Song Wenyan of the Xibei Administrative Commission. While they both concurred with Ma that there were problematic aspects of the original play, they felt his revisions were egregious examples of "characterizations full of loopholes," a script guilty of "preserving ahistorical, unrealistic mistakes, and seriously damaging a theatrical legacy."[41] Clearly, more was at stake than one play: the comments indicate that cultural workers feared traditional culture would sustain a serious blow if *West Lake* and other revisions like it were allowed to spread through the repertoire. They further castigated Ma for conflating superstition and ghost opera, and questioned his assertion that *Wandering West Lake* was banned under the GMD owing to its "superstitious" nature (the implication being that if the play were banned, it would have been banned on account of stirring up antigovernment feelings toward the Nationalists). Although the piece ended on a generally positive note—exhorting those involved in the excavation, adaptation, and preservation of China's literary gems to take care with their work—other contributors to *Literature and Art News* would not be quite so tempered in their remarks.

Zhang Zhen, who was and would remain a steadfast defender of ghost operas, both adapted and not, wrote another highly critical piece for the journal in late 1954. A prominent drama critic and writer, he was involved in elite groups from his youth, and would continue to circulate in the highest of cultural circles.[42] Zhang, like the quoted writers in *Literature and Art News*, took Ma to task for what he saw as revisions that weakened the realism of the play. The old classics, he argued, were exemplars of combining "romanticism and realism," which contributed to the very power of those works to transmit ideas of struggle.[43] This, he said, had been lost in the revisions, primarily through a weakening of the characters. However, Zhang's purpose was not simply to criticize what he viewed as an unsophisticated reworking; it was to criticize the very ideas underlying Ma's work. In particular, he took umbrage with the thought that there was a connection between seeing theatrical ghosts and popular belief that ghosts existed in the world. The critic bluntly stated that this was a misunderstanding of the role of fantasy and symbolism in art. Zhang went one step further than many critics, declaring that the mere idea that ghost plays were supporting superstitious beliefs was ridiculous: "Some people say that, at the very least, putting ghosts on stages enables the masses to believe that there are ghosts. Actually, if a person truly believes in supernatural beings, even if he doesn't see plays that have [them], he's *still* going to believe in them" (emphasis mine).[44] This problematic—the extent to which audiences were affected by what they were seeing onstage—was never sufficiently resolved, at least not until 1963. In that year, when ghost plays were finally banned, one justification by the Ministry of Culture was an insufficient level of ideological education and rational thinking on the part of most Chinese theatregoers. That is, they were simply too naïve, too unsophisticated, and too impressionable to be allowed access to potentially dangerous material like ghost opera, which could encourage belief in superstitions. This was a position that many critics throughout the 1950s and 1960s—including well after the ban—continued to oppose.

Zhang Zhen's essay joined others in cordoning off a celebrated section of Chinese culture, literature with potentially superstitious elements. A critical roundup that appeared in a 1955 issue of the influential journal *Play Monthly* made subtler critiques than Zhang's of the project of ridding ghosts from Chinese stages. But both just as Zhang Zhen had argued the year before, in the view of the critics and performers the author of the

Play Monthly piece surveyed, Ma Jianling's changes damaged the utility of the original. A Shanxi opera troupe member, for instance, complained that Ma's neat plot twist simply acquiesced to the wishes of the masses, and lessened the dramatic *and* didactic impact of the original.[45] In making revisions, Ma had fundamentally altered parts of the play that made it so emotionally powerful. One critic complained about the tempering of Li Huiniang's character: "Not only does [the revision] make Huiniang live, but she lives very well." It was much more difficult to grasp the essence of "oppression" that was important to justifying the original's continued maintenance. In short, Ma was being accused of having an ideologically less useful script than one written in the Ming dynasty.

In a pattern that would become quite familiar throughout the next decade, the critics stated that Ma was not being careful enough in making a distinction between "superstition" and "mythology." Righteous literary ghosts and subjects like them were not superstitious practices, but products of humans, and thus able to be staged. That is, he assumed that the "products of human imagination [found in drama]—gods, celestial spirits, buddhas, demons, fox spirits, and ghosts are all 'propagating superstition,'" which these critics strongly objected to.[46] The Tianjin drama critic Wu Tongbin flatly stated that Ma revised his drama "according to this incorrect point of view."[47] Wu, like many others before and after, held the opinion that *if* such "products of human imagination" were promoting struggle and illustrating the ills of feudal society, then they were emphatically *not* superstitious, and indeed could reflect the realities of oppression.

Ma Jianling may have been experimenting with what could be added and removed from a play with hundreds of years of history, but for many critics and artists, such experiments were ultimately a failure. In attempting to rid the original play of "superstition," these critics claimed Ma had made the play even more unbelievable. As one artist pointed out, while Ma tried to remove the ghost from the ghost play, his Li Huiniang still found herself dressed up as a ghost. Why is an actress dressed up as a ghost character more terrifying, or damaging, for audiences than an actress dressed up as a character dressed up as a ghost? If the claim was that it was less fearsome or frightening for audiences (because it was not "believable"), why then did Jia Sidao and his henchmen become frightened?[48] The implication was that if one believed that theatrical ghosts propagated superstition, surely characters masquerading as ghosts had the same effect.

Even the ideological underpinnings of some of the revisions were castigated, as critics pointed out that one of the foundations of *Red Plums*—Li

Huiniang's "love at first sight" reaction to Pei Yu—was an important critique of feudal society and marriage customs. Ma's contention that the Li-Pei love affair was lacking a foundation, thus the need to invent a backstory, was roundly derided. He must not have known, the critics opined, that in "feudal society," the idea of love at first sight *was* a form of resistance. Beyond the particulars of the love story, however, was the more unforgivable sin of making the characters dull. One critic noted that the new "West Lake" chapter—a key scene in the original that sets the stage for the tragedy to follow—consists entirely of "Pei Yu fingering his jade belt ornament [given to him by Li] and complaining tearfully, Li Huiniang holding her . . . fan [given to her by Pei] and complaining tearfully."[49]

Indeed, a comparison with Zhou Chaojun's Ming edition proves that in some cases late sixteenth-century drama could offer more biting social commentary—and less weeping—than modern revisions. Early in Zhou's play, Pei Yu and two friends are enjoying themselves at West Lake. After spotting elaborately painted pleasure boats, replete with beautiful women and musical accompaniment, one of Pei's companions comments that they ought to "withdraw quickly," since it is obviously the prime minister's party. The other student is indignant: "What kind of talk is that! West Lake belongs to everyone, if he can traverse the whole of it, why can't we? Get up on Broken Bridge," he orders his compatriots, intending to stand up to the corrupt minister.[50] Also importantly for the structure of the play, it is this defiant act on the part of students that allows Li Huiniang to catch sight of Pei Yu. She quietly remarks on his looks admiringly—"Oh, what a handsome youth! [*Ya, meizai yi shaonian ye!*]"—and it is for this spontaneous, innocent comment that she is murdered in the fourth act. Part of the injustice of Huiniang's death is that this murmured comment is so minor, Jia Sidao's outrage so outsized in comparison. That a woman could be brutally murdered for a one-off statement underscores the cruel nature of the prime minister.

In contrast, Ma's play begins with Pei Yu reminiscing on Huiniang, his childhood love, admiring the jade belt ornament that had been a gift from her. In the pivotal lake scene, Pei is once again accompanied by fellow students, one of whom yet again suggests it might be best to leave after spotting the prime minister's pleasure cruise. But this time, instead of Li Huiniang's reaction to a handsome stranger, she sees Pei Yu—just as he spots her—and says nothing. Instead, one of Pei Yu's companions, student Zhang, notes: "What a coincidence, very opportune—I never thought we'd run into Huiniang of all people."[51] Far from being a chance meeting of "love at first sight," it becomes almost a parody of youthful love and jealousy:

> ZHANG: Why, did you see how Huiniang was towards you?
> PEI: Oh, how exasperating—how annoying.
> ZHANG: What? What do you mean by that?
> PEI: You saw her silks and satins, her pearls and jade, arrayed in luxury—how could she remember me!
> ZHANG: Could you really not have seen her?
> PEI: I took one look and got angry, why look at her further?
> ZHANG: My god . . . what a person you are. I looked with my own eyes, her eyes were filled with tears, she gazed at you unendingly. . . .
> PEI: It might not be like that. (10–11)

Still, the brooding Pei agrees to follow Jia Sidao's boat. When the wayward students catch up with him, the silent, meaningful glances commence. Huiniang catches sight of Pei, and pulls out her white fan—a gift from him—"presses it to her chest, looks at the fan, looks at Pei, with limitless worry cries and says nothing"; Pei, meanwhile, looks at the fan and looks at this lover-turned-concubine, "with tearful eyes gazes upon them, and also with limitless concern, cannot open his mouth." The young scholar then states the obvious, apparently convinced: "Huiniang is too wretched!"[52] Although Ma may have reworked the plot to make it resonate more strongly with contemporary concerns about the "feudal" marriage system, he managed to remove not only the ghost but also the senseless tragedy from the original. No wonder Jia Sidao flies into a rage in Ma's version: not only is his party interrupted by students, at least one person involved has a deeply personal, romantic connection to one of his concubines.

Despite the minor concession of acknowledging what Ma "got right"—namely, getting rid of the scenes involving Yama, the underworld, and the slightly more lascivious points of the ghostly Li-Pei love affair, as well as trimming the plot of superfluous characters (all common features in revised dramas of the 1950s and 1960s)—there is no question that the critics were completely unimpressed with Ma's adaptation. The article ends on a damning note: "While the work of adapting *Wandering West Lake* has its good points, in speaking of the whole, it is . . . not good."[53] This criticism of Ma is striking on a number of levels, not least of which is the fact that the modern revision—by a noted author of contemporary drama on revolutionary themes—was compared unfavorably to the Ming original on an ideological level. But the critiques also exposed some of the anxiety these cultural workers must have felt in the face of attempts at remaking those works in a new, socialist image.

The criticism of Ma Jianling's ghostless ghost play illustrates that cultural production in the PRC was hardly a simple matter of "out with the old, in with the new." Despite popular campaigns aimed at stamping out superstitious beliefs, the cultural furor over *Wandering West Lake* should make us question the degree to which such campaigns crossed over into literary circles, and into more general ideas about cultural reform. Concern over "superstition," and the relationship between popular belief and popular culture, was not exclusive to the PRC; intellectuals had been fretting about the backwardness of Chinese culture and the Chinese people since the nineteenth century.[54] By the mid-1950s, however, many cultural workers argued that ghosts were not always symbols of China's backwardness; they could be useful tools to encourage and educate audiences, no matter how unsophisticated those audiences may have been.

The furor over *Wandering West Lake*, when read against antisuperstition campaigns, makes clear that there was no one set of categories that could be applied equally to cultural products, popular culture, social rituals, religion, and so on. There was in fact quite a lot of room to maneuver inside the bounds of what was considered appropriate for socialist society. This is not to say that the matter was settled; if anything, the pages and pages of ponderings on mythology and superstition, ghosts and gods, appropriate and inappropriate cultural forms, prove that cultural workers labored under a regime of arbitrary and constant redefinition, which in turn opened up a space for discourse and debate over what was or was not appropriate. Much as Ma Shaobo had, in 1951, critiqued the idea that a desire to stargaze during the Double Seventh Festival (discussed in chapter 1) meant actual belief in fairytales, many of those embroiled in the debate on ghost plays insisted that theatrical characters were, at worst, harmless.

The Hundred Flowers Movement and the Theatre World

As it turned out, political events were on the side of the critics who decried Ma's *Wandering West Lake* as an inappropriate adaptation that fundamentally misunderstood proscriptions for art and literature. By early 1956, overtures were being made to woo disenchanted intellectuals through motions to liberalize the cultural and intellectual spheres. Zhou Enlai outlined new policies at a conference in January, noting that the CCP needed to correct attitudes toward intellectuals, particularly those who were not party members.[55] On May 2, Mao made his famous speech from whence the Hundred Flowers Movement took its name. A few days later, Liu Shaoqi reinforced the message as it applied to the cultural realm: "Our policy is to let [a hundred] flowers bloom, to develop something new from the old. We cannot afford to erase certain things because they are old."[56] On the one hand, this stamp of approval on "old" culture freed—at least in theory—artists and cultural workers from the need to make the past resonate with contemporary events; on the other, this type of policy shift was exactly the type of sudden move that drove cultural workers to experiment (sometimes wildly) with form and content in an attempt to stay current with regulations.

The Hundred Flowers Movement had some positive, long-reaching effects in the theatre world, and despite the eventual blowback of the Anti-Rightist Campaign, many of the changes to repertoire and policies stuck. The actions taken to liberalize the theatre world were coming from the highest echelons, with the Ministry of Culture and the words of top leaders showing that this was a top-down checking of lower-level bans and suspect revisions. The words of CCP leaders sounded just like Ma Shaobo's cautionary words in the early 1950s. "There should not be any drastic revision of plays," Liu Shaoqi wrote in the May directive. "Any harmless play may be staged. Harmful ones may also be staged after minor alterations. . . . [Those] charged with duties to revise plays in . . . troupes should be warned against impetuosity."[57] Of course, such statements from the top ignored the fact that cultural workers and cadres had been attempting to negotiate confusing and often contradictory messages on what to perform since the establishment of the PRC (and in some cases, well before that). Considering the emphasis on fashioning "new" culture, it should come as little surprise that this backtracking left some cultural workers feeling unsettled, as cultural policy veered from one extreme to another.

The exhortation to "let a hundred flowers bloom, push out the old to bring in the new" had been a phrase familiar to dramatists since the founding of the PRC, and the connection to "let a hundred flowers bloom, let a hundred schools of thought contend" is clear. But "pushing out the old to bring in the new" was affirmed to mean an equal measure of preservation, at least in the mid-1950s. As Zhou Yang stated in March, "If we want to let a hundred flowers bloom, the first essential is to preserve and uncover the national heritage."⁵⁸ This point was made clear at the 1956 All-China Theatre Repertoire Work Conference, held in June. A particular emphasis was the necessity of "excavating and putting in order" traditional plays.⁵⁹ There was an explicit acknowledgment at the conference that old forms, even ones that some labeled "superstitious," particularly ghost opera and mythology plays, had value and could and should not be excised from the repertoire. This was not simply the point of view of critics feverishly debating Ma Jianling's revisions in *Play Monthly*, but one actively promulgated by cadres and cultural workers at a prominent event. The Ministry of Culture was essentially backtracking from its early 1950s limited spate of bans, and checking the "impetuosity" of cadres in charge of repertoires who were seen as doing serious damage to China's national heritage, their literary inheritance. However, the "impetuous" cadres had likely been trying to adhere to the spirit of regulations. As in other campaigns, the blame for problems was often placed on the lowest echelons of the government apparatus, with little (or no) acknowledgment of the high-level policy decisions that had led to the problems in the first place. In this case, the policies and limited ban discussed in chapter 1, ostensibly designed to rein in overzealous lower-level cadres, were interpreted by those further down the bureaucratic ladder as being "suggestions" for the types of plays not to be staged. Naturally, this list was much longer than the twenty-six plays specifically forbidden by the Ministry of Culture.⁶⁰

The 1956 conference set off a flurry of discussion and reportage in journals and papers. Articles from *Theatre Report* covered both the conference itself and broader themes brought up at the event. An essay by the editors of the journal was a broad declaration that China's theatrical inheritance needed to be preserved and "put in order" so as to enhance the theatre of the PRC. "The theatre arts of our country are not only elegant, refined," able to satisfy the tastes and wishes of the people, no matter how lofty, but they "also possess an amazing vitality."⁶¹ They went on to specifically address criticisms of "mythology" and "ghost plays," pointing to Ma Jianling's revisions in spirit, if not in name. Criticizing the point of view that "immortals [i.e., mythology plays] are acceptable, but all ghosts are put on the list of unacceptable [things]," the authors took issue with nonsensical revisions. "That strong avenging spirit in *Red Plum Pavilion* must be turned into a human, *Black Basin Stratagem* (*Wupen ji*, banned as a Peking opera entitled *A Strange Wrong Avenged* [*Qiyuan bao*]) has a ghost, it must not be staged. . . . In such a way, who knows how many scripts with healthy ideology they have killed?"⁶² For such destruction, they blamed individuals and cadres in positions of power who bypassed regulations in order to exercise their own tastes. That is, to declare a play unfit to be staged was supposed to be left to the Ministry of Culture; for a troupe or lower-level official to declare a play "banned" because of their personal dislike for a script was simply unacceptable. But for many people, it wasn't that they harbored "evil intentions of laying waste to our inheritance," but that they simply didn't understand what methods could be used to make art serve politics. "Art," the authors declared, "is not the same as a newspaper editorial, or a government report."[63]

The emphasis on inappropriate actions on a local or provincial level as the root of the problem is echoed in government documents sent from the Ministry of Culture in the autumn of 1956. One takes a close look at the situation in Shenyang, Liaoning, which they wanted to use as an example of how to enhance the repertoires of opera troupes. It explains that the overzealous banning of traditional plays happened "owing to an insufficient understanding of the special points and utility of theatrical arts on our behalf, as well as certain regional cultural departments."[64] Even by 1956, the Ministry of Culture was still battling with lower-level cadres who were creating an untenable situation for theatre troupes. As a result of such tensions, troupes were starting to take outlandish measures to be able to keep audiences coming in. In some cases, they would perform new works only while cadres were in the audience, but after the cadres had left, they would "return to the main story" of old plays.[65]

Of even more concern were literary abominations that were appearing. Performers, apparently quite desperate to broaden what they were allowed to stage, were surreptitiously putting scenes from banned plays back on the books by inserting them into "acceptable" plays. Thus, characters from plays set in the Han dynasty (206 BCE–220 CE) were stuffed into martial plays set during the eighteenth-century Qing dynasty. "The result of this sort of fraud and stealthy substitution is to cause many good traditional scripts to suffer harm. And so, at present, performed scripts are extremely lacking, dull, and at the same time maintain . . . a confused appearance, and have already caused a big [negative] impact on the lives of performers."[66] And yet, the desperation of troupes to take such measures indicates the anxiety that shifting regulations produced among cadres and cultural workers. It also speaks to the experimental and creative ways in which artists tried to preserve the repertoire (and their livelihoods) and work within often confusing and contradictory policy. The Shenyang Culture Bureau's response to this was what the Ministry of Culture wanted to see for *all* of

China, or so the directive claimed: they "broadened and enriched" what counted as appropriate plays. Clearly, the problem of "overzealous" cadres at the lower levels—discussed in chapter 1—had not been solved by providing a list of twenty-six banned plays. The solution was to throw the doors open, relatively speaking: precious few plays seemed to be explicitly off-limits, and this backed up the position of critics who had argued that ghosts (among other things) were *not* inherently unsuitable to be staged.

Alongside the changes to the repertoire, many artists spoke up in criticism of policies from the early years of the PRC. Tian Han, for instance, criticized the need for young artists to attend numerous political classes, as well as the "deplorable lives of celebrated old actors."[67] There were certainly many who felt aggrieved by party policies—particularly those that had forced actors from stages, as well as techniques and stagecraft that had been declared inappropriate for socialist stages—and they felt increasingly comfortable speaking up. In May 1957, the great *huadan* (young female role) Xiao Cuihua (Yu Lianquan) gave an impassioned plea to *People's Daily*, saying, "I want to sing opera!"[68] The star told an editor of the paper, "The Party has called for 'a hundred schools of thought to contend,' it wants us artists to speak our innermost thoughts and feelings, to help the party restore the mood to good order." Xiao claimed that the early restrictions on opera, including the art of *qiaogong* (using shoes that replicated the look and gait of a woman with bound feet), severely curtailed the plays he could perform; but it was the early opera bans that forced him off stages altogether. Still, it was hard to not perform, so he had decided in late 1956 that he wanted to sing again. However, three abortive attempts to see the director or deputies at the Beijing Culture Bureau came to nothing. Xiao optimistically said he "hasn't given up hope. I have faith, Chairman Mao called for 'a hundred schools of thought to contend,' and this will certainly get something done. . . . It will soon be half a year, and the Culture Bureau just brushes my requests off."[69] Xiao was unsuccessful, and the *huadan* never returned to performance, although he was allowed to teach and "even to record the details of performance techniques," which Siyuan Liu points to as evidence that "live performance was more dangerous than the printed archive."[70] In addition to artists who spoke up regarding ill treatment, Tian Han and others criticized "*waihang* (nonprofessional) Party control over the professional dramatists as 'dangerous.'"[71] Certainly, there was a sense that artists and cultural workers should be the ones in charge of repertoires and policies, particularly as they stood the most to lose if bureaucratic decisions hampered their ability to make a living.

As for ghost drama and banned plays, the increased openness and discussion during the Hundred Flowers had an ameliorating effect, but, as I have illustrated, it by no means launched the critical discussion on traditional opera in socialist society. The discussion that had been taking place in papers, speeches, and journals since the establishment of the PRC continued to flourish, and found an even more hospitable climate. The elite theatre world did not begin the discussion, but simply engaged in it even more; work on reforming and maintaining traditional drama also benefited from this more relaxed atmosphere, just as it would in the early 1960s. But Ma Jianling, Zhang Zhen, Liu Naichong, and the others were not the nonparty intellectuals the CCP wished to woo. Thus, the development of the ghost play debate may be seen as benefiting from the Hundred Flowers atmosphere, but should not be seen as deriving from it. The conversations that took place during the Hundred Flowers were already occurring prior to the relaxing of the cultural sphere.

Despite this "blooming and contending" throughout late 1956 and the first half of 1957, not everyone was advocating for an open atmosphere. Although a speech Mao gave in March 1957 seemed to represent a more inclusive attitude than, for instance, his talks at Yan'an, his new position was hardly the stamp of approval on traditional drama that Liu Shaoqi and others had spoken of in 1956. Delivering his talk to provincial-level organizations, Mao looked toward the eventual extinction of "feudal" dramatic traditions. In a general critique of "poisonous weeds," Mao was not advocating for their alteration, but rather suggested that they should be allowed to remain as negative examples. They would thus serve as a foil for the development of new revolutionary dramas. Paradoxically (and somewhat naïvely), he wished for a full saturation of the market with such plays, for the more of these plays that were performed, "people will start talking, and when more and more people start talking, then fewer and fewer people will come to watch, and these things will not be performed."[72]

Despite, or perhaps because of, these words, the Ministry of Culture continued the trend it had started in 1956 with *Black Basin Stratagem* and formally lifted the ban on all twenty-six plays.[73] This seems to simply have been an explicit declaration of what the directives of 1956 were talking around. Certainly, the previous year's discussion of *Black Basin Stratagem* hinged on its "appropriate reform," and no one was suggesting flooding stages with unadulterated "feudal" works. But as the criticism of Ma Jianling's adaptation showed, the changes that many wanted to see were minor deletions, not wholesale rewritings. Experimentation with trimming and changing forms was one matter—and certainly had a long precedent in the history of Chinese theatre—but attempting to align classical culture with modern, scientific, rational thought was, for many, quite another.

Even as critics debated and theorized, sidelined performers turned a hopeful gaze to the possibilities of this period of blooming and contending, and as the Ministry of Culture was lifting bans entirely, party leadership was beginning to plan their counterattack. As with many of Mao's decisions, loosening the reins had unintended consequences—in this case, the criticisms of the CCP were likely more numerous and more sustained than anticipated—and thus the country was in need of a sharp check. In early June, a series of editorials published in the *People's Daily* contended that the criticisms needed countercriticisms; "rightist elements" (that is, those people considered "bourgeois and reactionary," or working against the interests of the people and the party) were accused of "misusing the rectification campaign to turn back the clock and overthrow the Communist Party, the proletariat, and the socialist cause."[74] As it turned out, those intellectuals who had been wary of the 1956 calls to bloom and contend were proved right; the Anti-Rightist Campaign would punish many of those who had done just as they had been asked. Ai Qing, for instance, would be branded a rightist for defending the novelist Ding Ling, and banished to China's northwest for twenty years.[75]

Despite the political crackdown on those labeled "rightists," the lively discussion in the drama world did not entirely stop. If anything, the continuation of the ghost play debate illustrates that the discussion existed very much outside of the call for blooming and contending; this is another way the ghost play debates can get us outside of campaign time. In the summer of 1957—just as the reins were being hauled in on the Hundred Flowers Movement—the critic and editor Qu Liuyi published an important essay on ghost plays in *Theatre Report*. The distinction between mythology plays and ghost plays had not been particularly important in the first few years of the PRC; if anything, many writers conflated mythological characters and ghosts together when discussing why they should *not* be considered "superstition." But this was a distinction that would become increasingly important in the early 1960s, when some critics attempted to argue that mythology plays were inherently suitable for socialist stages, while ghost plays were emphatically not. Qu's essay was an early defense of ghost characters on stages; if anything, it argues that ghosts are more useful than mythological characters.[76]

In Qu's opinion, ghost plays and mythology plays were inherently similar, being products of human imagination; but the worlds of Sun Wukong, the Cowherd and the Weaving Maid, and other such subjects were always out of reach. Ghosts, on the other hand, represented people who had once been alive, just like the audience. According to Qu, these "two strange flowers" were equally as deserving of being on stages. Despite a distance of four years from Ma Jianling's ghostless ghost play, even this 1957 essay cannot resist a dig at the idea of "turning ghosts into people": he set out to show why such techniques were undesirable. Like others before him, he objected to "restricting artistic education to the principles of science education, as this really fetters artistic development."[77]

Qu provided a taxonomy of good and bad ghost plays; with the removal of banned plays as a category, the division between "good plays" (*haoxi*) and "bad plays" (*huaixi*) became the important factor for determining whether or not a play ought to be staged. However, as the existence of Qu's article may indicate, the definitions were also—unlike a ban that explicitly listed what should go—difficult to pin down. The critic did not advocate for a blanket approach to ghost plays one way or another, but careful study and revision if necessary (just like Tian Han's early 1950s suggestions on how to deal with the problem). This type of relatively permissive approach to plays with potentially suspect subject matter was, in fact, the dominant approach advocated by intellectuals from 1949 to 1963. The liberal atmosphere of the Hundred Flowers may have encouraged even more discussion of the topic, but the blowback from the Anti-Rightist Campaign certainly did not shut it down. As chapter 3 illustrates, even more attention was paid to reforming drama in the late 1950s and early 1960s.

Reghosting the Ghost Play: The 1958 Wandering West Lake

As Qu Liuyi's summer 1957 article indicates, the ghostless *Wandering West Lake* was still on the minds of drama critics, and time had not improved its standing. Perhaps owing to this continued criticism, in 1958 Ma Jianling, along with Huang Junyao, Jiang Bingtai, and Zhang Digeng, made yet another adaptation of *Wandering West Lake*. While they maintained some of the plot changes Ma had made in his 1953 revision, the ghost was restored to the ghost play. Just as in his original adaptation, Li Huiniang and Pei Yu were provided with an existing love story; in 1958, however, Li Huiniang was murdered, and returned as a ghost.[78] But even with this substantial change, the new *Wandering West Lake* was still not a critical success, though it seems to have been a generally popular play among audiences and troupes, even far from Shaanxi. Several years later, Yang Huasheng, a performer of Shanghainese farce (*huaji xi*), would remember that in the mid-1950s, *Wandering West Lake* was "praised in every possible way" when it was performed in Shanghai, to the extent that artistic leadership organized troupes to learn from the revised drama.[79]

It can be difficult to ascertain what exactly counted as a popular play. Until the advent of theatre yearbooks in the 1980s, it is uncommon to see in the archival record the precise makeup of a troupe's repertoire. In Shanghai, for instance, while yearly statistics of the general number of performances by opera type and lists of plays in the repertory were kept beginning in 1949, they by and large do not reveal how many performances of each play there were, nor how many people attended. It is entirely possible that for critics concerned about the future of theatre, "popular" meant simply being in the active repertory, and a play could have two performances or two hundred. The distaste by the critics writing in the premier publications related to literature and culture seems often to have been more on a theoretical basis—that is, the *idea* that such plays could be popular—than rooted in documented statistics. However, at least in terms of readership (a different, but related question, to audiences, to be sure), the combined publication numbers of Ma's original 1953 and 1958 versions *Wandering West Lake*—plus later reprints[80]—topped at least 100,000 printings over the span of eight years, giving some indication of its relatively widespread popularity.

Regardless of the concrete popularity of Ma's revisions to *Wandering West Lake*, critics were still unhappy with his tinkering. Liu Naichong, who was partially responsible for the highly critical 1955 article on the first revision of *Wandering West Lake*, returned in 1959 to offer his opinion on the reworking.[81] While he found the characterization of Li Huiniang as a ghost a very positive point, and now rather liked the idea of a prior Li Huiniang-Pei Yu relationship, he was largely unimpressed with the revised play, and again found the original superior in many ways. Ma's experimentation had produced a play that still could not reach the heights of the original.

His primary criticism was that the new revisions squandered the potential to elicit sympathy from the audience. Pointing to several classical examples of female protagonists who aroused the sympathy of audiences by being "unwilling to submit to humiliation," Liu maintained that Ma's milder Li Huiniang showed herself to be powerless, and thus was a much weaker character.[82] Although Liu stated in the beginning that he found the backstory of the Pei-Li betrothal an interesting and useful addition, it had a number of negative consequences: namely, that the political and ideological content of the play was extremely watered down. In the original, he maintained, there was a better representation of the oppressive nature of Jia Sidao's household, and more importantly, there was much more political content. Li Huiniang's return as a ghost had, in the Ming version, more of a political dimension, whereas the new revision removed this entirely. Li Huiniang exists in life and death for the love of Pei Yu.[83]

The concubine wasn't the only problem. In the original play, the altercation on West Lake between Pei Yu and Jia Sidao is primarily a political and ideological struggle: as seen earlier in this chapter, the students were angry about Jia Sidao's actions (and inaction). But the previous relationship between Li and Pei in the 1950s versions changed the dynamics of this scene. It is transformed from a political statement about the corrupt prime minister to a scene with a frustrated lover. Even Li Huiniang's utterance in the original—"Oh, what a handsome youth!"—is tinged with political overtones; Liu maintains she was referring not just to his attractive face, but to his moral stance and bravery in standing up to Jia Sidao.[84] With the emphasis on the previous relationship between Pei and Li, this entire political inflection was lost.

Liu's point, however, was not simply to critique the revised version; he again seemed genuinely interested in underscoring the utility of the original play in socialist society. As he set up the comparison, it was the *new* version of the play—written at least in part by a well-known proponent of revolutionary drama—that was more interested in romance than politics. He noted that "some comrades have said things like: 'In the past, *Wandering West Lake* was, in the hands of the dark ruling class, a play full of lascivious and fearsome [things]. Today, in the hands of the masses, it has finally brought out its descriptions of . . . oppressed people resisting the ruling class.' This," he continued, "is an extremely unfair remark." That is, the original *Red Plums* had of course been produced by a member of the literati; but even "elite" culture had uses and value in a society oriented toward the masses. He went on to admit that while the original certainly has its failings, it was excessive to say that the play is replete with negative elements. Most importantly, it was "truly full of a resisting spirit."[85]

In some respects, Ma Jianling was between a rock and a hard place. On the one hand, his first attempt at revising *Wandering West Lake*, in order to make it more politically suitable, had attracted criticism from cultural workers who focused on the excision of the ghost character. On the other, when Ma and others revised the play again, it still was not up to the standards demanded by critics like Liu: the play was *still* lacking in the political power of the original and had weakened the characterization of the main characters. Apparently, the man who had been so successful in creating contemporary dramas could not squeeze the same success from this classical work. Of all the plays that Ma wrote in his lengthy career, the 1953 *Wandering West Lake* receives little dedicated attention, probably because it was, at least as far as the cultural elites were concerned, a failure.[86] The "ghostless ghost play" would be trotted out again and again as the ultimate example of how *not* to reform traditional drama.

The Ma Jianling affair illuminates the first real debate over ghost plays, which in turn was built upon the earlier defense of mythological subjects. Many cultural workers, confronted with what was an eminently logical solution to the problem of "superstition," immediately set about "proving" that literary ghosts were *not* superstitious. The debate, which eventually resulted in the reinsertion of the ghost into *Wandering West Lake*, set the tone for years to come. Not until 1963 would the suitability of ghosts on stages be seriously challenged. This is not to say that early efforts at drama reform were entirely successful. Policies did force many plays (and their interpreters) off stages, some never to return.

Conclusion

One literary scholar has wondered why ghost stories—often appealing in times of trouble—"failed to appear more often in the first eight decades of the twentieth century."[87] But ghosts were a constant presence in the Mao years. Antisuperstition campaigns may have tried to stamp out the ghosts that inhabited people's daily lives, but there was a clear separation of *those* ghosts on the one hand ("superstition") and *theatrical* and *literary* ghosts on the other. Certainly not everyone agreed that such literature belonged in a socialist world; but by and large, critics and artists successfully separated popular custom and artistic ghosts.

A year after the premiere of Ma Jianling's 1958 re-revised *Wandering West Lake*, work began on yet another version of the tale of a corrupt prime minister, a righteous young scholar, and a tragic concubine. This time, the ghost would be making an appearance in a serious time of trouble: the disastrous famine resulting from the Great Leap Forward. Meng Chao's *Li*

Huiniang was as different from Ma Jianling's interpretation as a play could be, in both form and conception. And yet the stories of these two playwrights and their very different plays share more than a few similarities. But it was Meng Chao's *Li Huiniang* that represented the zenith and the nadir of the ghost play debate: from exquisite, celebrated literary works to thoroughly trashed "poisonous weeds." Li Huiniang would return with a vengeance in 1961, and this version would be fêted by the literary elite. But a terrible price would be extracted from those who put the righteous phantasm back on socialist stages in her imperial-era glory.

CHAPTER 3

Old Trees Blooming

Li Huiniang, *Ghost Literature, and the Early 1960s*

As the autumn of 1959 inched toward winter, Meng Chao, a veteran member of the CCP, lay in his Beijing home, wracked by illness. In his 1962 retelling, the weather was already turning cold; insects cried as a chilly wind blew through the season's fallen leaves. The scene was not unlike Li Bai's famous Tang dynasty meditation, "Thoughts on a Still Night," wherein moonlight pools at the foot of the bed and the poet's thoughts turn to the past.[1] Although his recollections do not mention it, perhaps being confined to bed had allowed this aging revolutionary to consider the situation facing the country: a mass movement in ruins, the countryside gripped by famine, and the party he had loyally served for over three decades seemingly unwilling to do anything about it. Perhaps his thoughts drifted to history, to men like Hai Rui who courageously stood up to corruption in the government. Perhaps he was simply feverish. Whatever the reason, his mind flitted back to his childhood in Zhucheng, Shandong, during the waning years of the Qing dynasty and the first years of the Republic. He thought not of politics and history, however, but of the plays he had loved watching as a boy. There were many famous characters from literature and antiquity that he had first seen at those performances, but one in particular had always captivated him. Now, decades later, she crowded back into his vision. Her name was Li Huiniang. And she was, in his recollection, beautiful beyond belief.

As Meng Chao recovered from his illness in 1959, he threw himself into an academic study of Zhou Chaojun's *Story of Red Plums*.[2] This was not an onerous job: although he had been a member of radical literary movements since the 1920s, his upbringing in an elite family had equipped him with a deep knowledge of and appreciation for classical culture. As he read, he thought of writing his own vision of that beloved character from childhood, a Li Huiniang for the current age. In his telling, the tragic ghost would not simply be driven by love for a living man. No, she would have a higher purpose—to speak for those who could not speak, for people who suffered under the rule of a cruel and corrupt prime minister. In Meng Chao's hands, her purpose would be clear: she would return to the world of the living seeking vengeance for the masses who suffered under a callous and cruel government. Thus was born Meng Chao's play *Li Huiniang*.

The genesis of *Li Huiniang* and other politically prominent "new historical plays" that emerged in 1961, primarily *Hai Rui Dismissed from Office* and *Xie Yaohuan*, has largely been read in the context of the disaster of the Great Leap Forward. Certainly, it hardly seems accidental that the story of an unjustly slain concubine, corrupt government leadership, and the suffering of the people reasserted itself in Meng Chao's imagination just as the Leap was descending into a tragedy of monumental proportions. So too for Wu Han and Tian Han, who turned to stories of upright officials and callous governments.[3] These plays have generally been analyzed in mostly political terms, suggesting that the authors penning revised dramas in 1959 and 1960 were responding primarily, or even solely, to contemporary political events. It is indeed not difficult, using Meng Chao's own depiction of his inspiration, loaded with words that lend a tragic impression to the scene, to turn such a connection into the author's preoccupation.[4]

But Meng Chao's play was not simply criticizing the wrongs of the present. Its structure, language, and positive reception made a strong case for the compatibility of even elite classical culture with a socialist present. Much as skill in calligraphy and poetic composition never fell out of style, classical language and literary heritage were still prized by many of the intellectual and literary elite.[5] Although many of Meng Chao's generation argued against maintaining what they saw as harmful, feudal relics, they nevertheless managed to bring both classical tradition and contemporary theories and trends into their writing. And indeed, many critics, as previous chapters have shown, argued vociferously for the utility of maintaining many aspects of traditional cultural production. *Li Huiniang* was intended to be a supremely elegant example of combining modern ideology with classical language and form. In much the same way as Ma Jianling had experimented with content—was the ghost necessary for a ghost play?—we can see Meng Chao's turn as another type of experimentation in his retelling of this old ghost story. Though quite different in methodology and form, ultimately both writers had the same goals in mind: taking a celebrated piece of Chinese theatrical heritage and making it suitable for socialist stages.

Critics took up *Li Huiniang* with zeal, and it is instructive to trace both the elements of discussion that are present, as well as what is not. Critical points of debate in the 1950s and in 1963, particularly the question of whether or not ghost plays ought to be performed, are nearly totally absent in their critiques. While not all of the early 1960s reviews agree on every point, the disputes tended more to concern minor stylistic issues. This is in striking contrast to both Ma Jianling's earlier revisions and to the way in which *Li Huiniang* itself would be treated in 1963 and after. The relative lack of political rhetoric, paired with the absence of debate over the suitability of ghosts, marks this period of the early 1960s as unique in the high socialist period. The relative success of those earlier 1950 defenses of keeping ghosts on socialist stages laid the groundwork for this discussion between 1961 and early 1963.

However, *Li Huiniang* was not the only prominent example of classical ghosts being repackaged for a socialist audience to appear in 1961: the play's premiere came after the publication of the state-sponsored *Stories about Not Being Afraid of Ghosts*, a collection of ghost tales drawn from classical literary compendia.[6] *Stories*, however, presented ghosts in an entirely different light than the ways in which theatrical ghosts had been discussed and celebrated. These two products, so similar in many respects, and yet so very different, reflect the tensions that had been inherent in the (re)production of classical supernatural tales since the earliest days of the PRC. While Meng Chao presented his ghost as a heroine to rescue common people from cruel and incompetent officials, the editors of *Stories* made it clear that ghosts were mere stand-ins for real world villains: capitalist roaders, landlords, enemies of the party. These competing narratives would be thrown into high relief in 1963, when ghost operas would be banned entirely from Chinese stages; but for the transitional period of 1961 and 1962, these divisions would not be quite so stark.

This chapter considers the production of these two prominent examples of ghost literature and connects them to the wider discussions on the role of classical culture that had been going on since 1949. The existence of *Li Huiniang, Stories about Not Being Afraid of Ghosts*, and the celebration of supernatural literature on a national stage by the cultural elite were, for a while, proof that such cultural production and socialist society could coexist comfortably. Meng Chao's revision, and the story of ghostly literature in the early 1960s, was not simply reflective of cultural and political discussions happening in the wake of the Great Leap Forward; instead, they show the high point of discussions that had been going on since the earliest days of the PRC. By contrasting *Li Huiniang* and *Stories*, I illuminate the fundamental dramatic question at the heart of the ghost play debate: Was the audience meant to *identify with* the ghost, as an expression of the masses' historical frustrations? Or should ghosts stand as metaphors for real-life *antagonists*?

The status of supernatural literature in the early 1960s provides an example of the unique, transitional atmosphere of that period, in which the de facto leaders of the country took little interest in remaking culture in a radical fashion. *Li Huiniang*, unlike the early 1950s experiments in how far classical culture could be pushed to resonate with the present, seems to be an exercise in establishing how little imperial-era culture needed to be changed to comment on contemporary affairs. Cultural workers and artists were largely left to their own devices, free of interference from officials. Correspondingly, many veteran cultural workers found themselves in a relaxed environment, a period when even plays celebrating the talents of imperial-era masters like Tang Xianzu could find favor on the pages of *People's Daily* and *Theatre Report*. The ghost that emerged from Meng Chao's illness-wracked autumn may have been looking for vengeance, but her words were honeyed poetry in a classical style. However, the convergence of two competing narratives about ghosts—ghosts as enemies, and ghosts as heroes—would set the stage for the increasingly hostile cultural and political climate that developed from the sanguine discussions of 1961 and 1962.

Diverging Discourses: Stories about Not Being Afraid of Ghosts

Meng Chao's *Li Huiniang* was not the first appearance of classical ghost literature in 1961. There was a production of an even more curious product, a compendium of classical ghost stories entitled *Stories about Not Being Afraid of Ghosts*. According to a later commentator, in the spring of 1959 (coincidentally, the same time work was being undertaken on *Hai Rui* and *Li Huiniang*), it was decided that a collection of "stories about not being afraid of ghosts" would be selected in order to disseminate Mao Zedong Thought, particularly antisuperstitious mind-sets and the idea that "all reactionaries are paper tigers."[7] Mao himself suggested edits to the collection and personally tapped He Qifang to write the introduction. Afterward, Mao again took a personal interest in the collection, meeting with He twice in January to suggest further edits to the introduction. Ghosts were thus on the radar of the Chairman himself at the height of the Great Leap Forward.

The preface to *Stories about Not Being Afraid of Ghosts* begins with a typical statement: "There are no ghosts. Belief in ghosts is a backward idea, a superstition and a sign of cowardice. This is a matter of common sense today among the people."[8] He Qifang continues: "What should amaze us today is not that there were so many believers in ghosts in those days but that . . . there was a minority who denied the existence of ghosts."[9] It goes on page after page, extolling the virtue of Mao Zedong Thought, while highlighting some of the stories contained within (a total of sixty-six, drawn from a wide variety of imperial-era sources), and explaining *why* ghost stories were apparently useful:

> There are no ghosts such as are described in the old stories, but there are actually many things in this world which are like ghosts. Some are big, such as international imperialism . . . , modern re-visionism, serious natural calamities and certain not-yet-reformed members of the landlord and bourgeois classes who have usurped leadership in some organization at the primary level and staged a comeback there. Some are small, such as difficulties and setbacks in ordinary work. . . . All these can be said to be ghost-like things. (4–5)

Therefore, these ghost stories were meant to teach people not to be afraid of things that perhaps looked fearsome, but had no substance. That is, the stories could teach the Chinese masses to overcome enemies of the party itself, just as the characters in the classical tales overcame ghosts.

Furthermore, *Stories* is, to say the least, an odd collection if one assumes its purpose was to encourage the masses of Chinese people to stand up to fearsome entities. The original publication consists of unadulterated originals in classical Chinese, augmented with copious notes (in many cases, the glossary section is lengthier than the original story). Even the physical layout of the initial February 1961 publication seems a consciously styled throwback: it is printed in a vertical orientation, being read from right to left.[10] Another edition from 1961, also in the vertical orientation, was published in October, featuring a pale blue cover with the title of the collection presented in an ancient seal script. Visually, they are striking in hewing to older printing conventions. While it is not uncommon to see such orientation in publications from the early-to-mid 1950s (Ma Jianling's ghostless *Wandering West Lake*, for instance, utilized this orientation), by 1961, newspapers, journals, and many books—classically accented or not—were universally published in the horizontal, left-to-right format. Later editions of *Stories*, published in 1978 and 1981, also adopt the horizontal format.

Apparently recognizing that many people would find reading stories in classical Chinese a challenging proposition, in April 1961 the People's Press published a much abridged version of the collection that included only ten of the original stories in classical Chinese with accompanying vernacular translations (and, unlike the original publication, printed in a horizontal format).[11] Even here, the notes are copious, and while this edition was certainly broader in potential reach than the highly literary original, it hardly seems to be the best vehicle for efficiently propagating Mao's political beliefs. In addition to several Chinese editions, selections from *Stories* (thirty-five tales in all) were also translated into multiple languages by the Beijing Foreign Language Press. The English edition, translated by Yang Xianyi and Gladys (Taylor) Yang, was first published in 1961 and handsomely illustrated by the noted artist Cheng Shifa. Copy on the flap notes that the stories "show the adroitness and courage of Chinese people in ancient times who dared to defy ghosts."[12] And yet, the very things being celebrated—classical ghost tales—were worlds away from socialist literary production. For foreign audiences, the collection highlighted cherished parts of the Chinese literary canon, but not the *socialist* literary canon.

In many respects, *Stories about Not Being Afraid of Ghosts* is well in line with the 1950s and early 1960s discussions on ghost literature. The very fact that a book compiling classical ghost stories was apparently encouraged, and production partially supervised, by none other than Mao himself affirms that ghost literature was not only *not* under attack for the most part, but was actively promoted by the state. It was part of official cultural production both for domestic and foreign audiences, as evidenced by multiple foreign language translations, including English, Russian, and Spanish. At the same time, *Stories* is markedly different from the products debated in the 1950s, and indeed from other ghostly products produced in the early 1960s. Unlike the celebrations of ghost characters and their virtues discussed in chapters 1 and 2—usually because brave ghosts could encourage resistance and struggle—the ghost characters in *Stories* are not the heroes. To the contrary, as the very title makes clear, the heroes are the people who are "not afraid of ghosts."

However, *Stories* was not universally praised, and some intellectuals noted with no little sense of irony the oddness of the collection. Liao Mosha, writing in the paper *Frontline*, was a major contributor to the *zawen* series "Three Family Village." *Zawen*, a form popularized by Lu Xun in the Republican period, underwent something of a renaissance in the early 1960s. Here, he commented on the "elegant joke" of *Stories* and criticized the foundation of the work. "The Chinese Academy of Social Science's Institute of Literature has published *Stories about Not Being Afraid of Ghosts*," Liao's essay begins. "Of course this is a good volume. But looking at it right now, one volume about 'stories about not being afraid of ghosts' is insufficiently useful; we ought to have one volume on 'stories about being afraid of ghosts.'"[13] Why was this so? As Liao pointed out, *Stories* was actually replete with people *being* afraid of ghosts, whereas the people "not afraid" of ghosts were rare. And, furthermore, he challenged the assumptions underpinning the introduction: "Regardless if [the characters] fear ghosts or don't fear ghosts, they all have one point of agreement: all of them know there are ghosts." Stories about people being afraid of ghosts would underscore the "superstitious" nature of believing in ghosts. In many respects, Liao's essay reads as an intellectual exasperated with the theoretical couching and justification of a compilation of ghost tales. Can we not simply enjoy these stories for what they are, he seems to be asking; does reading tales culled from great classical compendia really need to be justified with ideology? This would not be Liao's only contribution to the discussion on literary ghosts, however: he would return to the subject after the premiere of the most important revised ghost play of the socialist period, *Li Huiniang*. While work was taking place on *Stories about Not Being Afraid of Ghosts*, Meng Chao was writing away on what would become his most defining contribution to Chinese literature. Instead of celebrating the heroics of humans standing up to ghosts, however, his Kun opera would laud a brave ghost for standing up to an almost inhumanly cruel government official.

Meng Chao and the Move from Revolutionary to Postrevolutionary Writer

Today, Meng Chao lies mostly in obscurity. Little attention has been paid to the author of one of the three "great poisonous weeds," the plays heavily criticized in the lead-up to the Cultural Revolution. But during his lifetime, he was part of a small and elite group of party members and cultural workers. These few hundred people, both radical and liberal, occupied a very important position in the wake of the Great Leap Forward. The "liberal" camp, borrowing Merle Goldman's phrasing, included Meng Chao and more familiar names, such as Ba Jin, Xia Yan, and Mao Dun, plus patrons such as Zhou Yang, Chen Yi, and Zhou Enlai. The "liberals" generally embodied many of the values of the May Fourth Movement, particularly intellectual autonomy. Despite the dedication of many to the party and Marxist ideology, they were equally committed to addressing problems in the system with debate and critique.[14] In many respects, Meng Chao's story is typical of this camp: born in the last decade of the Qing dynasty to a prominent Shandong family, he came of age surrounded by ideas promulgated by May Fourth intellectuals, but also steeped in classical learning.

Born Meng Xianqi in 1902, Meng Chao grew up in Zhucheng, Shandong, the city that produced two other important figures in the Maoist period, Kang Sheng and Jiang Qing. Kang Sheng remains one of the most inscrutable people in the history of the CCP, "a sinister and shadowy figure even to his colleagues."[15] His position in the party had fluctuated wildly between the 1920s and 1950s: he served in Moscow in the 1930s, helped oversee the Yan'an Rectification Campaign of the early 1940s, was largely invisible in the early 1950s, but retained a seat on the Politburo.[16] However, he had proved a useful tool for Mao since the mid-1930s and is generally depicted by later chroniclers as an opportunist who "adroitly [changed] allegiances as the political winds shifted."[17] As it happened, he also introduced Mao to his fourth wife, Jiang Qing. Unlike Meng Chao and Kang Sheng, Jiang's family was not a prominent provincial family. However, she eventually made her way to Shanghai, became an actress, and then moved on to Yan'an due to her political activities, where she would marry Mao in 1938.[18] Throughout the 1950s, she held a number of posts for brief periods, most related to the performing arts. However, by the early 1960s, she began taking a much more active role in the cultural realm—a path that would eventually culminate in the launch of the Great Proletarian Cultural Revolution in 1966.[19] Kang Sheng and Meng Chao were friends from a young age, although it does not appear the playwright was acquainted with Jiang Qing in their youths. However, the political relationship that developed between Kang Sheng and Jiang Qing—one based in no small measure, at least initially, on hometown ties—would eventually prove to be Meng Chao's undoing.

As for Meng himself, like Kang Sheng, he hailed from a prominent scholarly family in Shandong. Attending middle school in Jinan, he was expelled at the age of fifteen for participating in a strike. After returning to Zhucheng, he joined literary societies and began cultivating relationships with other youthful radicals who would grow into prominent writers. Finally, in 1924, he moved to Shanghai with his old friend Kang Sheng to pursue literary studies at Shanghai University.[20] Here, Meng Chao, like many other young people, found himself in an environment suffused with Marxist sympathies, and he had extensive contact with some of the premier left-leaning intellectuals of the day.[21] This combination of scholarship and radical political activity set the tone for the rest of his career.

Meng joined the Communist Party in 1926, and by 1929 he was a member of the city's Culture Bureau. In addition to purely political work, Meng Chao was one of the founders of the "Sun Society" (Taiyang she) in the late 1920s, a radical literary group that advocated for proletarian literature, and would go on to join the League of Left-Wing Writers in the 1930s. In fact, he was one of the CCP members involved in preparatory discussions leading to the League's creation.[22] Sun Society members believed that May Fourth literature was just as elitist and remote as classical traditions.[23] Jiang Guangci, a fellow member, described the sort of "anti-individualist" revolutionary literature that was to be later outlined in Mao's 1942 Yan'an Forum on Art and Literature. "The duty of revolutionary literature," Jiang wrote, "is to show in this life struggle the power of the masses, to instill into people collective tendencies."[24] In keeping with such points of view, Meng Chao's literary activities in the 1920s and 1930s paint a picture of someone unquestionably dedicated to the cause of proletarian literature, part of which necessitated an attack on "tradition."[25]

Meng's political career marked him as a loyal and diligent member of the party. Although he was not part of the Long March or present at Yan'an, his activities for the party were numerous and took him all over China. After 1930, he was a committee member of the Zhabei (Shanghai) branch of the CCP and a member of the Shanghai labor union, as well as the All-China Work Union doing propaganda and recruitment work. He was arrested in March 1932 for his recruiting activities in a Shanghai cotton factory; after his release in 1933, he went north to Beijing and engaged in unspecified "cultural work."[26] Between 1935 and 1937, he worked at the normal school in Tancheng County, Shandong. Between 1937 and 1945, he produced anti-Japanese propaganda, published the journal *Weeds* (*Ye cao*), and taught in the southwestern Chinese cities of Guilin, Guiyang, Kunming, and Chongqing.[27] Meng Chao may not have been a true literary star, but his more radical literary and political activities did give him entrance into prominent circles. He counted among his friends a number of people who were or would go on to be important party members. Yet while his talents may have been initially turned toward new-style literature, such as his spoken language drama version of the May 30th events, he also had a deep knowledge of and appreciation for Chinese classical literature. Although his works riffing on classical themes—particularly his character studies of *The Water Margin* and *Plum in the Golden Vase*—dealt with what are considered "popular" novels, his later turn to Kun opera and high-flown literary language was not entirely unexpected.[28]

Unlike some of Meng's more famous friends, he never reached the heights of stardom, but he did carve out a comfortable career in the literary realm of the PRC.[29] After 1949, and nearly three decades of active service to the CCP, he settled down in Beijing, serving various posts in major publishing houses.[30] His editorial focus seems to have been theatre; although he was best known in the Republican period for his work as a poet and essayist, after 1949 he published with relative frequency in theatre journals. In the spring of 1957, he was appointed the deputy editor of the Chinese Theatre (Zhongguo xiqu) publishing house. Finally, in 1961, he was made a deputy editor of the People's Literature (Renmin wenxue) publishing house and appointed head of the drama division.[31]

While it might not be surprising that a well-educated intellectual with a demonstrated expertise in drama would once again return to the form, Meng Chao's turn toward Kun opera in the period after 1959 indicates just how far he had come from his position of the late 1920s and 1930s. Of all the types of Chinese opera, Kun opera is the most strongly associated with the social and cultural elite. The delicacy of the form meant that it was suited to the intimate settings of literati homes, and its mass appeal was questionable.[32] While even the supposedly "national" style of Peking opera could have surprisingly little reach in the PRC—a Shanghainese survey from 1963 indicates audiences were small and composed of older, well-educated people, and mostly northerners at that—Kun opera was the domain of elites, whether in 1561 or 1961.[33]

*Calling Forth the Ghost: The Northern Kun Opera Theatre
and* Li Huiniang

The genesis of *Li Huiniang* highlights, on a structural level, some of the contradictory nature of theatre practice in the high socialist period. It also helps explain how Meng Chao found himself undertaking a Kun opera, a form he readily admitted to having no experience writing. The story highlights how the interests of the Meng Chao, Kang Sheng, and the young Northern Kun Opera Troupe (Beifang kunqu juyuan) intersected to produce this peculiar development both in PRC cultural production and Meng Chao's own career.

In June 1957, the Northern Kun Opera Troupe was formally established by the Ministry of Culture. An undated book (probably from 1957 or 1958) commemorating the founding of the troupe lays out its history, the history of Kun opera, the troupe's repertoire, and also includes a number of essays on Kun opera and theatre work in the PRC, as well as congratulatory essays written by cultural elites, ranging from Yu Zhenfei to Tian Han.[34] The troupe was headed by operatic luminaries Han Shichang, Bai Yunsheng, and Jin Ziguang, and the opening gala was an affair attended by a number of cultural heavyweights and political elites. Indeed, it was Jin who "pestered" Meng Chao to make his play Li Huiniang a Kun script.[35] Despite the general emphasis placed on contemporary drama and local forms from the Yan'an period on, the commemorative book is a celebration of Kun opera's traditions. Photographs show Mei Lanfang and Han Shichang preparing "Wandering through the Garden" (Youyuan), as well as Mei and Bai Yunsheng performing "Waking from the Dream" (Jingmeng) at the opening ceremony, both famous acts from Tang Xianzu's Peony Pavilion.

In addition to hosting a performance, the extent of CCP support for the undertaking is immediately apparent in other photographs and materials. Shen Yanbing, minister of culture (better known by his pen name, Mao Dun), and Zhou Yang (at that time assistant minister of propaganda) are both shown giving speeches. The book reprints the text of several speeches given at the founding. Chen Yi, then vice-premier, exhorted the assembled artists to "preserve, on behalf of the people, the outstanding classical genre of opera, not allow it to disappear."[36] Certainly, others spoke to Kun opera's need to modernize and find better ways of reaching the masses—Zhou Yang, for instance, went on at some length—but such remarks are tempered by the explicit acknowledgment of Kun opera's long history, its place among other genres of theatre, and its traditions.[37] In this light, commissioning a new play that at once hewed to older conventions, while ostensibly measuring up to contemporary standards for art, was entirely logical, perhaps especially for such a young theatre troupe.

Still, it is worth pondering how Meng Chao, a veteran cultural worker with plenty of literary credentials, but no Kun librettist, wound up writing a Kun opera. There is another prominent figure present on the pages of Northern Kun Opera's commemorative book, and that was Meng Chao's old friend Kang Sheng, who had not yet risen again to the political heights he would reach in the 1960s, but who was nevertheless a member of the Politburo and an unrepentant fan of traditional opera. Despite his later activities during the 1960s, which would see him publicly attacking the Chinese theatre world for his own political gain, this was not at all the case in the 1950s and early 1960s. Once quoted as saying "I'll revoke the party membership of anyone who wants Ma Lianliang [a famous Peking opera actor and director] to put on contemporary dramas,"[38] he is featured prominently in materials that the Northern Kun Opera Troupe put together. The first three glossy pages of photographs and text are dedicated to Kang's calligraphy and a note he sent on the day of the founding, including the lines "The undertaking is very difficult! The future is very promising!"[39] In another photograph, taken after the opening performance, he is pictured standing between Mei Lanfang and Chen Yi, alongside other officials and artists (see figures 3 and 4).[40]

The friendship between Meng Chao and Kang Sheng dated back to their youth in Zhucheng; their relations only deepened over time, despite Kang Sheng's later assertions to the contrary.[41] It was Kang Sheng who would introduce Meng Chao to the latter's future wife, Ling Junqi, whose father happened to be Kang's financial support during their years in Shanghai.[42] Although their divergent activities in the 1930s and 1940s separated them—Kang Sheng would spend time in Moscow and Yan'an, becoming an important part of the security apparatus, in the same period that saw Meng Chao in Guilin and other parts of China—they renewed their friendship in the mid-1950s.[43] Meng Chao never mentions Kang Sheng by name in his postscript, but others writing after the Cultural Revolution, such as Lou Shiyi, Mu Xin, and Meng Chao's daughter Meng Jian, note the connections between the two, and especially between Kang Sheng and the production of *Li Huiniang*.[44] Kang Sheng advised his old friend on everything from the content of the play, to turns of phrase, to the color of fringe on the ghost costume for Li Huiniang.[45]

Despite the involvement of Kang Sheng, the production of *Li Huiniang* was not as carefully managed as that of *Hai Rui* or *Xie Yaohuan*, and *Li Huiniang* nearly missed becoming an important play. Cong Zhaohuan, a prominent *xiaosheng* (young male role) of the Northern Kun troupe during the 1950s and 1960s, noted that *Li Huiniang* was received by the

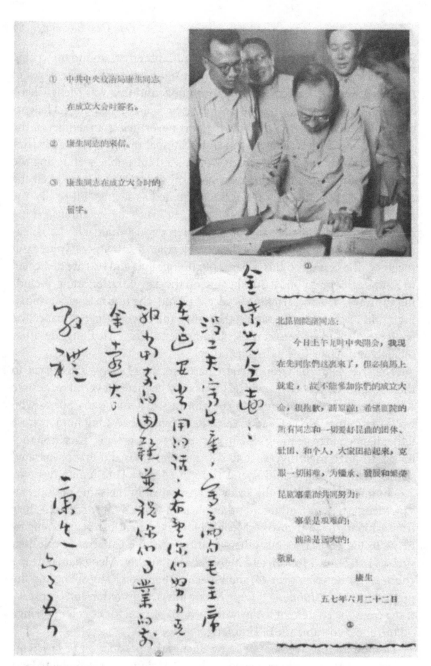

Fig. 3. Glossy photo pages from Northern Kun Opera Theatre commemorative book. Kang Sheng's calligraphy is prominently displayed alongside a photograph from him. *Source*: Beifang kunqu juyuan, ed., *Jicheng yu fazhan kunqu yishu* ([Beijing?]: Dongdan yinshuachang, n.d.), 3, 7. In author's personal collection.

Fig. 4. Glossy photo pages from Northern Kun Opera Theatre's commemorative book. (R) The top photograph features (L-R) Bai Yunsheng, Han
Shichang, and Mei Lanfang. The bottom photograph features (L-R) Li Shujun
(the actress who would bring Meng Chao's Li Huiniang to life), Mao Dun,
Mei Lanfang, Kang Sheng, Chen Yi, Han Shichang, Bai Yunsheng, Cheng
Yanqiu, and Qian Junduan. *Source*: Beifang kunqu juyuan, ed., *Jicheng yu
fazhan kunqu yishu* ([Beijing?]: Dongdan yinshuachang, n.d.), 3, 7. In author's
personal collection.

troupe in 1960, and the initial impulse was to have it performed only by
the student division.[46] It eventually made its way to the professional division, and premiered in the summer of 1961 (see figure 5), after months of
rehearsals (a mimeographed practice edition used by the troupe is dated
May 12, 1961).[47] Cong described how the performers wanted to energize
the performance of classical dramas, undertaking rehearsals with gusto. Li
Shujun, who played Li Huiniang, sought special tutoring in the execution
of the ghost step (a technique that made actors appear as if they were glid-

Fig. 5. Images from
the Northern Kun
Opera Theatre. Li
Shujun playing Li
Huiniang before and
after death. *Source*:
Meng Chao, *Li
Huiniang* (Shanghai:
Shanghai wenyi chu-
banshe, 1961).

ing or floating), and Cong practiced *shuaifa*, a technique of "swaying the hair" typically used by male characters who are in distress or humiliated.[48]

The two months of practice paid off as soon as the play made its debut: Cong stated that "very quickly, the Beijing Culture Bureau saw that this was a good play—the south had [the opera] *Fifteen Strings of Cash* [*Shiwu guan*, often cited as the paragon of a highly successful Kun adaptation], the north had *Li Huiniang*, and it was a paradigm for 'pushing out the old to bring in the new.'"[49] This old phrase from the Hundred Flowers was reenergized in 1961, and the problem of how best to "bring in the new" was a consistent feature of discussions on opera until 1965. The play was a hit not just with bureaucrats but also with cultural elites.

The reaction to *Li Huiniang* is, in many respects, an encapsulation of the cultural climate of the early 1960s. Writers like Meng Chao attempted to balance the reverence for classical language and culture with a professed desire to make them more relevant to contemporary audiences. At the same time, authors, critics, and artists threw themselves into "traditional" culture with zeal. One imagines that Meng Chao's play may well have been a pleasure for him to compose, an interesting challenge for the artists presenting it, and a delight for educated audiences. While *Li Huiniang* may not have been entirely free from attempts to make the content more "educational" by emphasizing political themes of struggle, it was nevertheless a play that seemed clearly aimed at the cultural elite. This is underscored by the exclusive run it received by the Shanghai Art & Culture Press in 1962: in contrast to Ma Jianling's *Wandering West Lake*, which saw a minimum of 100,000 copies printed from at least three different runs between 1953 and 1961, *Li Huiniang* received a single printing of merely 3,000.[50] Written in exquisitely literary language and performed in an elite style of opera, the play did not tamper with the potentially problematic (but emotionally powerful) core of the original: the murder of Li Huiniang and her return as a ghost.

Perfecting Perfection: The Reception of Li Huiniang

Following the premiere of the play, an enthusiastic discussion about its merits and shortcomings followed on the pages of newspapers and in drama journals. In examining the discussion over *Li Huiniang* in greater detail—and in particular by emphasizing its connection to broader 1950s discourses on the suitability of supernatural literature and theatre—I propose that, regardless of the potential criticism of the present that may have been found in *Li Huiniang*, and whether or not audiences saw in Meng Chao's adaptation a criticism of the Great Leap Forward and party leadership, the discussion about his play indicate that there were other issues at stake that intellectuals and performers enthusiastically took up. The discussion surrounding *Li Huiniang* in 1961 and 1962 underscores these points, particularly the balance between the necessity of adapting drama and maintaining literary traditions. I do not suggest that coded criticism of the Leap was not part of the creation and reception of the play. We would not expect to see open acknowledgment of such a point in reviews, nor could we expect Meng Chao to discuss such a use of his opera openly. Despite Mao's retreat in the wake of the failure of the Leap, no one was openly disparaging party policies. The most "open" critics, such as Deng Tuo, utilized their *zawen* series, published in major newspapers, and their critiques were still cloaked in allegorical language, designed to be understood only by a limited circle of people.[51] Meng Chao himself was a talented writer of *zawen* and participated (under a pen name, Chen Bo) in a 1962 essay series, "The Long and the Short," published in *People's Daily*, along with Wu Han, Xia Yan, Liao Mosha, and Tang Tao.[52] This seems a more natural avenue for expressing his frustration with policy than Kun opera, which he readily admits to having no experience writing.

Despite his inexperience with the form, however, critics received *Li Huiniang* in an overwhelmingly positive manner. Zhang Zhen, the supporter Meng Chao mentions in his postscript, and who had taken an exceptionally dim view of Ma Jianling's "ghostless" *Wandering West Lake* several years before, was extremely enthusiastic in his *Theatre Report* review. Zhang praised the portrayal of the unlucky concubine, as well as the extensive edits Meng Chao made to the original storyline.[53] He took an approving view of Meng Chao's lyricism, as well as the "*zawen* techniques" he brought to the revisions.[54] Making much of the actors' artistic qualities, he mentioned that Li Shujun's ghost step was learned from Xiao Cuihua, one of the great *huadan* of Peking opera, and the same artist who had been forced from stages in the 1950s and complained mightily of it during the Hundred Flowers. Zhang also pointed to Cong Zhaohuan's *shuaifa*, noting that such traditional skills really helped bring characters to life.[55] He seemed exceptionally pleased with a play that, by many accounts, hewed very closely to its Ming predecessor.

Much of the discussion centered on comparing various revisions of the *Red Plums* story. Yang Xianyi, the well-known translator and no stranger to China's illustrious classical traditions, took up the long history of revisions. Yang, who had studied at Oxford in the 1930s before returning to China in the early 1940s, translated into English, along with his British wife Gladys, some of the most famous pieces of the classical literary canon, including *The Peony Pavilion* and selections of Pu Songling's *Strange Tales*. The pair had also been responsible for the English translation of *Stories about Not Being Afraid of Ghosts*.[56] He noted in *Play Monthly* that Meng Chao's adaptation was truly the best of the numerous versions of the story, and the best Kun opera representative since *Fifteen Strings of Cash* of the order to "let a hundred flowers bloom, push out the old and bring in the new."[57] Like many other reviewers, Yang pointed to the streamlining of the play as a highlight of the new version—perhaps, in some respects, the most basic aspect of adapting drama. "While writing plays, these feudal period literati often forgot that plays were meant to be staged so people could watch," he noted. "[They] didn't give much thought to the structure of the libretto, and on the contrary, often made the plots excessively complicated . . . the result being there was no way to stage the whole play, only excerpt a few scenes." Yang suggested that "most Ming-Qing *chuanqi* could be handled in the manner of *Fifteen Strings of Cash* and *Li Huiniang*. After discarding the useless and preserving the good, we would invariably discover many good plays to stage."[58]

Yang, like many other cultural workers, saw the value of preserving many aspects of traditional culture; he did not see the "ghost" in "ghost plays" as something to be discarded. On the subject of Ma Jianling's 1954 ghostless adaptation, the esteemed translator praised certain aspects, such as the typical trimming of "superstitious" scenes involving Yama. But Yang criticized the decision to change Li Huiniang from an unjustly slain concubine-turned-ghost to a concubine faking death and dressing up as a ghost as "spoiling the fun" and "really detracting from the atmosphere of the original script."[59] Beyond Ma's version, Yang considered other revised scripts, which overwhelmingly shared an impulse to strip away superfluous elements while adding other confusing elements and plot twists. In outlining why *Li Huiniang* was the superior adaptation, Yang emphasizes the short length and concentrated plot above all other things. If anything was lacking, Yang opined, it was that Meng Chao's version fails to capture the *romanticism* of the original, and the narrative foundation of the Pei Yu-Li Huiniang love story is unstable![60] This was a criticism that was repeated many times by reviewers, including those who otherwise found *Li Huiniang* a shining achievement. This was not a question of political suitability. Rather, it seems that Meng Chao had, in his efforts to improve the ideology of the play, downplayed a beloved aspect of the plot. It is an echo of the critiques of Ma Jianling's attempt to deal with Li Huiniang: the changes had fundamentally altered the emotional *and* didactic powers of the original story.

Huang Qiuyun, writing under his pen name of Zhao Yan,[61] also picked up the theme of other adaptations. In an issue of *Literature and Art News*, he drolly noted that poor adaptations were cases of "the remedy being worse than the illness, touching gold and turning it to iron." Huang was appreciative of Meng Chao's talent for preserving Kun opera's traditions, calling the "Hatred" (*youhen*) chapter a particular achievement, written as if it was of the same generation as the great Yuan playwright Bai Renfu or Tang Xianzu. Just as Meng Chao displayed deep reverence for Tang Xianzu's achievements, so too did many critics display an appreciation for the revisions that maintained "elegant" and "traditional" (and exceedingly complex) language.

This achievement of Meng Chao's, capturing both the literary quality of the original, as well as the ideological spirit of the PRC, is a constant undercurrent in the reviews of *Li Huiniang*. Indeed, his libretto is extremely lyrical and poetic, fitting expectations for Kun opera quite well. It is little wonder critics found much to celebrate. Consider his supremely elegant poetic preface, a standard feature of traditional drama that sketches the plot of the drama to follow:[62]

> Crossing the river to the south, the mountains are rugged,
> The dissolute still hold sway in Lin'an.[63]
> In a bamboo hut, I am fond of reading "discourses on ghosts,"
> My intentions and energy link to a long rainbow,
> My vigorous brush punishes treacherous officials.
> Drawing from the wisdom of my predecessors,
> I express my own humble views,
> And give the old play *Red Plum* a new turn.
> I have carefully studied the tender emotions of youths, the feelings
>   of personal enmity.
> I write of a flourishing dream being cut off,
> I write of northern horses neighing at the banks of the Qiantang.
> Jia Sidao endangers the state and harms the people, but there is
>   music and song at evening banquets;
> His smile hides a dagger, and a chance for murder appears;

Pei Shunqing, indignant, speaks bluntly—the source of his
  misfortune,
Pleasing the hearts of people, extending righteous justice,
Li Huiniang is a heroic spirit after death, avenging injustice! (1)

Here, Meng Chao hews to classical literary conventions in structure and
turn of phrase and consciously styles himself as an erudite hermit in an
ancient mold. The image of reclusion (particularly for Confucian scholar-
literati "withdrawing" from the world of court politics) in Chinese literature and painting has a very long history, and Meng Chao here plays on
some of the ambiguity of a hermit's life, at once withdrawn from political
life, while at the same using his "vigorous brush" to criticize officials.[64] Perhaps more importantly, through his language and classical references, his
preface makes it clear that the play to follow is going to be a lyrical throwback to the great dramas of the imperial past. Meng Chao underscores his
research and preparation, his connection to his classical "predecessors,"
and explicitly links himself to a "long rainbow." Rudolf Wagner mentions
that he is unclear on what the rainbow signifies, though he assumes "it
refers to the link between the present and the 'discourses on ghosts' that
the poet read."[65] "Discourses on ghosts" (*guibian*) can be read in several
ways, I think: as a reference to classical discussions (what Wagner is suggesting), or the "discourses on ghosts" of the 1950s and earlier, which
Meng Chao himself did not participate in, but could hardly have been
ignorant of. It could also be read as a type of synecdoche, with "Guibian"
(the last act in part one of *Story of Red Plums*, which forms the last act of
Meng Chao's revision) standing in for *Red Plums* or classical works as a
whole. In any case, it seems obvious that Meng Chao is connecting himself
and his adaptation to a myriad of classical antecedents.

It is not only the preface that is highly literary. In the act "Hatred," the
scene that marks Li Huiniang's return as a ghost, she describes the situation she is in with hauntingly poetic language:

I am a masterless spirit,
Wandering aimlessly . . . ,
Like a kite with a cut string,
I have floated to this silent, fragrant place.
I watch the fireflies flit about,
The fallen leaves rustle through the empty courtyard. . . .
That music and song over there—an alluring, bustling dream.

I am here, all alone, hiding in the shadows—wanting to cry but
  unable to make a sound. (26–27)

Even when writing of less poetic subjects than chilly, moonlit autumn
nights, Meng Chao's language is elegant. Pei Yu, the young student who
stands up to Jia Sidao, makes his entrance in the libretto through a poem
he sends to the prime minister:

Foreign dust darkens the sun and war drums ring out,
But those who sleep soundly by scenic lakes and hills will not go
  out to battle;
While they are ignorant of strategic spots and vantage points,
Farmland lays fallow, for the common people are injured. (10)

Critics enthused about Meng Chao's revisions, the reverence with which
he treated traditional drama and literature, his sublime language, and his
overall success in updating a classic for the modern age, all without taking too many liberties with the core of the original. His ability to distill
the essence of Zhou Chaojun's play, in both content and language, while
dispensing with the unnecessary (or politically problematic) sections is
applauded again and again.

  This is especially clear in a review in a December issue of *People's Daily*.
Here, Tao Junqi and Li Dake took up the subject of the inadequacies of the
many adaptations of Zhou Chaojun's original play.[66] Unlike many of the
others, however, Tao and Li consistently praised the original for its art-
istry *and* its ideological content. In their opening, they chastised others for
not paying enough attention to the original or criticizing it as being "not
very bright." The problem was not with the original per se, but with many
adaptations. Tao and Li opined that adaptations generally expunged the
story of political struggle between Pei Yu and Jia Sidao, choosing instead
to focus on the twin love stories of Pei Yu and Lu Zhaorong and Pei Yu and
Li Huiniang. According to them, Meng Chao had preserved the essence
of the original, while deleting the weak segments; they provided historical
justification for the strengthening of the characters' political resolve.

  The robust discussion of *Li Huiniang* in journals and newspapers was
mirrored in numerous meetings and conferences. In August 1961, the Beijing Federation of Literary and Art Circles brought together the director
and theorist A Jia, Meng Chao, the Northern Kun Opera director Bai Yunsheng, actress Li Shujun, and others for a meeting to discuss the success

of *Li Huiniang* as an adaptation.[67] The *Beijing Literature and Art* write-up of the meeting proves illuminating on the subject of the work of adaptations more broadly. The title of the piece, "Making Perfection Even More Perfect," aptly described the discussion that ensued. Despite the effusive praise for *Li Huiniang*, there was a clear tension between the mandate to improve ideological and political content (which Meng Chao seems to have been generally successful at) and preserving favorite aspects of the play, the love story in particular. But while discussants criticized the love story as being built on an unstable base, no one could offer an example of a play that managed the balance better. In some respects, dramatists were, even in a more relaxed period, in an impossible position, as the article makes clear. Critics wanted plot lines that "improved the ideological thinking" of characters, and love stories that melded with the theme of political struggle. At the same time, they yearned for those love stories to seem "believable," while remaining true to historical circumstance.

This emphasis on the love story is reflected in Meng Chao's postscript to the play, which was published in book form by the Shanghai Literature and Art Press in 1962. Responding to the discussion of his play, Meng Chao addressed the specific criticisms of the lack of romantic love between Pei Yu and Li Huiniang. The romance was intended to be "relatively veiled," to better fit with his conception of Li Huiniang and her strength of purpose in saving the masses (versus simply rescuing Pei Yu). And yet, as he pointed out indignantly, he had no intention to avoid the love story, asking, "Can you say [a line such as] 'I sleep in a withered tomb, lovelorn, [hearing] a lone jade flute!' isn't 'love'?" Admitting there were areas where he could have played up the romantic elements, he added that he was unable to bear the idea of handling his own characters in a rash manner.[68] His Li Huiniang met with death on account of being moved by Pei Yu's righteousness; her motivation after death was to save the masses as well as Pei Yu, and love emerged by degrees from a place of respect and justice. This debate over literary romance is one that certainly deserves more attention than it has gotten. Haiyan Lee has argued that conceptions of "romance" or "love" experience a total shift after 1949: "a socialist subject 'loves' another socialist subject for his or her class belonging, not for his or her moral qualities, intellectual prowess, economic standing, social status, or sexual appeal. Love ceases to be an affair of unique persons and singular hearts."[69] In this framing, romantic love only returns to the literary world in the post-Mao period. But what, then, do we make of ghosts moved by the bonds of love and the discussion of the romanticism of these plays?

However, despite this good-natured debate over romance or lack thereof, the piece that *Li Huiniang* and Meng Chao have been most strongly identified with—both by Cultural Revolution–era critics and later scholars—is a short essay written by Liao Mosha, the same intellectual who gently poked at *Stories about Not Being Afraid of Ghosts* in the "Three Family Village" *zawen* series. His "some ghosts are harmless theory" (*yougui wuhai lun*) was not a critique of Meng Chao, but a powerful, brief defense of ghost plays and ghost characters, as well as a guide for how audiences *should* interpret ghost characters such as Li Huiniang. According to his own accounts, Liao Mosha may have been a semidisinterested participant in the debates on history on stages and theatrical ghosts, but he defended both—and by extension, defended the value of classical culture in modern society. In the context of the generally positive back and forth of 1961 and 1962, Liao's essay is an outlier: it was highly critical of those who would ban ghosts from stages. Like Meng Chao, Liao Mosha had been active in the Republican Shanghai literary scene and was known as a talented writer of *zawen* (and indeed, the two would both publish essays in the 1962 series "The Long and the Short"). Unlike Meng Chao, however, Liao had achieved a good measure of literary and political prominence beginning in the 1930s. By the 1960s, he was director of the United Front Work Department of the Beijing Party Committee and part of the central Propaganda Department.[70] A cursory glance at his collected works makes it clear that he was a prolific writer who weighed in on a number of critical issues of the day, including the discussion on new historical plays. However, his entrance into the ghost play debate would have a lasting impact on Liao, Meng Chao, and the cultural world at large.

In his 1978 essay on the genesis of "Ghosts," Liao Mosha explained that Meng Chao's supporters wanted him to craft a similar essay to one he wrote on the subject of Wu Han and *Hai Rui*.[71] Liao's piece on *Hai Rui* was written as a relatively lighthearted, congratulatory note to an old friend, Wu Han. Of course, the subject itself was weighty: the relationship between history and theatre had been one of Wu Han's "major preoccupations during the period 1959–1962."[72] Liao wrote positively of his old friend's efforts, noting that "[w]ith your *Hai Rui*, at long last the doors of the two families of 'history' and 'theatre' are beginning to be broken down [i.e., historical scholarship is combined with drama in a thoughtful manner] . . . This is a very difficult thing, a very creative type of work."[73] Thus, the *Hai Rui* essay very obviously extended beyond the bounds of a single adaptation, and instead raised questions relating to the creation of historical dramas more broadly. The one thing never up for discussion was whether or not historical dramas should be on stages. Rather, the critics simply assumed they *would* be performed, which would assuredly not be the case by 1963 and 1964.

So, at the behest of Meng Chao's supporters, the *Beijing Evening News* gave Liao tickets to see *Li Huiniang*. But when he sat down to write his review, he was apparently at a loss for words. He spoke with editor Hou Qi, who "mentioned that ghost plays were unable to be accepted by some of the audience."[74] This apparently reminded Liao of Mao's words on theatrical monsters that the Chairman referred to as "ox ghost–snake spirits" (*niugui-sheshen*). Liao quoted part of Mao's words in his "Some Ghosts" essay: "Recently, some *niugui-sheshen* have been staged. Some comrades look at this situation, and they are very anxious. I say, a little bit is fine. . . . Of course I am not *recommending* monsters [be staged], I simply say 'a little bit is fine.'" He quoted from the speech further, but left out a few critical lines: ". . . within a few decades such ghosts and monsters will disappear from the stage altogether, and you won't be able to see them even if you want to."[75]

Liao sketched connections between the *Hai Rui* essay and "Ghosts," and there is a fair amount of similarity between the two pieces. Both were published under the pseudonym Fan Xing[76] in *Beijing Evening News* ("'History'" in February 1961, and "Ghosts" in August that same year). And, like his letter to Wu Han, the piece on ghost plays came down firmly in the camp of the adaptation; as such, the pieces were more than a defense of a single author. Rather, Liao penned a defense of a large part of the classical canon. Liao noted a question he attributed (somewhat tellingly) to "youth": "Since these are adapted scripts of contemporary authors, why are we preserving the superstitious component of old plays, allowing ghosts to appear on stages—how can this not be propagating superstitious thought?"[77] He did not address this right away. Instead, he noted that the percentage of classical literature that involved ghosts and spirits in some capacity was quite significant. If one removed the ghost from plays that involve or reference ghosts, "it fundamentally cannot be considered as a play. People say, 'Without coincidences there would be no stories.' As it happens, these types of plays [illustrate that] 'without ghosts there would be no plays.' Thinking of *Li Huiniang* or *Story of Red Plums*, if after strolling around West Lake, Jia Sidao returns home and cuts Li Huiniang down in one blow, and her ghost did not then appear—now, what interesting play is left to watch?"[78]

The catchphrase that "some ghosts are harmless" pointed to Mao's words in the Hundred Flowers period that "a little is okay," while ignoring Mao's prediction that such things would soon cease to exist. In arguing that *Li Huiniang*, like other adapted plays, was "not only *not* disseminating superstition, but precisely the opposite—it was really one type of encouragement of struggle against oppression," he added his voice to many others that argued against blanket condemnation. "It's not whether Li Huiniang is a human or a ghost," he wrote, "it's about who she represents and who she resists. To use a phrase children often want to ask while watching plays: Is she a good ghost, or is she a bad ghost?"[79] In large part, Liao's theory was nothing novel: ghosts had been justified on similar merits for more than a decade. But Liao's essay was unusual in the context of the ghost play discussion it appeared alongside: others simply took for granted that *Li Huiniang* was a *good play*, never mind that she was a good ghost.

At the time that "Some Ghosts Are Harmless" was published, the play and the author were facing no serious criticism. To the contrary, *Li Huiniang* had been well received, and there was no indication that the debate on ghosts would take a serious turn for the worse. There was no *actual* debate over ghosts on stages, at least not publicly. Liao's preemptive defense of ghost opera was also a defense of nonsocialist Chinese culture at large. The recognition that banning ghosts on stages could lead to a whole host of ramifications in the literary field was one that would only become more widespread in following years. Furthermore, Liao seems alert to the possibility that ghost characters could be used for much more sinister purposes than "encouraging a resisting spirit." It is possible to have a "good ghost" is the ultimate point of his essay: a very different take than seen in the introduction of *Stories about Being Afraid of Ghosts*, where there are no "good ghosts."

"Some Ghosts Are Harmless" was not the last word in the debate. One of the strongest critiques of Meng Chao's interpretation of *Li Huiniang* appeared in the May 1962 edition of *Theatre Report*—though, to be clear, this was not an attack on the suitability of ghosts on socialist stages. Much as some critics in the early 1950s took a dim view of ghostless ghost plays, Li Qingyun criticized the overly political nature of Meng Chao's plot; the point of contention underscores the general nature of the discussion, which never relied on broad condemnation. Li focused on a minor change that Meng Chao had made between the 1961 publication of *Li Huiniang* in *Play Monthly* and the 1962 publication of the play in book form. In Meng

Chao's script, as in many other versions, Li Huiniang first sees Pei Yu as he unleashes a verbal tirade on Jia Sidao:[80]

> I ask you:
> Why do you plunder the people's salt, practicing usury with large
>   profits?
> Why do you occupy the people's fields, oppressing, exploiting,
>   plundering?
> Why do you increase taxes, and seize them with brutal force?
> Why do you abuse the law codes, pressuring good people, killing
>   people like flies. . . . (17)

Li Huiniang, who has been present for the heated exchange, comments:

> This powerful speech—
> It is exactly the poem the youth of the Pei family inscribed . . .
> It seems this marvelous upright youth
> Defies power,
> And has the courage to display the righteousness of the world. (19)

And then, in the 1961 *Play Monthly* version, she sighs: "Oh, handsome youth!" (*mei zai shaonian*), a nearly character-for-character repetition of Li Huiniang's innocent comment found in Zhou Chaojun's original script.[81] The next year, it was appended to "Oh, righteous youth! Oh, handsome youth!" (*zhuang zai shaonian, mei zai shaonian*), which Meng Chao added because he felt that "righteous" better expressed the admiration Li Huiniang had for Pei Yu.[82] Li Qingyun's critique focused almost exclusively on the four-character addition, querying that while the concubine's "ideological level has improved, has the power of her image been enhanced or not? Is the new work more moving to people or not?" Li bluntly questioned whether or not the changes had improved the play in any respect other than the "political grounding" of the characters.[83] Although this is a relative outlier in the positive reception of *Li Huiniang*, it is a point of commonality between both Ma Jianling and Meng Chao's versions. Just as dramatists attempted to push the limits of revisions—in two different directions—skeptics questioned whether the didactic function of such revisions ultimately overpowered the very reason for their utility as tools.

Li's point is also an echo of the criticisms of Ma Jianling's invention of

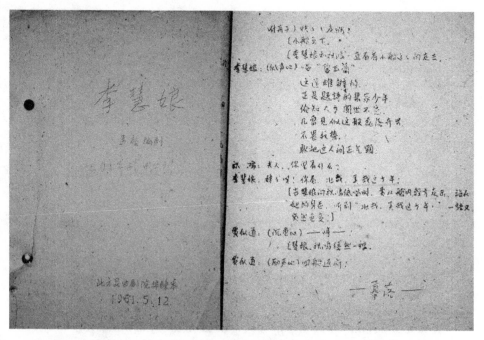

Fig. 6. Practice edition from the Northern Kun Opera, dated May 12, 1961. The line that would become rather contentious: "Righteous youth! Handsome youth!" (underlined heavily in pencil—the only such marking in the text). This is in the practice edition and the 1962 book publication, but not the July–August printing of *Play Monthly*. In the author's personal collection.

a preexisting love affair for Li Huiniang and Pei Yu. In the Ming original and its many adaptations, Jia Sidao's wrath is aroused simply by Huiniang's impulsive comment on a handsome young stranger. Ma Jianling gave the two a deep prior relationship, and it is partly for this reason that Jia Sidao's fury is stoked. In Meng Chao's revision, she sighs not just about his attractiveness but about his "righteous" courage as well. Interestingly, while this addition is not found in the July/August appearance of the script in *Play Monthly*, it *is* found in the practice edition (*pailianben*) of *Li Huiniang* used by the Northern Kun Opera theatre, dated May 12, 1961, several months before the play's textual "premiere" in the journal (see figure 6). Furthermore, the line is underlined heavily in pencil—the only line in the entire script to receive such attention.[84] Although the reasons for this emphasis are unclear, it seems likely that special significance was attached to the addition, which is reflected in the changes between the original script, as prepared by the Northern Kun Opera, and its original print version.

In most versions of the play, Li Huiniang is murdered for a minor offense, her almost involuntary comment on the attractiveness of a young man. But in the two prominent socialist revisions, she is struck down for another offense that critics often found too "understandable," and thus not a clear enough signal of the arbitrary power of the feudal elite. As for Meng Chao's particular twist, by her comment that Pei Yu is a "righteous youth," Li Qingyun argued that Huiniang is making a pointed, considered statement disapproving of Jia Sidao and his inaction. "To put it plainly," Li commented, "isn't this [sort of statement] looking for death?"[85] That someone could be killed in the "old society" for opposing a powerful official would not be a revelation for audiences.[86] Finally, Li Qingyun stated that, while reforming drama is an admirable goal, not all works can have political thought grafted in without damaging the artistic integrity and usefulness of the pieces. Li concluded rather provocatively that, at least in the case of *Li Huiniang*, "new people are not equal to the old."[87] That is, ideological "improvements" had not actually *improved* the play, but were rather changes that harmed the emotional, and thus didactic, power of the original.

The final word of this 1962 debate came from Feng Qiyong, who grounded a critique of Li Qingyun's position on a historical survey of the story.[88] He took particular issue with Li's assertion that Li Huiniang's death was an obvious consequence of making a politically defiant statement in the old society, and that this lessened the impact of the play on the audience. Feng's impassioned argument—built on the numerous adaptations of the original story—defended Meng Chao's revisions. Wasn't it possible, he asked, for multiple works to pull from the same foundation, but for each to have a different emphasis and method of expressing their point? Feng ended his essay with a critique of Li's statement that "new people are not equal to the old." Such a statement not only negated Meng Chao's revisions, but anything that deviated from the Ming original, which included a whole host of regional adaptations spread over four centuries. Feng ended that he thought Li's "conclusion is still up for debate." There would be more debate, but not precisely in the way Feng suggested.

Conclusion

Meng Chao's *Li Huiniang* and *Stories about Not Being Afraid of Ghosts*, despite their shared origins in classical ghost literature, represented two fundamentally different usages of the ghost trope, and are representative of two competing narratives that would become increasingly important politically after 1962. In *Stories*, the selections were aimed at combating superstitious thought, as well as illustrating the necessity to stand up to "ghosts," whatever "real world" phenomena they might be. *Li Huiniang*, on the other hand, was framed as a tale that encouraged people to resist by associating themselves *with* the ghost, not placing themselves antagonistically against the character. In contrast to the heroic humans who stand up to "ghost-like things" in *Stories*, in Meng Chao's recounting of Zhou Chaojun's play (and indeed, in the original play itself), it is *humans*—not ghosts—who prove the most fearsome enemies of the people. The titular apparition of *Li Huiniang*, on the other hand, declares herself to be a "ghost bodhisattva," returned to the land of the living in order to offer aid to those who suffered under the strain of Jia Sidao's callous policies.

The divergent discourses on ghosts highlighted in this chapter represented tensions that had been simmering since the first debates on "mythology" and "superstition." Cultural workers and critics had successfully argued for the inclusion of many ghost plays in repertoires, based on their didactic and literary merits, evidenced by the glowing praise heaped upon *Li Huiniang* and its author. But the idea that ghosts represented dangerous evils would come to the fore in 1963, when a total ban on ghost opera was enacted by the Ministry of Culture. There would be more debate on the subject, but the political winds were shifting, and along with them, the fate of writers and artists who brought righteous phantasms to life would shift dramatically, as well.

CHAPTER 4

Resisting Spirits
The Ghost Play Debates of 1963

If one looks only at the articles published in 1961 and 1962, it would seem that *Li Huiniang* and its creator were destined to be a success story of cultural production in the Mao years. The reworking of the ghost play was the high point of more than ten years of heated discussions on the place of such works in socialist China, and it seemed that writers like Meng Chao, Tian Han, Liao Mosha, and the rest had emerged from a turbulent decade to bask in a more relaxed cultural environment. While some in the leadership poked fun at pedantic plays and encouraged writers to create true entertainment—not just ideology lessons dressed up as traditional plays—some writers reveled in highly literary Chinese, and critics debated the finer points of balancing political ideology and romance.

But the balance that had been maintained from 1950 to 1962 was upset in 1963, when the Ministry of Culture banned all ghost plays from stages for "spreading feudal and superstitious thought among the masses."[1] This action marked the first step in the increasing radicalization of the cultural world that would culminate in the all-out attacks on Wu Han and Tian Han in late 1965 and 1966. This did not, however, mean that the "ghost play issue" had been totally resolved. To the contrary, despite the first blanket ban, a robust debate played out on the pages of elite publications and in troupe meetings. Writers like Li Xifan, who had written copiously on the subject of historical drama, now wrote pages and pages on theatrical ghosts. Between the two poles of "some ghosts are harmless" and "no ghost is harmless," writers and artists struggled to "decide" the future of drama in China, and, by extension, the fate of traditional culture. The terms of the debate had changed, and much larger forces were at work as Mao returned to the political fray and his wife, Jiang Qing, took on new importance behind the scenes. No longer was it simply a question of whether or not certain subjects belonged on stages; from 1964, authors became the subject of stiff criticism. By 1965, with the vicious political attacks of the early Cultural Revolution period already in planning or under way, there was no lively debate, only strident calls to take down people seen as promulgating antiparty, antisocialist tendencies.

In many respects, the 1963 debate served as a testing ground for Jiang Qing and her clique—she successfully insisted on a total ban of ghost plays, put into practice by the Ministry of Culture, and engineered criticism of ghost plays and Liao Mosha's "some ghosts are harmless theory." At the same time, many intellectuals seemed uncomfortable with this attack on traditional drama, and were not afraid of sharing their opinions. Jiang Qing may have been prepared to take on the whole of the cultural realm, but many people objected to a whole-scale remaking, both in public and in more private spaces, from Shanghai to Beijing. An overwhelming scholarly focus has been on the 1965 criticism of Wu Han's *Hai Rui*; the attack on the author and play is often read as the "prelude" to the Cultural Revolution. However, the criticism of Wu Han and *Hai Rui* came only when lesser artists and more suspect plays had been thoroughly trashed.

This chapter considers the last 1963 debate on ghost plays, with special attention to the series of essays published that autumn in the *Guangming Daily*. I argue that, in addition to narratives that emphasize the connection of reformed drama to the Great Leap Forward, the 1963 debate should also be seen as intimately connected to discussions that stretch back to the 1950s. I also underscore the connection between elite politics and culture and the grassroots; the 1963 troupe meetings, a direct result of the *Guangming Daily* publications, reveals the full toll that the years between 1949 and 1963 took on theatre artists. The debates on ghost plays and traditional drama, within the bureaucracy and on the pages of elite publications, were not simply thought exercises. The instability of the drama world took a very real toll on the artists and cultural workers tasked with carrying out quickly changing directives over a long period of time. The year 1963 was a pivotal, transitional one: though critics and artists still carried on debates that dated back well over a decade, the position of supernatural literature—and soon, the status of the writers and artists who brought it forth—was rapidly changing. Increasingly, the narrative—seen in *Stories about Not Being Afraid of Ghosts*—that emphasized that ghosts needed to be resisted would become the dominant one. Writers and artists themselves would be turned into ghosts, in the form of *niugui-sheshen*—ox ghost–snake spirits—not exemplary artists, but antiparty, antisocialist thought enemies of the CCP and the people.

Banning Ghosts

By 1962, Mao was increasingly displeased with criticism focused on him, a fact that was relayed to the screenwriter Xia Yan by Jiang Qing that year.[2] Jiang joined forces with Zhang Chunqiao and Yao Wenyuan, "natural allies in their common animus" directed at the elite cultural apparatus, which "had criticized and blocked their efforts to achieve prominence in the cultural realm."[3] In the summer of 1962, Jiang suggested a ban on Wu Han's *Hai Rui*, which was ignored.[4] This failure prompted her to turn elsewhere. It is possible that Jiang Qing saw in ghost plays an opportunity that was hard to pass up: ghost opera had been a subject of serious debate even before 1949, and was reasonably easy to criticize as bourgeois, individualistic, and feudal. Mao had never urged anyone to act like a ghost, but he had encouraged people to be more like Hai Rui. Perhaps most importantly, Meng Chao, the author of the celebrated ghost play's newest revision, lacked Wu Han's political connections. There was no Peng Zhen or Zhou Yang on his side. Meng Chao had only Kang Sheng, ally of Jiang Qing—and a dangerous friend to have. The man who had played matchmaker for Meng Chao and his future wife, and who had encouraged his old friend in rewriting a Ming ghost play, would help bring him to ruin.[5] Kang Sheng, perhaps the most inscrutable of all the players in the great drama of 1960s Chinese politics, also began agitating behind the scenes that summer, sensing political opportunity with Mao's increased displeasure at the state of the cultural world. His cryptic messages to Meng Chao, criticizing ghost opera, represented quite the reversal. He himself had played a key role in bringing *Li Huiniang* into existence and was an unrepentant fan of traditional drama.[6] Indeed, in the months prior to sending his ominous warnings to Meng Chao, Kang Sheng and Jiang Qing had spent time in Hangzhou, where they apparently demanded many performances of banned plays, or plays the local troupes had on their own decided not to stage.[7]

It was political expediency, not any great love for contemporary theatre, that propelled Kang and Jiang's activities in 1962 and 1963. The pair understood that there were "political opportunities" in the wake of the

Tenth Plenum, where Mao focused on class struggle and the demand that it be talked about "every year, every month, every day."[8] However, taking advantage of them would require disavowing their interest in traditional drama.[9] According to Li Zhisui, Mao's personal physician, Jiang and Kang's new position on traditional drama was not immediately apparent even to people in Mao's inner circle. Mao did not see *Li Huiniang* until early 1963, despite the fact that a show at Zhongnanhai had been arranged in 1961 for top party officials.[10] In his doctor's recollection, the chairman apparently did not like this revised ghost drama. Li posits that the critical scene where Li Huiniang cries out in admiration of "righteous" and "handsome" Pei Yu struck too close to home, making Mao recall unpleasant events with younger women. While Mao may have sulked, the true villain of the story seems to be his wife. Li, no great fan of Jiang, paints a picture of a woman on a cultural rampage. He quotes Mao's primary bodyguard as saying "We're in big trouble. Jiang Qing thinks *Li Huiniang* is a very bad opera, a big poisonous weed."[11] Although the new historical plays, including *Li Huiniang*, were produced in a tense political atmosphere, there is no hint of a critical political reading when looking at reviews from the plays' premieres, and Meng Chao was assuredly not offering commentary on Mao's love life. But, if we take Li Zhisui's account at face value, is it possible that Jiang Qing saw a political opportunity in Mao's irritation at the drama, whatever its source? Meng Chao and his *Li Huiniang* are conspicuously different from Wu Han and his *Hai Rui*, Tian Han and his *Xie Yaohuan*. Wu and Tian were much more politically well connected than Meng Chao, despite his inclusion in a relatively small group of cultural and intellectual elites, and *Li Huiniang* is a play that was intimately bound up in a genre that had been hotly debated since the founding of the PRC and before: ghost opera.

In March 1963, the Ministry of Culture published a directive that formally banned ghost plays, and once again made it clear that artistic matters were to be firmly subsumed to political ones: the "thaw" was over.[12] It asserted that a ban would help the drama world put into practice the policies of art and culture serving socialism and the masses and "letting a hundred flowers bloom, pushing out the old to bring in the new"—the same slogan, of course, that had been applied to the reworking of *Li Huiniang*, and drama reform more broadly. While noting that the most "poisonous" of ghost plays had already been banned in the early years of the PRC, the directive expresses some alarm at the popularity of ghost plays, especially in light of the "profusion of praise" *Li Huiniang* received from critics, and Liao Mosha's idea that "some ghosts are harmless."[13] While this seems a sharp rebuke to critics who enthusiastically took up the defense of traditional drama, of equal (or even greater) concern was the fact that ghost plays were "spreading feudal and superstitious thought among the masses."[14] Despite all the campaigns and education of the past fourteen years, audiences still loved theatrical ghosts. Mao had claimed during the Hundred Flowers that "poisonous weeds" did not need strict regulation, as they would eventually fall victims to their own success. This had not happened, and so his wife stepped in to set the cultural world straight and expunge undesirable elements from stages once and for all.

Compared to later statements, the Ministry of Culture's announcement was remarkably even-tempered. It affirmed that there were some "comparatively good" ghost plays, particularly in regard to artistic achievements.[15] Even the criticism of *Li Huiniang* was muted. Meng Chao was never mentioned, and neither he nor his play was discussed with the vituperative rhetoric that would plague them during and after 1964. Certainly, there is no hint of an accusation that the work and its author were fundamentally "antiparty, antisocialist thought." As presented by the Ministry of Culture, the problem simply boiled down to one of negatives outweighing positives. Ghost plays may have indeed provided examples of oppressed people resisting and struggling against their oppressors, but it was "impossible to ignore the fact that they all affirm the superstition that after death, people turn into ghosts."[16] In contrast to people who claimed that the ideological level and general knowledge of the common people had been drastically raised since 1949, the directive espoused the belief that the masses were still far too uneducated, too unsophisticated, and too impressionable to be allowed access to such dangerous material. For purposes of rooting out superstition among the people, ghost plays had to go. Nevertheless, theatre and education work units would still be permitted to stage otherwise banned plays internally with permission from the ministry. That is, what was unfit for public consumption was, at least in theory, perfectly acceptable for cultural workers in the confines of their work units, or presumably for leaders still interested in seeing the traditional repertoire. Clearly the Ministry of Culture was primarily concerned with reactions of the "superstitious" masses.[17]

The announcement also underscored the problematic distinction between superstitious ghost plays and other types of traditional tales: here, mythology plays and legends (*chuanshuo*) not involving ghosts were specifically excluded from the ban. While the announcement noted that troupes should take care not to play up "superstitious aspects" or put on "fearsome" scenes, there was no explanation as to why many other plays featuring miraculous subjects would be any less likely to "promulgate superstition" than ghost opera. The likely answer, of course, is that plays based on subjects like *The Legend of White Snake* and *Journey to the West* retained political utility, even for cultural radicals.[18] The distinction between ghost plays and mythology plays dated back to the 1950s, but many people did not find it entirely convincing. Indeed, critics and artists would continue to argue against the ministry's intervention. The analogies that ghost plays were to superstition and "legends" were to mythology remained as unconvincing in 1963 as they were in 1953.

"Separating Wheat from Chaff": Debating Ghosts in the Guangming Daily

If the ban was a fairly temperate method of chastising writers who were overstepping their bounds, the discussion that followed was a bit more critical, particularly where Liao Mosha's "some ghosts are harmless" theory was concerned. However, in contrast to essays organized between 1964 and 1966, critics in 1963 were not attacking writers and artists directly. *Li Huiniang*, for instance, would be criticized as a poor didactic tool and inappropriate for the masses, just as the Ministry of Culture announcement of the ban had highlighted; its author's political motivations were never questioned. Opponents of ghost opera claimed that the popularity of the genre reflected broader problems in society, particularly what was presented as too much affection for "old" and "traditional" works. Supporters of ghost literature, on the other hand, continued to argue that such plays held great artistic and didactic value. And those who defended ghost opera pointed to a dangerous precedent being set by banning an entire genre, and argued vociferously against the idea that theatrical ghosts had a connection to real life "superstitious" beliefs. The print debate ultimately underscores how many cultural workers were unwilling to silently watch an important and beloved genre disappear. If they could not reverse the ban, they would at least voice their displeasure and concern about the actions of the Ministry of Culture.

Critics of Liao's essay, by and large, claimed that his distinction between "good" and "bad" ghosts was a spurious one, because *all* ghosts were bad. One of the first pieces to appear after the ban was published in *Literature and Art News* in April, and it showed clearly that the general terms of the debate had, not surprisingly, shifted. No longer were reworked ghost plays a case of perfection needing a touch of polishing: 1963 marked a return to an earlier type of discourse, one that took up whether or not theatrical ghosts had any redeeming value. The author, dramatist Zhao Xun, stated that regardless of whether a ghost was "good" or "bad," when it came to acknowledging or promoting the existence of ghosts, "they were all the same."[19]

In May, two months after the announcement of the ban, an article highly critical of the "some ghosts are harmless" theory and *Li Huiniang* appeared in the Shanghai-based *Wenhui Daily*.[20] Like later attacks in 1965, this essay was organized by Jiang Qing (in this case, through Ke Qingshi, mayor of Shanghai).[21] However, while the lengthy essay clearly targeted the two pieces, the author Liang Bihui (pen name of Yu Minghuang, minister of the East China propaganda bureau[22]) criticized broader cultural trends. "It's a pity that in recent years, a small number of comrades have advocated 'history for the sake of history,' 'tradition for the sake of tradition,' believing that this [work] cannot be corrected, that [work] cannot be changed—this is pushing out the old and not bringing in the new [*tuichen buchuxin*], to the point of pushing out the old to bring in the old [*tuichen chujiu*]."[23] If there is one unusual feature of this essay, it was the lack of response from the two writers under attack—indeed, they were conspicuously absent from the 1963 debates. In Meng Chao's case, this was probably due to the warning from an editor of *Wenhui Daily* that "the article came from 'an authoritative side' and that [Meng Chao] should not reply."[24]

Still, many published pieces, in contrast to the essays that would begin appearing in 1965 and 1966, were critical of specific works, but did not yet attack specific authors. However, it is still possible to see the relatively gradual undermining of cultural workers who had defended or been engaged in the work of remaking and repurposing certain types of traditional theatrical culture, as in one essay published over three days in May, "The Harmfulness of Ghost Plays."[25] Authored by dramatist and critic Jing Guxie, who himself was involved in the work to adapt traditional drama, it also illustrates the intimate connection between 1963 criticism and the discussions of the 1950s and early 1960s. Jing sought to offer a primer to the ghost play "problem," and so introduced readers to major pieces of Chinese criticism of the 1950s, as well as more classically Marxist-Leninist approaches to "superstitious" literature and drama. Jing did not describe the plays as a threat to the party or the political elite, but rather castigated them as poor teaching tools and inappropriate for the masses. On the subject of *Li Huiniang*, Jing's criticisms have little hint of the venom that would plague the play and its author in following years. Instead, he asked whether or not the "improvement to the ideological content" of the Li Huiniang character had any effect on the course of the play. Despite the fact that Li Huiniang wreaks havoc for Jia Sidao, he opined that her "political struggle—just as before—is a failure!" Simply paying lip service to political issues was not enough; to have value, works needed to show a positive outcome for struggle.[26] These few articles did not snowball into something larger, though some would receive rebuttals later that year. The publication and dissemination of "Liang Bihui's" article did not lead to wider outcry, which may indicate that Jiang Qing and her coterie remained relatively politically weak. While some writers advocated for the same position espoused by these radicals, there was also a notable amount of opposition in public and more private venues. At stake was not simply whether or not ghosts should be reinstated on Chinese stages, but the future direction of China's artistic policy: the criticisms of *Li Huiniang* were merely the opening volleys for criticism of better-connected, better-protected playwrights and cultural workers.

Although isolated articles on the problem of ghost plays appeared in newspapers and journals throughout 1963, September proved a high point for the discussion. In August 1963, the Ministry of Culture, the Playwright Union, and the Beijing Culture Bureau convened a meeting to talk about a number of problems: the policy of "letting a hundred flowers bloom, pushing out the old to bring in the new," the feudalism and affinity to the people (*renminxing*) of traditional plays, historical plays, and ghost plays, among other things.[27] This was not a discussion confined to a high level meeting or two; it was to be the basis of discussion for several months, and the *Guangming Daily* would be the primary platform for debate.

On September 9, a lengthy piece kicked off several months of articles on drama. While the piece was published as an "editorial note," ostensibly by the paper's editors, it was created under the auspices of Zhou Yang, members of the Central Propaganda Ministry, heavily edited, and finally approved by Mao himself.[28] Although it is largely an unremarkable essay, the effect of the seemingly mild criticism was to summarily shuffle plays like *Li Huiniang* and *Hai Rui* from the category of "good play" to "bad play"—yet another example of the quick shifts in cultural policy seen in preceding years.[29] Such reversals were hardly novel for intellectuals and artists who had survived the 1950s. Much of the rest of the piece simply repeated the same things that had been published since the founding of the PRC: drama needed to incorporate socialism and patriotism and improve political awareness. It ought only to "suit the wishes of the people, keep pace with the forward progress of the age."[30] Of course, those who engineered the essay did not mention that, by and large, it seemed that "the masses" were more than happy with the traditional repertoire of various local opera forms! Despite this official intervention, many involved in implementing policy or involved in the cultural world did not simply reverse their opinions and begin publishing self-criticisms. Instead, a rich debate took place in print. Mu Xin recounts that between September and December, the paper received five hundred and thirty-two submissions related to the subject, totaling nearly two million characters. Illustrating the popularity of the "ghost play problem," nearly a third—166 responses—were on the subject of theatrical ghosts.[31]

One of the most frequently referenced articles was published by noted critic Li Xifan in the *Guangming Daily*.[32] Appearing six months after the ban on ghost plays, Li's essay was published alongside a much longer primer on the problem, authored by the *Guangming* editors. Li's essay criticized ghost plays on multiple levels, yet still attempted to cordon off a safe area for more useful "mythological" plays like *Journey to the West*. He tried, as authors had done before, to make distinctions between these various kinds of plays; however, his argument can seem contradictory and confusing. For instance, he insisted that stories such as *The Legend of White Snake* and *The Cowherd and the Weaving Maid* had utility: they encouraged individuals to use their own power to resist and did not rely on ideas of predestination and fate. Of course, *Li Huiniang* itself was celebrated for the very same reasons the previous year. This was an old argument that had never been satisfactorily settled, but people who favored a more nuanced, individualized approach to regulating plays found the broad distinctions between "ghost" and "mythology" plays suspect at best. Summarily declaring one type of play "bad" and another type of play "good" would mean leaving many important, valued, and didactically useful plays out of the repertoire entirely.

In the same edition of the *Guangming Daily*, a piece appeared criticizing Zhao Xun's essay of months earlier.[33] In particular, "Ruo He"—nom de plume of Chen Gongdeng, a student at East China Normal University—strongly critiqued the idea that people who wrote about ghosts were people who believed in ghosts, an echo of the superstition debates of the mid-1950s. Leaving aside romantics like Li Bai, Pu Songling, or Wu Cheng'en, the author pointed out that even realists like Du Fu, Guan Hanqing, and Lu Xun wrote of ghosts—and "almost-but-not-quite" ghosts also appeared in such vaunted socialist works as *The White-Haired Girl*.[34] He further contended that the idea that getting rid of ghosts on stages would somehow stamp out superstition among the masses was preposterous. He pointed to Mao's own words, in his 1927 report on Hunan peasants, that "idols were erected by peasants, and at the right time, peasants will use their own hands to tear the idols down, there is no need for anyone else to do it prematurely."[35]

Many authors pointed out the suspect logic that connected ghost plays and "actual" superstition among "the masses"—or at least, the problem of pinning the blame on ghost plays. One essayist called the ban a case of "giving up at the slightest obstacle," arguing that a lighter hand was called for, so as not to toss out perfectly good plays with the bad. As an example of the good type of ghost play, the author stated that Meng Chao's *Li Huiniang* was "perfect and without fault" both in terms of its ideology and its art.[36] Another flatly stated that as many ghost plays were, or had been, included in the "mythological play" designation, arguments that applied to ghost plays likewise applied to mythology plays. If one was going to claim that ghost plays spread superstitious thought, one really had to say the same thing about mythological plays. Why, there was apparently a certain place in Shanxi where the locals kowtowed and burned incense to a snake—yet *Legend of White Snake* was not banned.[37]

The discussion may have been stacked in favor of the naysayers, but those who found the arguments unconvincing or downright ridiculous at times still published critiques. From a distance of several decades, arguing that *The Peony Pavilion* was merely a case of "borrowing the form of a ghost to express the author's ideals" (thus, a "special," acceptable kind of ghost play) seems a stretch, and it is not difficult to understand the irritation many supporters of revised dramas felt.[38] One author argued that the heavy-handed approach to ghost plays was ideologically suspect: "The Marxist approach to criticism is not to wholly negate [something], to toss it out entirely, but to carry out concrete analysis, to separate the wheat from the chaff."[39] According to Mu Xin, even more expressed dissatisfaction with such "indiscriminate attacks" privately. One anonymous person who "could not abide by the current outrageous criticism of the Kun opera *Li Huiniang*" went so far as to send a poem to the paper, asking that it be forwarded to Meng Chao.[40]

Although the March ban set a firm policy on ghost opera, the robust debate in *Guangming Daily* underscores that many critics and writers were not convinced as to the ban's wisdom, necessity, and theoretical underpinnings. The fact that nearly one-third of the responses submitted to the paper explicitly addressed the ghost play problem indicates the cultural prestige these products held. To ban ghosts entirely from stages was to remove an important part of China's literary heritage, and, in the views of many, was an ineffectual way to address problems of real-life "superstitious" behavior. While the blanket ban was a fait accompli, those skeptical of the policy change were not content to remain silent; instead, they took on critics and cultural radicals like Li Xifan in print. They would not have many more opportunities to do so.

Managing "Gusts of Wind": Troupe Responses to Changes

It was not only writers, students, and other critics who took up the issue of ghost plays and drama reform. In light of the August discussion in Beijing and the ensuing *Guangming Daily* debate, the theatre world in Shanghai was instructed to discuss a number of artistic and political problems.[41] In addition to internal troupe discussions, a number of meetings were convened that involved cadres from the Shanghai Culture Bureau, as well as various district branches, plus artists from troupes all over the city. Particular emphasis was put on the issue of "pushing out the old to bring in the new," reform of drama and ghost plays. The documents produced after these meetings shed light on the nonpublic behavior and thoughts of performers and cadres. They also illustrate that even in light of the March 1963 ban on ghost opera, performers were divided on this action for a wide variety of reasons.

In thinking of the drive toward the Cultural Revolution, much has been made of the increasingly radical Shanghainese leftists, such as Yao Wenyuan, whom Jiang Qing found to be eager and willing participants in her struggle for cultural dominance. The troupe discussions underscore that while there may have been a "debate between Shanghai and Beijing," at least where elite intellectual and political maneuvering was concerned, the reality for those tasked with carrying out cultural directives was much murkier.[42] While there are many voices that appear to be in line with the radicals, there are also large numbers of dissenting or apathetic views. And, since these discussions took place behind closed doors, not on the pages of elite publications, they prove illuminating in several respects, particularly in highlighting the reach of published discussions, the practical concerns brought up by those directly impacted by shifts in policy, and the sheer exhaustion many artists felt after years of reversals and changes.

While many points of view echo published articles, performers and cadres brought up a number of very basic concerns. Although writers and critics, who could be somewhat removed from the day to day business of making a living as members of opera troupes, often debated on largely abstract terms, theatre artists did not have that luxury: a ban meant serious changes in active repertoire for many styles. Many participants also seemed upset by the apparently arbitrary nature of decisions on art and culture, perhaps because they were the ones who actually had to implement changes. Most importantly, statements were also made that do not appear in print. Outright criticism of the often-contradictory nature of party policy is not seen in *Guangming Daily* essays. However, unnamed members of the Xinghuo Pingtan troupe questioned the uneven application of supposedly "antisuperstitious" rules such as the banning of ghost plays, since the early 1960s collection of classical ghost tales, *Stories about Not Being Afraid of Ghosts*, was still being printed.[43] Members of the Feiming Yue Opera troupe wondered why "old struggles" of 1956 were being revived in 1963.[44] If ghosts were so bad, why had no one criticized *Li Huiniang* in 1961 or 1962? Further, the performers often seem more attuned to the potential ramifications of banning ghost plays. Some noted that several great dramas, including *The Peony Pavilion* and the *Injustice Done to Dou E*, were useful tools for teaching. Beyond that, even a play branded "dangerous" by the Ministry of Culture had its fine points: *Li Huiniang* was singled out for having a lot of artistic value due to its arias and dance techniques. During the course of a two-day meeting at the Shanghai Yueju Theatre, the dramatist Xu Peijun underscored that the banning of ghost plays could be a slippery slope—were Pu Songling's *Strange Stories from a Chinese Studio* (*Liaozhai zhiyi*), or the poetry of Qu Yuan and Li Bai next?[45]

The Xinghuo Pingtan troupe brought up an intriguing question, and one not usually addressed in discussions on ghost plays: What, exactly, was the meaning of "ghost"? What did it encompass? More saliently for the discussion on the ban: When was a ghost not a "real" ghost? Drawing on the example of the revolutionary opera *The White-Haired Girl*, they queried how to interpret the famous line that "the old society turns people into ghosts, the new society turns ghosts into people [*jiu shehui shiren bian gui, xin shehui shigui bian ren*]."[46] The documents provide no answer for the question, but the question is illustrative of the challenges facing artists and writers. Even a term that seemed like it should be easy to define was extremely malleable.

A similar train of thought showed up in another meeting. Fu Jun, who had written *Bloody Handprint* (*Xie shouyin*) for the Hezuo Yue opera troupe, insisted the play was not problematic, as it featured "a person dressed up as a ghost." Fu claimed this was very different than a ghost character, and thus the play was *not* a ghost play (and not subject to the ban). But some of the audience disagreed, stating it was a small step from people dressed up as a ghost to a ghost character.[47] Here is an echo of the 1954 arguments about Ma Jianling's ghostless adaptation of *Wandering West Lake*, when critics wondered how a person dressed up as character dressed up as a ghost was any less frightening to audiences than a person dressed up as a ghost character.

In keeping with the robust and varied discussion, many of the voices do speak approvingly of the ban and a less permissive approach to drama. In general, such agreements took the same form: ghost plays were fundamentally flawed at best, and at worst were dangerous and harmful. Theatrical ghosts supposedly encouraged superstitious behavior among the masses, gave the impression that there was an afterlife, and were not in keeping with the goals of socialist art. However, some performers pointed out that the ban was due more to audiences than the plays themselves. "If we performed a ghost play for the senior cadres of central party," Wu Chen, assistant director of the Shanghai Yue Theatre, stated, "there wouldn't be a problem."[48] That is, senior members of the party were assumed to be sophisticated and educated enough not to fall into "superstitious" thinking and beliefs due to seeing opera featuring ghosts. This is in fact echoed in the Ministry of Culture directive, which provided an explicit loophole for the performance of ghost plays in theatre and research groups. It is unclear how often (if at all) requests to perform ghost plays were made or granted, but the fact that it was mentioned at all reinforces the idea that this was—from the point of view of the CCP's cultural apparatus—a problem of audience.

Even though a diverse set of opinions is evidenced in these discussions, there is one rather constant undercurrent: simple exhaustion with trying to keep up with changes in the cultural realm. This is one aspect that is difficult to uncover in the published essays on the subject. During one meeting, Zhu Haizhou expressed his frustration with nearly a decade of policy changes and the impact on art by bringing up the numerous hotly debated changes to the character of Li Huiniang: "At first it was ghosts being changed into people [referring to the 1953 Ma Jianling version, *Wandering West Lake*], afterwards the people were turned into ghosts—why do we want to change like this and change like that? The [political] thought [behind all of it] is unclear."[49] Some members of the Puguang Huai opera troupe succinctly stated their position on ghost play problem: it had "already been decided by the central party—what's left to discuss?!"[50]

The Shanghai performers often seemed to grasp the reality of the situation in ways that their counterparts in more removed situations did not: there was, in fact, not much left to discuss. Though many of the critics and performers would not have known it, not only had the Ministry of Culture spoken, but Mao was once again critiquing faults he saw in the cultural realm. He declared in September that "pushing out the old to bring in the new" required new forms, and old forms needed an internal transformation if they were to be of use. In November 1963, he strongly criticized *Theatre Report* and the Ministry of Culture: the journal was disseminating ox ghost–snake spirits, while the Ministry of Culture had been paying no heed to culture. A great many feudal things had taken root, and the Ministry ignored it all—if the Ministry was unable to change, Mao suggested changing its name to "the ministry of emperors, generals, and ministers" or "the ministry of scholars and beauties," or even "the ministry of foreigners and dead people."[51] This was well in keeping with Mao's increasingly radical leftist line and emphasis on class struggle, and a far cry from the relatively sanguine attitude he displayed during the Hundred Flowers. Cultural production was still an incredibly important part of transforming the masses, and Mao was ready for more dramatic action to be taken. Traditional drama was not driving itself to extinction, and something had to be done.

Conclusion

For all the sharp criticisms of the 1963 ghost debates, they paled in comparison to the attacks that would be coming in 1965 and 1966. The discussions of 1963 were true debates, and cultural workers talked seriously of what to do with drama. Even the more radical participants often expressed a desire to maintain traditional drama in some fashion. Although the torturous logic employed to differentiate plays with ghostly characters from ghost plays can seem less than convincing several decades after the fact, the 1963 discussion was very much in keeping with the general tone and structure of discussions of the 1950s. Yet the Shanghai troupe discussions illustrate that not everyone was interested in debate: some critics must have felt the same fatigue as many of the Shanghai troupes.

The increasing power of the cultural radicals around Jiang Qing was largely invisible, even in Shanghai. The East China Drama Festival in late 1963 and early 1964 would be a sign of growing power, but the Festival of Peking Operas on Contemporary Themes in the summer of 1964 marked the overt beginning of serious attacks and criticism of traditional drama and its proponents. But the end of the year saw a subtle shift in the theatre journals like *Theatre Report* or *Play Monthly*, with political musings on socialist thought and contemporary themes crowding out the lively discussions on traditional or classical subjects that had largely dominated until 1963. However, even with increasing power and visibility, proponents of radicalizing the cultural sphere would not find an entirely receptive environment in which to peddle their new wares. The year 1963 marked the last time ghosts appeared on Chinese stages until 1979, but it by no means marked an end to the high cultural and political drama.

In the wake of the 1963 ban, criticism and persecution of authors, performers, and the plays themselves—particularly Meng Chao's *Li Huiniang*—intensified and took on an increasingly personal dimension. The climax of the story of ghost plays, historical drama, and traditional theatre in the Mao years was the Cultural Revolution. Yao Wenyuan's November 1965 criticism of Wu Han and *Hai Rui Dismissed from Office* has conventionally been regarded as the "prelude" to the Cultural Revolution.[52] However, it may also be seen as the pinnacle of the early Cultural Revolution: the attack on *Hai Rui* and Wu Han was the penultimate step in the increasingly radical critique of liberal cultural workers (the March 1966 attack on Tian Han and *Xie Yaohuan* would be the critical pièce de résistance).[53] Criticism of Meng Chao and his *Li Huiniang*, and the ghost debate more broadly, paved the way for the later criticism of better protected, more politically connected intellectuals. In this respect, the ghost play debate of 1963 and the targeted criticism of Meng Chao in the first months of 1965 was a much earlier indicator of the increasing radicalization of the cultural and political spheres.

CHAPTER 5

Ox Ghost–Snake Spirits and Poisonous Weeds
The Origins of the Cultural Revolution

Writing in 1979, the author Lou Shiyi recalled his relationship with the author of *Li Huiniang*, dwelling for some time on the period before the Cultural Revolution. In the piece, published in *People's Daily*, he recalled that "everyone," from bathhouse attendants to fellow intellectuals, was worried about Meng Chao, who grew more and more hunched as the attacks on himself and his ghost heroine intensified after 1963. "Beautiful Li Huiniang," he noted, "had become a 'vicious' ghost," and Liao Mosha, author of "Some Ghosts Are Harmless," had been branded an ox ghost–snake spirit. "For a short while," Lou recalled, "a ghostly atmosphere flickered, and we saw ghosts everywhere—everyone was afraid of ghosts, deathly afraid."[1] The fear was not misplaced: Lou records the brutality visited on Meng Chao by "young path-breaking revolutionaries" after 1966 with chilling detail. No longer were literary ghosts seen as righteous figures standing up to great evils; now they were simply embodiments of evil, and their authors and defenders were made to be ghosts—ox ghost–snake spirits, bad elements par excellence—as well, literally and figuratively.

This chapter considers the activities of the theatre world leading up to and during the early Cultural Revolution. Cultural discussions quickly shifted from the type seen in 1963, which were relatively robust debates on the suitability of traditional plays, to a much more one-sided valorization of theatre on contemporary themes and demonization of traditional operas of all kinds. The discussions of 1963 did not alter the course of radicalization, and the discussion quickly moved beyond ghost plays to a more general critique of traditional theatrical forms. The criticism of the "status quo" in the theatre world, encompassing not simply productions, but institutions and people, likewise became far more general, using far more negative terms. I also examine both the high-level actions aimed at priming the cultural sphere for a new, much more revolutionary era, as well as the impact on theatre repertoire. I consider the discussions surrounding drama between late 1963, with published accounts of the East China Spoken Drama Festival (Shanghai, December 1963–January 1964), and summer 1964, when the Festival of Peking Opera on Contemporary Themes was held in Beijing. This period was key for Jiang Qing and her allies to establish themselves as leaders in the cultural realm (never far from politics). The Peking opera festival in particular marked a coming out of sorts for Jiang Qing, with her first major public speech, and the first example of high-level political and cultural leaders getting on board publicly with her program of drama reform.

However, the high-level political maneuvering and battles that played out in the pages of *Theatre Report* and leading newspapers are only one part of the story. As documents from the Shanghai Culture Bureau show, the cultural radicals faced not only private opposition from political and cultural elites. They also found themselves attempting to reform the repertoires and performance habits of troupes, as well as the tastes of audiences, in a very short period of time. The preference of audiences and performers for traditional subjects bore little resemblance to the grand narratives spelled out in the speeches given at the large drama festivals that lauded the eagerness of the cultural sphere for new dramas on contemporary themes.

I also examine the specific criticisms aimed at Meng Chao and his supporters, as well as at Tian Han and Wu Han, in order to illustrate the influence the 1965 and 1966 attacks have had on readings of pre-1965 events. While Yao Wenyuan's attack on Wu Han is well-traversed ground for historians of the socialist period, there has been far less attention paid to the attacks on Meng Chao, which occurred a full eleven months before those against Wu Han. I analyze these criticisms in large part to illustrate that Cultural Revolution–era discourse on cultural production signaled a sharp break from its predecessors in the 1950s and early 1960s, and that it has had the effect of coloring post-1976 interpretations of the pre-1963 cultural sphere. It is, in fact, from the 1965 and 1966 criticisms that an overwhelming emphasis on the Great Leap Forward as the impetus for the creation *Li Huiniang*, *Hai Rui*, and other reformed drama derives. As previous chapters have illustrated, the debate on ghost opera and traditional drama extended far beyond the period of the Leap—a fact that can be difficult to discern in the criticisms of 1965 and 1966.

Radicalizing Culture: Festivals on Contemporary Themes,
1963–1964

As evidenced by the reversals of 1963, the cultural world needed, in the opinion of Mao, to be whipped into shape and mobilized on behalf of party goals. He wanted to ensure that intellectuals were "drummed into service on his side," which would first require getting them back in line after a relatively open period in the wake of the Leap.[2] As seen in the previous chapter, he sharply rebuked *Theatre Report* and the Ministry of Culture for ignoring their duty to promote socialist art. Mao set his sights on the cultural elite at large, stating in December 1963, "In many departments . . . very little has been achieved so far in socialist transformation. The 'dead' still dominate. . . . Isn't it absurd that many Communists are enthusiastic about promoting feudal and capitalistic art, but not socialist art?"[3]

Mao's irritation turned into outright hostility, and in early 1964 he criticized the role of cultural workers throughout history and further ordered that "'actors, poets, dramatists, and writers' be 'driven out of the cities,'" going so far as to say that "only when they go down will they be fed"—a return to 1940s-era rhetoric regarding the need of urban intelligentsia to work among ordinary people.[4] Just as he had said at the famous Yan'an Forum on Literature and Art, "Our writers and artists have their literary and art work to do, but their primary task is to understand people and know them well."[5] That arguing among themselves on the pages of *Theatre Report* and the *Guangming Daily*, to say nothing of penning highly literary adaptations of Ming dynasty plays to be performed in arcane styles like Kun opera, did not qualify as "knowing the people well" hardly needed to be said. Despite the warning signals that had been coming since 1962, and despite the fact that numerous senior members of the party leapt into action with Mao's increasingly irate commentary on the state of the cultural realm in mind, many cultural workers were under the impression that any attempt at shaking up cultural production would be yet another "gust of wind" (*yizhen feng*), a term that performers used to describe the occasional periods of intense socialist artistic production in the 1950s.[6] However, Jiang Qing, Yao Wenyuan, Kang Sheng, and the growing group of cultural radicals attached to them, most based in Shanghai, would ensure this would be no mere gust.

In late 1963, political criticism of theatre took a sharp turn, becoming ever more personal. In contrast to the theatre debates published throughout the spring and fall of 1963, which focused on the content and form of plays, not the purported ideological stance of the authors, by December writers and artists themselves were increasingly the targets for criticism. This was evidenced not just in the published discussion, but at two major drama festivals organized in Shanghai and Beijing in late 1963 and 1964. The first, held in Shanghai, was the East Chinese Spoken Language Drama Festival; five months later, the Festival of Peking Opera on Contemporary Themes was held in Beijing. The press was full of laudatory articles about the new, appropriately socialist turn the theatre world was taking, but the tone was increasingly aggressive. Publicly, there were open, named attacks on dramatists like Meng Chao. In more private settings, unlike the autumn 1963 ghost play meetings (largely dedicated to discussing issues as opposed to individuals), there were criticisms of specific people at meetings designed to discuss "general" issues in theatre. While these were not the struggle sessions of the Cultural Revolution, they do reflect an important change in how political battles were impacting the cultural world.

The Spoken Language Drama Festival, held from December 1963 to January 1964 under the auspices of the Shanghai Propaganda Department, was a celebration of the new.[7] Spoken drama lagged seriously behind traditional theatre in popularity, and the goal of the festival was to introduce new plays, new performers, and new writers to supposedly eager audiences. Ke Qingshi's opening remarks attacked, without naming names, the established drama world. According to him, problems in the theatre world were the fault of writers and performers who produced plays that harmed the people by promulgating feudalism, capitalism and bourgeois values, old class structures, old habits, and old thoughts.[8] Wei Wenbo's remarks, which closed the festival, largely echoed Ke's emphasis on newness. He noted that the festival brought out "many new people, new dramatists, new actors. . . . For some it was their first time writing a play, for some it was their first time setting foot on stage."[9] However, to describe this impact, he relied—somewhat ironically, considering the circumstances—on a line from the Tang dynasty poet Li Shangyin, opining that "the cry of a young phoenix is more pure than that of the old" (*chufeng qing yu laofeng sheng*), illustrating that expunging "the dead" from culture was harder than it might first appear.[10]

The emphasis on new productions designed to serve the masses and socialism, as well as the critique of the cultural establishment, continued with the Festival of Peking Opera on Contemporary Themes, held in Beijing from June 5 to July 31, 1964. This was on a cultural and political plane far above the earlier Shanghai festival. Notably, it was significantly more politically pointed than its predecessor and in many respects laid the foundation for Jiang Qing's model operas, as well as the all-out political attack on the old guard of performers and cadres. The festival was an impressive affair, and China's political and cultural elite turned out en masse, along with troupes from all over China. Zhou Enlai and Peng Zhen presided over the events, while cultural heavyweights were in prominent attendance.[11] The main emphasis of the festival was on the failings of the cultural world. In Peng Zhen's speech, which hewed closely to the line that had become popular in late 1963, he criticized the theatre world for sticking too closely to stories of "emperors, generals and ministers, scholars and beauties, old men and their wives, princes and ladies."[12] The masses, particularly young people, he claimed, "don't like this performing of emperors, generals and ministers and not putting on revolutionary contemporary plays, and long ago expressed this. The method of expression was quite simple, they just didn't buy your tickets. Old Peking opera audiences [are smaller than] those for local forms, and this is because [local forms] put on revolutionary contemporary dramas."[13]

This was simply untrue, at least in one major market. While Peng was correct that local forms were preferred in many locales over Peking opera, the idea that this was due to a plethora of revolutionary dramas found in local forms is suspect. A year before the Peking opera festival, the Shanghai Culture Bureau undertook a small survey to assess the popularity of the genre in the city and its outskirts. In one respect, it proved Peng Zhen correct: young audiences were largely disinterested in traditional opera of any stripe, including operas on revolutionary themes, preferring contemporary spoken drama.[14] Among the few people who counted themselves as Peking opera fans (primarily educated cadres from the north), they largely wanted to see famous actors in traditional roles. But, as the Culture Bureau discovered, most Shanghai audiences simply preferred local forms by a huge margin, some expressing that they found the language and dramatic conventions of Peking opera difficult to understand. As one older woman from Shanghai's Jing'an district said, "The more you listen to Yue opera, the more comfortable it becomes; a sentence of seven words is a sentence of seven words . . . in Peking opera, one word can become ever so long."[15] In fact, many people from the outskirts were described as thinking Peking opera so unintelligible that it must have been some sort of "foreign play" (yangxi).[16] Furthermore, for most Shanghainese genres, the repertoires were made up overwhelmingly of traditional drama.

Regardless of the veracity of politicians' claims about the popularity of drama on contemporary themes, the festival was a major affair on multiple levels, and it signaled a sharp shift in the discourse surrounding theatre. Jiang Qing's speech, for instance, was the "first major public speech of her life."[17] Her comments were rather tempered, particularly considering the remarks of others like Kang Sheng: while stressing the creation of opera on revolutionary themes, she noted that those on historical themes "before our party came into being are also needed."[18] It seems likely that Jiang Qing's idea of "appropriate historical themes" and the opinions of many cultural workers on what constituted suitable themes diverged rather greatly (namely, "historical" came to mean in her usage "history of the party")—and it was, of course, Jiang Qing's interpretation that won out in the end, at least for a period. Kang Sheng did not hold back in his criticisms of the very same play he had encouraged his old friend Meng Chao to write. "In the past fifteen years," he declared, "we have not put out any good plays. On the contrary, we've only produced bad scripts like *Li Huiniang* and *Xie Yaohuan*."[19] Kang Sheng was nothing if not a political opportunist, and a friendship of fifty years meant very little in the face of the possibilities presented with Mao's leftist turn.

The Peking opera festival was not entirely made up of speeches and performances. As the summary from the Shanghai Culture Bureau documents, there was much discussion going on behind the scenes that the public would have found unsavory. The Shanghai contingent was a significant one: Zhang Chunqiao, a close collaborator of Jiang Qing, headed the delegation, with operatic luminaries Zhou Xinfang and Yu Zhenfei as deputy heads. Jiang had also spent much time in Shanghai prior to the festival working on the operas *Taking Tiger Mountain by Strategy* (*Zhi qu weihu shan*) and *The Legend of the Red Lantern* (*Hongdeng ji*), which were duly trotted out at the festival.[20] Probably owing to the close collaboration with Jiang Qing, the delegation enjoyed a certain level of prestige at the festival. But there were indications of significant divisions in the Shanghai theatre world, particularly the idea that performance of contemporary-themed plays was simply a "brief gust of wind," as some performers described it. The impression that the focus on contemporary themes was yet another temporary cultural fad was "not just present among the old generation of Peking opera practitioners," the report complains, "but also among some of the younger members." The young actress Li Bingshu "still had a thought of finding several teachers [in Beijing], so as to study more traditional plays, to improve her performance of 'The Broken Bridge' [*Duanqiao* from *Legend of White Snake*] and those types of traditional plays."[21]

Considering the clear preference audiences had for traditional drama, it is little surprise that artists, even in the midst of a festival on contemporary themes, made time to polish performances of traditional works. Shanghainese statistics collected in 1964 give a strong indication both of audience preferences and how cadres interpreted them. The statistics include Yue opera (by far the most popular type of opera, at least as far as sheer numbers of plays performed), Peking opera, Kun opera, Hu opera, Yang opera, Huai opera, Tong opera, and Xi opera—all relatively local styles, with the exception of Peking opera. The troupes included in the statistics are all Shanghai-based troupes. While non-Shanghai troupes had general statistics listed for themes, they did not tally the types of nonlocal troupes coming through, although nonlocal performances made up a not insignificant 30 percent of plays performed. Despite the efforts of 1963 and 1964, the Shanghai survey makes it abundantly clear that there was hardly overwhelming interest among audiences and performers for these new drama trends of contemporary and revolutionary themes. Throughout 1964, plays on contemporary themes never comprised more than 40 percent of plays performed, and were not even a quarter of the active repertoire of Shanghainese and other local opera forms.[22]

However, the same survey tallied historical data from 1958 through 1963, illustrating why many cultural workers may have believed that the 1963 and 1964 efforts were just one more shift in a period that had experienced many "gusts." In 1958 and 1959, for instance, drama on contemporary themes made up nearly 30 percent of plays performed. In 1960, they declined to less than 25 percent, and by 1961, they comprised barely 10 percent. The nadir of contemporary-themed drama was 1962, where they made up a mere 8 percent, with traditional plays making up 84 percent of plays performed. Yet, in the next year, the numbers "equalized," and returned to numbers seen in 1959.[23] Much like the discourse of 1963—which many writers seemed to think was simply another change of direction, a pendulum that would eventually swing back to the other side—one could imagine that performers and cadres of the cultural sphere would find fluctuations a normal part of business. And, in some respects, Shanghai seems to have been far ahead of Beijing in terms of performances on revolutionary themes. Colin Mackerras has stated that in Beijing, traditional pieces made up 97 percent of performances in 1960, 83 percent in 1961, and all plays in 1962.[24]

Just as important as the performances, the Peking opera festival was also an opportunity for criticism. The delegation's report records several instances of discussions to debate failures of years past. When the topic turned to the problem of promoting traditional drama, several stars of the Shanghai theatre world—among them, Zhou Xinfang, Yu Zhenfei, and Yan Huizhu (Yu Zhenfei's wife)—were the focus of criticism, and "all remained totally silent." Li Shizhao, editor of the journal *Shanghai Theatre*, likewise simply held his tongue when accused of propagating "ghost plays."[25] And even when discussion moved away from individuals, there were wide criticisms for most anyone who was part of the current system of theatrical productions. The Peking opera community (and surely, this could be extended to the opera world more broadly) was described as "preserving the feudal student-teacher relationship, the feudal trade association relationship, relationships of feudal factions—all of these are placed above the party and proletariat."[26] For all the relatively accommodating words of the public speeches, behind the scenes it certainly appeared that factions of the political apparatus were preparing for quite a fight—to not simply promote drama on contemporary themes, but to tear down the theatre world as it existed. It was obvious by the summer of 1964 that matters had become ever more political, and ever more personal, in the world of cultural production.

Tearing Down the Garden: Criticism and the Remaking of the Theatre World

Ultimately, Mao was in fact quite right in declaring little "progress" had been made since 1949. Despite the effort poured into reforming traditional drama and promoting new forms of entertainment, in the major cultural center of Shanghai, reformed traditional scripts like *Li Huiniang* comprised a mere 2 percent of operas performed in 1964.[27] In some ways, this shows how small the reach of the soon-to-be "poisonous weeds" were. Audiences were, by and large, not watching adaptations; Shanghai audiences watched scenes from *Story of Red Plums*, not Meng Chao's *Li Huiniang*. But it also highlights the potential challenges of fixing the system, and explains some of the drastic measures taken in 1965 and the years following. The gradual method had not produced significant results, except perhaps in filling the pages of elite journals and newspapers.

And so, if audiences and troupes would not choose to give up their preference for traditional drama, the choice would be taken from them. However, the shift (at least in Shanghai) challenges perceptions about how this took place, and what it looked like. Liu Ching-chi has argued that following the 1964 Peking opera festival, "There was no time . . . to write, rehearse, and perform many contemporary operas [in other regional styles]. . . . Contemporary drama was still unable to take the place of traditional drama."[28] Only in 1966, he states, were wholesale changes able to take place, with traditional operas finally being replaced en masse. This may have been true elsewhere, but was not the case in the case of Shanghai. Massive changes, including the creation of new scripts, happened very quickly and without much time to prepare.

In 1965, traditional plays simply disappeared from official reckoning of what had appeared on Shanghainese stages. Even accounting for the possibility that Shanghai's municipal Culture Bureau cadres were hiding whatever traditional plays had been performed (which there is no evidence of), there is no doubt that troupes and audiences experienced a massive shift. The drop in plays performed is impressive: from 1,051 plays performed by local, Shanghai-based troupes in 1964 to 276 in 1965. In fact, when the same play being performed by multiple troupes of different types is taken into account, the number drops to 148.[29] Even when we keep in mind that a great number of traditional opera plays were in fact the same story, overlapped heavily in source material, and were performed as multiple excerpts per performance, there is still an incredible constriction of repertoires in 1965. The themes were consistent, even if the titles were not: *American Invaders, Get Out of Vietnam!*, *Taking Tiger Mountain by Strategy*, *Ode to the Dragon River*, *The Red Doctor*, and so on. They were apparently red and revolutionary to the core, and most were created in the span of a year. And yet, despite this sudden narrowing of the theatrical sphere, Jiang Qing's projects—spoken language drama, Peking opera, and the plays that would become the model operas—continued to find comparatively little favor vis-à-vis local forms and other takes on revolutionary themes. Shanghai audiences may have been forced to watch contemporary themed drama if they wanted to attend the theatre, but they were generally going to see Yue opera, Hu opera, or Huai opera—local forms that were deeply rooted in Shanghainese culture—and not Peking opera or spoken language drama.

In addition to the massive changes effected on local levels, high-level discussions of plays, their authors, and performers also underwent a sharp shift, though less speedily than the repertoire was reformed. Although Mao was increasingly (and publicly) displeased with the drama world, senior cadres were hardly rushing to satisfy Jiang Qing's wishes in regards to overhauling Chinese theatre.[30] Many important members of the party are attributed with a variety of disbelieving and negative comments about Jiang Qing's forays into creating her model operas. Peng Zhen, despite his comments at the 1964 festival, is supposed to have said that the plays were "still at the stage of wearing trousers with a slit in the seat," and wondered "What the hell are these [model operas]? I'm head of arts in this place, and I know nothing of models." The cutting comment that "you just see a bunch of people running to and fro on the stage. Not a trace of art" is attributed to Deng Xiaoping.[31]

Still, Mao's words in late 1963 complaining about *Theatre Report* were certainly indications that the cultural and political realms were undergoing a major shift.[32] Other signs of the gathering storm were much more subtle: Kang Sheng's terse notes to Meng Chao in 1962 and the cold shouldering of Tian Han at the East China Spoken Drama Festival in late 1963, where the senior dramatist was denied the seating his position ought to have accorded him.[33] The slight notwithstanding, the early published attacks, from 1963 to late 1965, focused largely on Meng Chao and *Li Huiniang*—and it was this thorough attack on the old writer and his ghost that would lay the groundwork for the 1965 and 1966 criticisms of Wu Han and Tian Han.

The change in discourse in just a year is dramatic. In 1963, the socialist credentials of authors like Meng Chao were not under direct attack; even the Jiang Qing and Ke Qingshi–directed essay by "Liang Bihui" is relatively tempered in its tone. The criticisms that appeared in 1964 and 1965 were hardly so genteel, as Meng Chao's views took center stage. The play was not a "poisonous weed" simply because of its form and theme, it was poisoned thanks to the incorrect, *antisocialist* viewpoints of its author. This was indicative of a large change in the approach to "fixing" the cultural world: it was simply insufficient to concentrate on the plays without considering the people writing these "weeds." A wholesale change of personnel was necessary.

In the summer of 1964, coinciding with the opening of the Peking opera festival, a lengthy screed was published in *Literary Criticism* that is representative of the highly personal attacks levied at writers and intellectuals in the Cultural Revolution. The author, Deng Shaoji, was a thirty-one-year-old Fudan University graduate and specialist in ancient literature at what is now the Chinese Academy of Social Sciences.[34] His article drew primarily from Meng Chao's postscript to *Li Huiniang*, as well as the substance of the play itself, to launch a personal attack on the author and his supporters.[35] Now, the operating assumptions were that the author *clearly* held antiparty, antisocialist thought beliefs, had held such beliefs for decades, and the play was simply a way to express such dangerous views. No longer was Li Huiniang a righteous ghost; she was a dangerous ghost, a mask for her even more dangerous author.

The introductory paragraph quoted from numerous positive reviews, as well as Liao Mosha's "Some Ghosts Are Harmless." The target was not a singular ghost or one author, but the whole project that had supported revisions like Meng Chao's. To "refute the absurd idea that ghost plays are not only *not* harmless, but have good points" was one goal. To underscore Meng Chao's sin of "individualism" was another, as well as his lack of support for the socialist project. Deng also describes him as "gloomy" during the Great Leap Forward (based on Meng Chao's postscript), reading criticism of the CCP into such a mental state.[36] These points would be repeated time and again. However, unlike later pieces, Deng turned to one of the playwright's earlier pieces to divine more evidence for his antiparty thoughts. In 1949, Meng Chao published *A Guide to the Heroes of Liangshan Marsh*, a collection of twenty-nine character sketches from *The Water Margin*. Originally published under the pen name "Grassroots Historian" (*caomang shijia*), it seems an innocent—indeed, actively supportive of the CCP, according to some—project of a well-trained literary scholar and writer. As Meng Chao's old friend, the writer Nie Gannu, wrote in the preface to the 1985 republication of the collection, "Of his *Li Huiniang*, some said it was a case of 'using the past to allude to the present.' I think this little book really is using the past to comment on the present. This book is an ode to Liangshan Marsh, in reality it's an ode to Yan'an— Liangshan alludes to Yan'an, those writing *zawen* in GMD-controlled areas during the war of resistance often employed this tactic."[37]

How to attack an innocuous, or even actively supportive, piece, then? "Whether or not we can call him a historian is not under discussion," Deng declared. "But he cannot be considered some grassroots person, he is quite clearly a cadre of the country. That is to say . . . how can he pose as a rustic person? Isn't this a lie? We know Meng Chao enjoys engaging in word mongering, but he cannot possibly *not* know the meaning of these two characters [*caomang*]."[38] In the author's view, a pen name selected in 1949 or the years before clearly indicated Meng Chao's expression of individualistic leanings and his dissatisfaction with his current position, as if he were part of a faction that was out of power. His pen name was, in Deng's opinion, just one more example of the antiparty, antipeople feelings found in *Li Huiniang*, dating back to the 1940s. Considering the numerous materials available to Meng Chao's critics (particularly his *zawen* of the early 1960s), the *caomang* criticism is a somewhat baffling diversion from the *Li Huiniang* problem. It perhaps explains why later authors would stay away from attempting to divine anything from his pre-1949 works.

In January 1965, an article appeared in *Theatre Report* under the name Qi Xiangqun. Like the later criticisms of Tian Han and Wu Han, it is likely this was a pen name for a group of people and that the essay was carefully crafted with input from Jiang Qing and others. It would provide a model for the criticisms to follow in later months.[39] It was a vicious political attack on Meng Chao; the subject of the piece, as in Deng's essay, was the political motivations of the dramatist. The essay was not, unlike many of the 1963 anti-ghost-play essays, a particularly sophisticated piece of work. Whereas many of the earlier publications (to say nothing of their forerunners) were erudite, if radical, literary critiques, the Qi piece often reads as a muddled essay. Certainly, there was little effort to build a truly cogent argument: the essay was teleological in the extreme. Since it was a foregone conclusion that Meng Chao harbored antiparty, antisocialist feelings, there was no other reading of his play or postscript that was possible.

It often reads as a rather confused diatribe. For instance, the author states that Meng Chao's portrayal of Li Huiniang's "strength after death" could give the impression that "not only do people turn into ghosts after death, but further, ghosts are stronger than living people, living has no meaning, and only after death is there any power." By this logic, Meng Chao was neglecting his duties as a socialist author to stamp out superstition and encourage struggle among the living. On the other hand, there was an echo of the 1963 criticisms of the play: namely, that Li Huiniang was *ineffective* in her "struggle," and so lost power as a teaching vehicle.[40] While one doubts that having an especially strong ghost would have saved Meng Chao from harsh criticism, it does appear that—at least for purposes of the critical essays—the first crime of Meng Chao was in not being didactic enough. Returning to the 1962 postscript, the author underscored this lack of teaching on Meng Chao's part by discussing his apparent lack of concern for discussing the proletariat or opposing feudalism: "If he considers himself a proletarian author, why doesn't he clearly point out the evils of feudalism and the righteousness of opposing feudalism?"[41] The answer was a simple one, and one that Meng Chao addressed in his postscript— which was gleefully pounced on later in Qi's piece. In his postscript to *Li Huiniang*, Meng had no positive words for *overly* didactic plays, the type that were crammed full of "dry, turgid, and insipid language" and sent audiences fleeing.[42] This statement was framed not simply as an attack on certain dramatists, but as an attack on "socialist life" and evidence that Meng Chao was "dissatisfied or hates it."[43]

In the final section of analysis, questioning whom Meng Chao intended to encourage, the authors argued that *Li Huiniang* was hardly a reflection of contemporary society. The authors used one of Li Huiniang's arias[44] in the act entitled "Hatred":

> My worry is for the bitterness of refugees of disasters,
> My worry is for the resentment of those forced to wander.
> The lakeside scene glitters,
> But the howling of the people of Lin'an[45] is more desperate than the
>   howling of ghosts.
>
> Under the hand of Jia Sidao,
> Even after death, it's difficult to find peace!
> . . .
>
> I want to be as Guanyin, a ghost bodhisattva [*gui pusa*]
> Relieving suffering and assuaging difficulty.
> For hurting people, there is you [Jia Sidao]—
> For saving people, look to me! (27–28)

Here, Li Huiniang is describing the situation of the late Southern Song: the masses suffering under oppression, while the prime minister is only interested in his own pleasure on the shores of West Lake. The authors of the essay attacking Meng Chao declared that people in the PRC faced no hardships and there were no "bitter refugees of disasters." More damning, Meng Chao was supposedly harboring reactionary class thought, and accused of using Li Huiniang to express that. Meng Chao, they said, was *not* encouraging others like him to "wait until death to resist," as they "all know that resistance after death is fantasy. . . . It is actually describing the strong resistance to socialism by capitalist-individualist people, the state of mind of an exploiting class that is unwilling to withdraw from the historical stage, and describing their death struggle."[46]

Among the most important articles that year, which trod rather standard ground in many respects—1965 not being marked by a plethora of diverse viewpoints on the pages of leading journals and papers—is Bu Linfei's February essay, first published in the *Guangming Daily*, and reprinted in *Theatre Report*.[47] The primary issue was Meng Chao's "defense" of his "incorrect thought and theory," a typical enough discussion. However, Bu did make a rather intriguing suggestion: one of *Li Huiniang*'s greatest crimes was encouraging "escapism," a truly bourgeois idea in Bu's telling. How could the result be anything but a work of art that opposes socialism? Bu ended his attack by stating that there was no grand socialist purpose to Meng Chao's *Li Huiniang*, as revealed by the author's own writing: to the contrary, it was a "written declaration of war" on socialist thought.[48]

The suggestion that escapism was, at least in part, the real appeal of these works is tantalizing indeed. Is it possible that Bu Linfei, hardly the most sophisticated of the radical critics, had cut to the heart of the matter? Ghosts and gods and ancient generals offered an escape, a way to maneuver within a constrained literary system. They offered ways of linking back to a Chinese literary past—one that was not tied to official language or Marxist theory, and therein lay the problem. Meng Chao, for instance, was at his literary best when writing of his ghost. His lyricism and mastery of classical culture shine through in full force, in a way they do not even in his *zawen* (which themselves are extremely sophisticated little pieces, just like those of fellow writers). If ghosts have historically been vehicles for fantasies of many kinds, could this not be another kind of fantasy, one of escapism or resistance to the present? To read his poetic preface to *Li Huiniang* is to see a Marxist writer consciously styling himself as a scholar in a more ancient mode. Likewise, his postscript, which radical critics consistently deployed to attack him, is an elegant discussion of highly literary topics; even his criticism of the state of drama, circa 1962, is lyrical. He does not take much interest in defending his play on socialist merits; instead, he seems most eager to show himself one of the heirs of a great literary tradition.

One imagines the postscript must have been a pleasure for him to write, just as the play surely was, and not simply because of the topic and what might have been a satisfying, subtle critique of his party. But the core of the work, its language, is itself a world away from his essays expounding on the problems of revising drama and poems celebrating Chinese achievements of the Leap or climbing Mount Everest. It was a reminder to himself and to others that they could exist outside a socialist worldview; he deliberately links himself to a literary tradition that was beyond the boundaries of what was, for many, "appropriate" for socialist art. So too for his audience: it is difficult to believe that the play was so well received merely on the basis of its being a criticism of the Leap. This was literary escapism on multiple levels. The setting, the theme, the form, the language: it was not, despite arguments to the contrary, very socialist at all, and therein lay its appeal. There were plenty of other vehicles for criticism. But public methods of submersing oneself in literary production with so classical a bent were few. And to write a play—to use one's literary talents in a creative manner—is a very different exercise than writing an academic essay. Unfortunately, this literary escapism would have deadly consequences.

In addition to attacks from radical critics, at least one former supporter came forward to publish a self-criticism and repudiation of his earlier views. In March 1965, Liao Mosha appeared again as Fan Xing, writing on the "some ghosts are harmless" theory. Writing in the *Beijing Evening News* (though the essay itself would be reprinted in multiple places), the paper that had originally published his 1961 essay, this time he penned a self-criticism that was part examination of his own "incorrect" points of view, and part criticism of Meng Chao's motives.[49] Liao claimed he had "forgotten that our socialist society still harbored . . . class contradictions and class struggle, and still had the two road struggle of socialism and capitalism," which led to the folly of defending ghost plays. He criticized himself for ignoring that art was to serve the masses and socialism, and needed to "struggle with capitalist and feudal art that opposes socialist artistic improvement." Of course, self-flagellation was only a part of his public self-criticism; much of the essay was made up of an attack on Meng Chao (though one doubts that Liao had any choice in the content to be covered, to be sure). His approach was largely the same as the one seen in the Qi essay. Using Meng Chao's 1962 postscript, he questioned what "spirit of the age" Meng Chao was attempting to draw out. The spirit of the Southern Song? No, because while Jia Sidao was a real historical personage, Pei Yu and Li Huiniang were not. The spirit of the Ming? How could Meng Chao hope to grasp that period that was 450 years before his time? The answer, then, was that "it was Meng Chao's own 'era,' his own 'feelings.'"[50]

It was evident to those close to targets of criticism that the growing cultural and political firestorm was taking its toll. Lou Shiyi would later write that Meng Chao in this period, the man he had described as an "old tree starting to bloom" during the premiere of *Li Huiniang*, was now "an old, flowering tree nearly cut down for firewood."[51] When Liao Mosha's repudiation of "some ghosts are harmless" was published, Lou noted that everyone was very frightened, and saw ghosts everywhere: What did the future hold?[52] This was clearly not a simple cultural "gust of wind" that would pass in a few months or a year. Liao Mosha's defense of "good ghosts"—the acknowledgment that to slough all ghosts into a "bad" category could be highly problematic—now seemed needed, at the same time it was being attacked in the press and repudiated by the author himself. For now it was cultural workers who were not simply writing, performing, or defending theatrical ghosts, but *becoming* ghosts themselves—ox ghost–snake spirits, not even worthy of being called "human."

The criticism of Meng Chao in the early part of 1965 was followed by relative calm before the storm that would be unleashed by the publication and promotion of Yao Wenyuan's attack on Wu Han. However, *Li Huiniang* and its author were unquestionably linked to the criticisms of Wu Han, Tian Han, and their respective historical plays, the "three great poisonous weeds" of the early period. In November 1965, Yao's criticism of *Hai Rui Dismissed from Office* was published. Wu Han, unlike Meng Chao, was not simply hung out to dry in the face of the radicals' criticism. Deng Tuo and other intellectuals wrote comments supporting the historian that appeared in the same publications Yao's article had appeared in. He published a self-criticism in late December, but "it was already out of date," and Mao was ready for a fight.[53] Intellectuals and senior party members may have thought the leftist turn of the past few years was simply another "gust of wind," but they were quickly realizing that a storm was brewing. Peng Zhen, who not even two years earlier had delivered remarks at the Peking opera festival supportive of Jiang Qing, made herculean efforts in early 1966 to check the direction the leftists were heading in.[54] Mao, however, was having none of it, and by late March, he had condemned Peng Zhen, who was left exposed thanks to the travels of his patron Liu Shaoqi.[55] The final assault on the Beijing establishment, not simply on a handful of intellectuals and traditional culture, was on.

While high-level political shakeups were taking place, discussion on the failures of CCP intellectuals and performers continued. In the wake of the Yao Wenyuan article on *Hai Rui* and Wu Han, Tian Han was finally put in the crosshairs of the radicals.[56] In February 1966, Yun Song's "Tian Han's *Xie Yaohuan* Is a Great Poisonous Weed" appeared in *People's Daily*, filling an entire page, and it was republished in other top papers and journals.[57] And, although the focus of the new round of criticism was most definitely Wu Han and Tian Han, far more valuable political targets than Meng Chao, he and his ghost had not faded from public memory. In Feb-

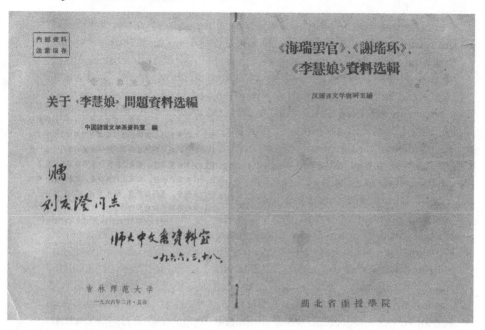

Fig. 7. On the left, a February 1966 compilation on the "*Li Huiniang* problem": Zhongguo yuyan wenxuexi ziliaoshi, ed., *Guanyu* Li Huiniang *wenti ziliao xuanbian* [A selection of materials relating to the *Li Huiniang* problem] (Changchun: Jilin Normal University, 1966); on the right, a contemporaneous volume dealing with *Hai Rui, Xie Yaohuan*, and *Li Huiniang* (Hanyuyuan wenxue jiaoyanshi, ed., Hai Rui Baguan, Xie Yaohuan, Li Huiniang *ziliao xuanji* [Selected materials of *Hai Rui Dismissed from Office, Xie Yaohuan, Li Huiniang*] (N.p.: Hubei sheng hanshou xueyuan, 1966). In author's personal collection.

ruary, for example, the Chinese language and literature department at Jilin Normal University put together a handy guide of "a selection of materials related to the *Li Huiniang* problem" (see figure 7).[58] It included the 1965 essays, a 1963 *Theatre Report* article on the ghost play problem, the full text of *Li Huiniang*, Meng Chao's postscript, Liao Mosha's "Some Ghosts Are Harmless," the positive review of the Northern Kun Opera performance by Tao Junqi and Li Dake, a 1956 piece on ghost plays, and a concise bibliography on the ghost play problem from 1956 on. Similar compilations appeared elsewhere, often drawing together criticism of all three of the "poisonous weeds."[59]

In the press, Meng was explicitly pulled back into the fray by a senior drama critic and producer, Liu Housheng. Liu's attack on the three authors, "[t]he anti-party, anti-socialist thought community—a discussion of *Li Huiniang, Hai Rui Dismissed from Office*, and *Xie Yaohuan* together," appeared in the March 1966 issue of *Theatre Report*, the last issue before the publication ceased printing for over a decade.[60] It is a truly sophisticated piece of writing, especially compared to the early criticism lobbed at Meng Chao in 1965, and is one of the best examples of critical essays that scholars have "read back from" in the decades since the Cultural Revolution. In general, the prime importance of *Li Huiniang* and other plays have been discussed primarily in terms of their political criticism of the Leap, a reading that overlaps heavily with the Cultural Revolution–era critiques. In the introduction, Liu noted that he sought to elucidate the numerous points of mutual interest and common foundations of all three pieces. It was first and foremost an attack on the three authors, but, more broadly, it attacked the group of cultural liberals and political moderates that enjoyed a period of relative freedom in the early 1960s.

Many of the points that Liu enumerated echoed those of the 1965 essays, particularly the vilification of what he saw as the reverence for "individualism" and "romanticism," as opposed to *revolutionary* romanticism, found in the plays.[61] Revolutionary romanticism was to draw on "real life" as it *should* be, not as it was.[62] The romanticism of Meng Chao, Wu Han, and Tian Han depicted a "reality" in which rulers were tyrants, where peasants starved after having their land seized, and only a handful of people were willing to defy authority in order to "plead for the people," pleadings that were generally unsuccessful. Liu criticized this approach, and says the authors were each the type of person who, when "writing and speaking the pronoun 'I' . . . surely [want] to use capital letters."[63] The settings of the plays—noble households and those of high-level officials—as well as subjects such as ghosts and dreams were clear evidence of the sensibilities of the authors, in opposition to socialist ideals for art.

However, underneath much of the trite phrasing is a surprisingly perceptive reading of many of the factors that led to these three authors facing the brunt of Jiang Qing and her clique's early wrath. Speaking of the plays, Liu noted the authors "use beautiful poetry and lofty language to glorify themselves and flatter each other."[64] Indeed, there seems to be little doubt that the exquisite literary language employed by Meng Chao, or the obscure historical references found in Wu Han's work, were designed to be read, understood, and enjoyed by a small subset of society—the cultural elite. (The limited reach of adapted dramas confirms that the audience was in fact rather exclusive.) Meng Chao's reverent references to Tang Xianzu and his careful use of the classical poetry canon were hardly aimed at a proletariat of a humble educational background.

Liu's essay also addressed the disaster of the Great Leap Forward in much starker terms than his 1965 predecessors. While those essays questioned why Meng Chao was "gloomy" and unhappy during what the radicals attempted to present as a very positive period of socialist history, Liu did not attempt to put such a pleasant gloss on the Leap and resulting famine. He specifically referred to the "three years of hardship" (*san nian kunnan*), and drew connections between the "hardship" and the emphasis of all three plays on the "miscarriage of justice" (*yuanyu*), particularly "the forcible seizure of the people's land bringing about one type of 'tragedy'"—a clear reference to collectivization.[65] Returning to the question of just what these three adapted plays were designed to encourage, Liu declared that they were encouraging people like themselves to resist the government. To the authors' claim that it was possible to have "history for history's sake," Liu said this was simply not possible; the authors were in fact using history to advance their own opinions on the present. Considering the deft use of historical and literary allusions in the early 1960s *zawen* written by Wu Han, Meng Chao, and others, Liu would seem to be on target with his criticism.

In many ways, Liu successfully cast a more sinister shadow on the activities of the literary elite in the late 1950s and early 1960s than earlier essays. He noted that the Anti-Rightist Campaign proved that "using [contemporary-themed] plays . . . was a comparatively hard road to walk" in criticizing the party, which thus led the authors to select historical plays as their subjects. He criticized the pre-1949 activities of the literary elite, who had accessed "feudal and bourgeois education to become intellectuals." They had made a show of understanding the proletariat, but were never able to fully enter into the struggles of the people. "They were able to write good works," Liu wrote, "but they were not able to truly hear the words of Mao Zedong . . . they held on to their own capitalist worldviews."[66]

From a distance of several decades, knowing what was to come, Liu's criticisms seem unfair: many writers from "bourgeois" backgrounds had suffered mightily for the party prior to 1949, and to accuse them of being "antiparty" seems outrageous. But if the artistic debates of the 1950s and early 1960s proved anything, it was that many cultural workers held fast to ideals that had been shaped in the environment of May Fourth artistic production. They were not willing to totally relinquish their intellectual and artistic freedom, nor were they willing to sacrifice their artistic "inheritance" for what they considered works of dubious quality. As it turned out, many of them paid a greater price than they ever could have imagined for their views. By 1966, no longer was it simply a matter of fixing forms or content; the cultural workers producing the content needed to be brought to heel. This increasingly began to mean that they needed to be swept aside entirely, with public denunciations, struggle sessions, and imprisonment—or worse.

The criticisms that appeared between 1965 and 1967 have in large part been read back into pre-1965 events, coloring perceptions of how works and debates were perceived in earlier periods. As previous chapters have illustrated, the debate on traditional drama—ghost plays in particular— went far beyond the narrow, post–Great Leap Forward readings that Cultural Revolution–era screeds may imply. In fact, the earliest published criticisms of Meng Chao's *Li Huiniang*, as well as Wu Han and Tian Han's work, do not hew as closely to the narrative that has been promulgated in the decades after Mao's death as one might expect. Liu Housheng's 1966 attack on the three authors exemplifies the position that we have assumed was the driving force behind those early criticisms: that the plays were written in response to the CCP's mishandling of the Great Leap Forward and the resulting famine. But this was the final phase of the formal criticism, and many of the earlier essays are not such elegant critiques. Nor do they draw direct connections between the contents of the plays and the tragedy of the Leap: Meng Chao was instead accused of having a lack of positive attitude during what was described as a dynamic and exciting period of socialist history. But it is Liu Housheng's 1966 criticism—which made a direct connection between the "three years of disaster" and the theme of governmental "miscarriage of justice" found in the three plays— that has stuck.

Unlucky Stars: The Fate of Artists and Writers during the Cultural Revolution

In the early months of the Cultural Revolution, people in the political and cultural realm reacted much as they had to more minor policy changes in former years: with confusion and hesitation. The earliest phases took place largely behind closed doors—the May 16th Notification was circulated at a Politburo meeting, but not publicly disseminated until 1967. A document plagued with typos and inconsistencies, it was at least consistent on the

need for upheaval; it was "to be by far the most ambitious attempt at dealing with revisionism ever attempted by the CCP."[67] But with the appearance of the first "big character poster" at Beijing University in June, the
movement was taking a much more public turn. As the conflict played
out in an increasingly high-profiled and frenzied manner, with rallies and
struggle sessions and the appearance of the Red Guards, ever more high-
level members of the CCP apparatus fell from power.[68] By the end of 1966,
influential "revisionists" like Peng Zhen, Wu Han, and Liao Mosha were
dragged out again and again in front of crowds of tens of thousands to
be struggled against and humiliated.[69] Meng Chao was apparently saved
some of the grandiose public humiliations; still, there are occasional chilling details that surface in the historical record. A mimeographed practice edition of *Li Huiniang*, produced by the Beijing Kun Opera Theatre
(while it is Meng Chao's script, his name appears nowhere on the copy),
features the title crossed out—a standard trope of Cultural Revolution–era
criticism—with "poisonous weed" written above, and "material for criticism" written below (see figure 8). The interior text is clean of any anno-
tations, but it makes one wonder: Who—or what—was being criticized,
how, and when? Or was this defacement perhaps intended to save it from
complete destruction, by marking it as material "necessary" to carry on
the struggle against artists and writers?

The defaced practice edition of *Li Huiniang* is a reminder that criticisms spread far beyond highly visible targets. Ma Jianling, who had tried
so hard for decades to write thoroughly socialist scripts for the people,
not for cultural elites, seemingly anticipated the turn events were taking
in 1965. That year, Ma was branded a member of an antiparty, antisocialist thought group that included the already-deceased Ke Zhongping, his
old People's Troupe collaborator from the heady Yan'an days. Apparently
intimating the even darker days to come, Ma—the man whom Mao had
praised for his earnest theatrical revisions in the 1940s, and who had
earned the ire of critics in the 1950s for trying to "fix" a ghost play to
make it more appropriate for socialist China—committed suicide.[70] Lou
Shiyi recalled after the Cultural Revolution that in the early days of 1966,
he "rejoiced" at being a minor literary figure, thinking that because he
had not written anything of particular prominence, he had "escaped [criti-
cism] by sheer luck." As it turned out, he did not elude the fate of his old
friend, and soon found himself branded an ox ghost–snake spirit and put
into a "cowshed" (*niupeng*) at a cadre reeducation school alongside Meng
Chao.[71]

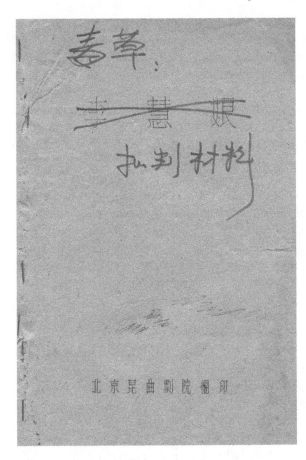

Fig. 8. Defaced practice edition of *Li Huiniang*, from the Beijing Kun Opera. In author's personal collection.

And yet, even while their targets suffered in reeducation camps or were held in private prisons, radicals still brought forth echoes of the 1950s and early 1960s debates and discussions on theatre broadly, and ghosts specifically. In the midst of the radical period between 1966 and 1968, time was taken to collect and review statistics from years earlier as critics attacked the artistic world broadly. In Shanghai, this manifested in at least one article in the July 1967 edition of the *Culture War* newspaper that took the "ghost play problem" to an entirely new level. The article included a nearly full-page list of "ghost plays" performed in Shanghai between 1949 and 1963 (see figure 9).[72] The list includes brief plot synopses of over fifty plays and notes on which troupes staged them. A shorter list details plays staged between 1959 and 1963, and a small chart illustrates the waxing and waning of the popularity of ghosts on Shanghainese stages (peaking in 1957). While not all the information is surprising (*Red Plum Pavilion* and its many derivatives are listed, including *Li Huiniang*, which is described as "the big poisonous weed concocted by Meng Chao"), some of the list does prove revelatory. Most interesting are two types of plays: first, traditional plays that would rarely have fit into any negative category before the Cultural Revolution. *The Peony Pavilion,* for example, had long occupied a privileged position; even critics after 1963 were willing to give credit to Tang Xianzu's masterpiece, while perhaps wishing it off socialist stages. Also included were several versions of the "Uproar in Heaven" episode from *Journey to the West*: a somewhat odd inclusion, since the icon of Sun Wukong was still very much in use, and as Wagner has persuasively argued, "the language and fantasy of the Cultural Revolution were strongly influenced by [*Journey to the West*]."[73] It might be remembered that literary critics went to extreme lengths to safely isolate "mythology" plays like *Journey to the West* derivatives from "ghost plays" like *Story of Red Plums* in the discussions of 1963 and 1964. Much like the early years of the PRC, when the central government had a difficult time reining in cadres who enthusiastically banned anything with the merest whiff of superstition, some things were still open to interpretation, and it was difficult to check the ideological excesses of radicals.

The second type of play that appears somewhat curious are plays that, either due to form or content (or in some cases, both), would not have been discussed as "ghost plays" prior to this period. The very first play listed, for example, is a 1962 spoken language drama called *Mount Everest* (*Zhumulangma*), which is rather obviously neither traditional Chinese opera nor concerned with "historical" subject matter. Its setting was entirely contemporary, being based on the 1960 Chinese ascent of Everest. However, the play included "five mountain spirits" as well as the ghost of a "foreign explorer."[74] The debates on ghost plays of the 1950s and early 1960s confined themselves to discussion of traditional drama, primarily adaptations of Ming *chuanqi*; spoken drama, with or without ghosts, drew no notice. Likewise included were a number of plays with what appear to be questionable ties to "ghosts" as had traditionally been defined. A number of plays listed are stories relating to *jiangshi*, the "reanimated corpses" that are more analogous to vampires and zombies familiar to Western literature than to ghosts. Even with this relative broadening, a number of classic plays were not represented, including seemingly obvious stories like *Legend of White Snake*. Still, the evidence of "inappropriate" artistic

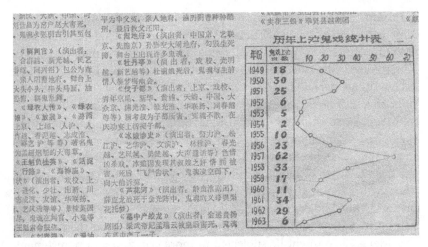

Fig. 9. From the *Wenyi zhanbao* discussion of the "ghost play problem" in Shanghai. On the left, part of the list and explanation of various "ghost plays" performed; a chart listing the numbers of "ghost plays" performed between 1949 and 1963; on the right, partial lists of plays performed in 1962 and 1963. In author's personal collection.

production found in statistics and charts would have been cause for a self-criticism at most in previous years. They were now ammunition for more serious charges and punishments.

The tales of suffering during the years of upheaval are familiar territory, and there is no doubt that people with far less power or influence than the senior cultural workers also suffered mightily. Still, fame had some significant downsides. Tian Han, last to face severe public criticism, died first on December 10, 1968, having been confined to a prison under the control of Kang Sheng.[75] His final plea was reportedly "Please, please let me see my mother one more time. Just one last time," and his mother waited for him in Beijing, dying four years later, still not knowing the fate of her famous son.[76] Wu Han, having been dragged about, humiliated, and mistreated in 1966 and 1967, was held along with his wife at a cadre school, although they were allowed to return home occasionally. In March 1968, he, too, was imprisoned, and died a year and a half later.[77] But what of the third writer and his ghost? Meng Chao, never achieving the prominence of Tian Han and Wu Han in life, has slipped further into obscurity in death (one wonders if this might not be, at least in part, because his story does lack the emotional punch of the outlandish abuse endured by his compatriots). The last ten years of Meng Chao's life come down to us largely through a grief-stricken essay by his daughter Meng Jian, affection-ate reminiscences by often-jaded fellow writers, and the memoirs of Mu Xin, the assuredly jaded former editor of the *Guangming Daily*. Although such writings were, of course, written after the fact and were certainly not unbiased, they do provide a picture of the fate of *Li Huiniang*'s author.

Meng Chao suffered a multitude of private tragedies, not well-publicized humiliation. Even so, he found his situation intolerable, and in the 1960s, he, like many others, attempted suicide. He was rushed to the hospital after swallowing poison, his case handlers hot behind him. The doctors inquired whether or not this was someone they "want[ed] or not?" The handlers responded, "This person is a very big traitor, and you mustn't allow him to die!"[78] The doctors dutifully did their work so that Meng Chao might be subjected to more criticism and punishment. At the cadre reeducation school, he was, according to Lou Shiyi, a special target of the "young pathbreaking revolutionaries" who frequently burst into their cowshed, crying "Which one of you is Meng Chao?" Having no choice but to show himself, he submitted to the abuse. He "never made a sound, and took the beatings with his head bowed low," scenes that made Lou's blood run cold with fear.[79]

As it turned out, Meng Chao's old friend Kang Sheng was in charge of his case—a fact of which he was unaware when he submitted two letters from Kang Sheng praising *Li Huiniang*, hoping to stem some of the criti-cism. The letters disappeared, and of course had no impact on the disposi-tion of his case.[80] He must have figured out his old friend's role at some point, though. Lou Shiyi recalled one evening at the "cowshed," when they had acquired a little bit of alcohol. Emboldened perhaps by the liquor, Lou asked Meng Chao: "Didn't you have that 'master of theory' [*lilun quanwei*, a sarcastic sobriquet often used after 1976 to refer to Kang Sheng] you grew up with? He was really good to you that day we went to see the pre-miere of [*Li Huiniang*]. He specially congratulated you and invited you out to eat Peking duck! Why don't you write him a letter and appeal, maybe you can be released a little early." Meng Chao was silent, and simply shook his head. Lou did not bring the subject up again.[81]

By the time the cadre schools were eventually dissolved in the mid-1970s, Meng Chao, Lou Shiyi, and the others were allowed to return home. Meng Chao's wife was dead and he was left to a small Beijing *hutong* flat. "I went to see him when I had time," Lou Shiyi recalled a few years later. "He was alone, reading the *Selected Works of Chairman Mao*. All of his books had been confiscated, only this one book was left." Jiang Qing and "the Gang of Four" were still clinging to power, and there was no change in his case or status, and there would be no change until the rehabilitations of 1979.[82] During his final months in 1976, Meng Chao cried to one of his daughters that he had been wronged, that someone had hurt him. His words to her—"the injustice!"—were a fitting echo of Li Huiniang's cries, and mirrored the feelings of many.[83]

And yet—the fierce criticism, persecution, and trauma of the Cultural Revolution was not quite the end of the story. Li Huiniang, whose socialist career was a mere hiccup in a theatrical legacy that stretched back centuries, would once again rise from the ashes, even if her authors could not. In the wake of Mao's death, the end of the Cultural Revolution, and the fall of the Gang of Four, the beautiful woman born under an unlucky star returned to Chinese stages with a vengeance, her story now tinged with even more immediate meaning. Perhaps her star wasn't as unlucky as it appeared in the dark days of 1965 and 1966.

Conclusion

Although Yao Wenyuan's November 1965 essay on Wu Han and *Hai Rui* has traditionally been read as the "prelude" to the Cultural Revolution, it ought to be read as the culmination of years of effort in the wake of Mao's increasingly radical line taken at the 1962 Tenth Plenum. The first important parts of the cultural world to fall were theatrical ghosts in the spring of 1963, and it was Meng Chao and *Li Huiniang* that bore the brunt of early 1965 criticism. Less politically connected and protected than either Wu Han or Tian Han, Meng Chao had only his old friend Kang Sheng—one of the people, alongside Jiang Qing, who was bent on remaking the cultural world, sensing the political opportunities presented by Mao's radicalism.

Prior to 1965, the "new historical plays" had never been discussed in relation to the Great Leap Forward. Of course, we would hardly expect to see such acknowledgments in print in the early 1960s. Further, I am sympathetic to readings of these plays that give them a political inflection; ghosts, after all, have often reasserted themselves in literature during times of crisis. However, Meng Chao and Wu Han had other avenues to express dissatisfaction with CCP policy or the present reality through their use of *zawen*. As illustrated in chapter 3, the discussion of Meng Chao's *Li Huiniang* was primarily focused on its artistic and literary merits. Was

Meng Chao's preoccupation really with the Leap? From reading essays on the play published in the early 1960s, and Meng Chao's own postscript, the cultural workers participating in the discussion seem most eager to prove their literary and artistic talents, and the connection of socialist cultural production to great literary traditions. The idea of the playwright's total preoccupation with criticizing the Leap, in fact, seems to derive far more from 1965 and 1966 essays than anything written in the years prior. It is this reading—wherein the primary purpose of the plays was coded political criticism—that has taken hold in the historiography, often to the exclusion of any other consideration.

CHAPTER 6

"Is It Not Fate?"
Li Huiniang *and the Post-Mao Milieu*

Following the 1976 fall of Jiang Qing and the so-called Gang of Four in the wake of Mao's death, a wave of discontent swept the cultural world. The pages of drama journals, resuming publication after a ten-year hiatus, were filled with attacks on the Gang of Four, lamentations for those who suffered during the Cultural Revolution, and the deification of Zhou Enlai, exalted as a party knight in shining armor. Gradually, such unrest died down, and critics and artists turned once again to topics of more literary interest—although politics remained, as ever, deeply intertwined with art. By 1979, the literary elite was enmeshed in debates over what lessons to draw from the Cultural Revolution, as more and more people came forward with bitter criticisms of a party that had betrayed them, their family, or their friends.

In the press, photographs of Jiang Qing's model operas were gradually replaced with those of traditional dramas, most of which had not been staged for a decade or more. A new discourse surrounding the "great poisonous weeds" of the Cultural Revolution gradually emerged, as those who had been intimately involved with the persecution of fellow intellectuals, or who had themselves been persecuted, attempted to find some meaning for the years of chaos and upheaval. As they parsed the responsibility of Mao and the rest of the party that had been so tainted by the radical excesses of the Gang of Four, they absolved themselves of all responsibility, or at the very least, abstained from publicly admitting to their roles in the events of the preceding decade. The result of a prominent 1978 gathering of famous literary theorists and critics, designed to examine Yao Wenyuan's essay on Wu Han and *Hai Rui*, was clear: the blame for the Cultural Revolution should rest entirely on the Gang of Four.[1]

The discussion—laid out in detail in *Theatre Report*—ultimately concluded (whatever it was worth) that there should be "democracy for scholars and artists," and their right to expression, within limits, should be protected by law. In delineating the line between "criticizing present reality" and being "antiparty, antisocialist thought," the assembled literary critics essentially admitted that the attacks on Wu Han, Meng Chao, Tian Han, and many others had been unfounded. The disgraced authors had not been trying to subvert the party or to criticize the foundations of socialist thought; they wished only to critique the dark days of 1959, all in hopes of bringing about a better future.[2] Naturally, the participants did not admit their own complicity in joining the early fray, and placed the blame squarely on Jiang Qing, Yao Wenyuan, and others for allowing cultural critique to spin wildly out of control. Helpfully, the anointed villains of the story were either dead or had already been imprisoned. Of course, those who could have most benefited from these pronouncements, the three men who had borne the brunt of early, vicious criticism, were by this point all dead. Even Meng Chao, who had managed to survive until 1976, outlasting Wu Han and Tian Han by nearly a decade, had "gone to see Marx," as the saying went, still wearing his "bad element cap."[3] So it was left to those who remained behind to vent their anger and move forward.

This chapter considers the fate of artists, writers, and ghost literature between 1976 and the early 1980s. Meng Chao's *Li Huiniang*, alongside *Hai Rui* and *Xie Yaohuan*, was put back on stages at the same time those persecuted during the Cultural Revolution were rehabilitated. However, while the plays found themselves in a more relaxed political environment, they could not escape the didactic imperatives that had haunted them in the 1950s and 1960s. In contrast, a brand-new production of another version of *Li Huiniang* by the Suzhou Peking Opera Troupe revealed an entirely different type of discussion: one that focused on novelty and artistic daring, without fretting about elements that would have been considered highly problematic in the high socialist period. Finally, I close with a consideration of what drove writers and critics to take up ghostly subjects in the 1950s and 1960s.

Reviving Spirits: The Many Lives of Phantoms

In October 1979—eleven months after many cultural workers, including Meng Chao, Ma Jianling, and others, had been publicly rehabilitated in *People's Daily* and other publications—Lou Shiyi recorded his memories of his time spent with Meng Chao in a *People's Daily* essay. The piece, which included descriptions of their life in a Cultural Revolution–era "cowshed," was sarcastic and literary in the extreme, and took aim at those who had begun the persecution of literary subjects. Why, he wondered, had a play that was "anti-Jia Sidao" come to be considered "antiparty" in 1965? "Don't tell me," he wrote with more than a touch of bitterness, "that our great, righteous, glorious, and honorable party harbored a Jia Sidao."[4]

Time and posthumous rehabilitation did not necessarily dull feelings of anger and injustice. Meng Jian's heartbreaking essay was written in 1980 for the republication of her father's most famous literary product. She recounted his anguished cries (echoes of Li Huiniang herself) two months before his death—"I've been wronged! Someone has hurt me!"— and his steadfast refusal to name his persecutor.[5] Although Meng Chao, like many others, had been rehabilitated in December 1978, his daughter bitterly wondered why she was supposed to be happy. Posthumous rehabilitation could not change what had happened to her father and their family. Meng Jian tells of standing in front of her father's urn and silently cursing Li Huiniang. Even merely in print, it is a harrowing scene to take in: a bereaved daughter, standing in front of what remained of her father, blaming a fictional ghost for the family's severe troubles. But though it is her father's literary creation she curses, Li Huiniang seems here a mere stand-in for the real villains of the story, whom she declines to name outright: most prominently, Kang Sheng (in this period, referred to sarcastically as a "master of theory," the sobriquet used in Lou and Meng's essays, and in many others).

The outrageous suffering of people like Tian Han and Wu Han has had the effect of burnishing their legacies. That Meng Chao has slipped into obscurity, despite the very visible role criticism of him and his play took in the early Cultural Revolution, probably has something to do with the less gripping nature of his story. He was persecuted, yes, but was saved the grandiose public humiliations many of his colleagues suffered through. Crying to his daughter of generalized injustice lacks the emotional punch of the pleas of the imprisoned Tian Han, only days from death, to see his mother one last time. Certainly, many other people suffered far more for having done far less than Meng Chao. And yet his daughter's grief sums up the feelings so many must have had. All the elegant intellectual debates over who was to blame, all the rehabilitations and lashing out at Jiang Qing, Kang Sheng, and others, could never replace what had been lost. She ends her essay on her father and his ghost on a melancholy note, at once deeply personal, and yet able to speak for many:

> For a long, long time I did not dream; the strange thing is that recently, I've dreamt often. In dreams I see my father, wearing a half-length Chinese padded jacket, a long, camel-colored scarf wrapped around his neck three times; he rests on a walking stick, his body short and thin and weak. As before, his back has a bit of a hunch to it, he drags his leg that was hurt during his persecution, and in his mouth he keeps the end of a long, long cigarette—one, then following that, another. He hobbles towards me, but is always, always unable to reach me. . . . .
>
> Waking up, I know that it's simply an empty dream. But—I miss him, I really miss him. (128)

Meng Jian speaks not to abstract ideological fallout, but the high personal costs borne by so many people.

Still, Lou Shiyi offered a hopeful interpretation of *Li Huiniang*'s ultimate import. He closed his essay with a reflection on Meng Chao's heroine in the form of couplets, befitting an old friend, a good revolutionary, and participant in the heady cosmopolitan days of Republican Shanghai.[6] Meditating on this ghost who brought an old workhorse of the party to great ruin, Lou noted that it also provided him with another life after death:

> Right now, *Li Huiniang* is back on stages. I just received an official notice that there's going to be a memorial service for comrade Meng Chao at Babaoshan [Cemetery]. I thought—as a reply—I ought to send funerary couplets. I thought for a long time, and finally came up with these two lines:
>
> *While living, you were made to be a ghost; for this we should whip the corpse of Jia Sidao three hundred times.*
> *Though you have died, it is as though you still live; for this we should offer solemn song to Li Huiniang.*

Lou was entirely correct in many respects. Although the authors may have had only one life, their literary works could live again and again—and they would, being set to new purposes in the cultural realm. Beginning in 1979, many actresses stepped once more into the long-sleeved gowns of ghost characters and brought them back to life. Among the "three poisonous weeds," it was Wu Han's *Hai Rui* that was initially revived, but *Li Huiniang* premiered again with the Northern Kun Opera Theatre, the troupe that had commissioned Meng Chao twenty years before, on April 27, 1979. Based on a December 1978 practice edition, corresponding precisely to the month when the author and play had been publicly rehabilitated, the re-premiere had been in preparation for at least four months.[7] A blurb in *People's Theatre* made note of the performance and offered one of the great understatements of its value: "As everyone knows, this is a good play" (*zhe shi yige haoxi*).[8] Of course, as everyone *also* knew, *Li Huiniang* had been declared the very antithesis of a "good play" for many years. But these formerly "poisonous weeds," like their authors, had been rehabilitated and were being celebrated once again. The April issue of *People's Theatre*, for instance, prominently featured photographs of performances of *Hai Rui*, *Xie Yaohuan*, and *Li Huiniang*. In the photograph of Meng Chao's ghost opera—featuring Li Shujun, the originator of the role, as Li Huiniang and Zhou Wanjiang as Jia Sidao—Li seems to be wearing an ever-so-slight smile, even as she places a hand on the sword that Zhou brandishes. Likewise, in two similarly prominent photographs of the revived *Xie Yaohuan*, performers Du Jinfang and Yuan Shihai are both captured midmotion, smiling. It was, perhaps, an accident of timing. Yet the performers themselves, at least in the photographs selected for inclusion in the journal, look just as pleased to be performing old roles as audiences apparently were to see them.

Of course, the play, its author, and those associated with the Northern Kun Opera troupe were indelibly linked to the Cultural Revolution–era criticisms, although now they—or those that remained, at least—returned to theatres to acclaim, albeit often cloaked in political language. In June, *People's Daily* contained a brief note on the return of *Li Huiniang*, stating that the play that had once captured audience interest in the early 1960s was now able to be seen again in the capital. Noting that Bai Yunsheng, original director of the troupe, and Meng Chao had both been "persecuted to death" during the Cultural Revolution, the short announcement ended on a more positive note, if one tied intimately to the rise of Deng Xiaoping and the era of reform and opening. The cultural workers of the Northern Kun Opera Theatre, the announcement declared, were now "determined to work even harder to carry forward and develop the art of Kun opera, in order to passionately support China in realizing the Four Modernizations."[9] What, exactly, *Li Huiniang* would be doing in order to support Deng's reforms went unsaid. But it would be doing *something*, apparently.

One imagines audiences were rather less interested in watching formerly banned plays for their contemporary political merits, and rather more in the "pleasure and satisfaction" of watching good theatre that Chen Yi had referred to in 1961, after another period of great political and social upheaval.[10] Still, the enthusiasm for the revived ghost and her new historical play comrades was probably due in no small part to the fact that their return suggested that other, more recent specters of the past were now off cultural and political stages alike.[11] While it can be difficult to determine the exact origin of plays with similar stories and similar names, Meng Chao's Kun opera ghost—or ones partially inspired by her—seems to have enjoyed a popular revival in the years immediately after the rehabilitation of its author. In 1981, for instance, the Jiangsu Kun Opera troupe put on a total of 223 performances. Roughly 50 percent were productions of *Xi Shi*, a classical tale of a beautiful woman—but 40 percent were of *Li Huiniang*.[12] Whether or not the play was Meng Chao's version is not particularly important. Although *Red Plums* had always been a popular play in several styles of opera, it took on even more meanings in the wake of the Cultural Revolution; it was now inextricably linked to the vicious criticisms of 1965 and 1966 and the ensuing chaos.

It was not simply Kun opera troupes reviving or re-creating the ghost heroine. A sampling of practice editions purchased from Chinese secondhand booksellers reveals an astonishing number of versions, most simply titled *Li Huiniang*, from all over China appearing in 1979 and 1980. Several explicitly reference their high socialist predecessors: Meng Chao's Kun *Li Huiniang* and, more frequently, Ma Jianling's 1957 *qinqiang* revision of *Wandering West Lake*. In January 1979, scant weeks after Meng Chao, Ma Jianling, and others had been posthumously rehabilitated, a Xiang *gaoqiang* version for the Hunan Xiang Opera troupe, prepared by the Hunan Opera Workshop and the Hunan Xiang Opera Theatre, explicitly stated it was "revised according to the 1957 *qinqiang Wandering West Lake*."[13] Several months later, in May 1979, shortly after the re-premiere of Northern Kun Opera's *Li Huiniang*, the Hubei Chu Opera troupe put together their own *Li Huiniang*, "adapted according to the *qinqiang*."[14] In December of that year, an unknown Dian (Yunnan) opera troupe saw their own version, revised by Wang Zhichi, with a script "arranged according to *qinqiang*, Chuan, Kun, and Yu opera versions"—giving some indication of

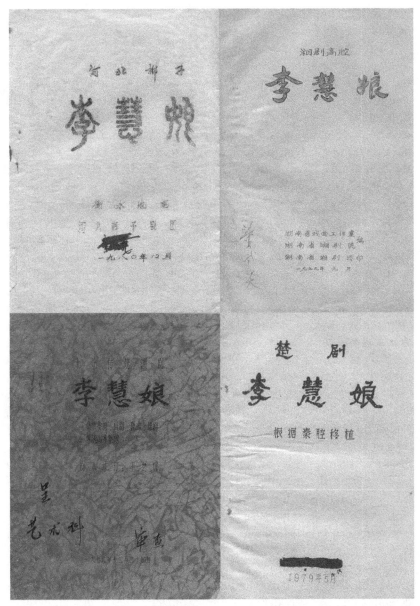

Fig. 10. Four of the numerous versions of *Li Huiniang* staged in 1979 and 1980 (from upper left, clockwise: December 1980 Hebei *bangzi*, January 1979 Xiang *gaoxiang*, May 1979 Chu opera, December 1979 Dian opera). In author's personal collection.

how common *Li Huiniang* and variants were in a number of styles (see figure 10).[15]

Even with the revived stagings, the ghost play debate had still not been satisfactorily resolved, although everyone seemed ready to agree that the Cultural Revolution–era accusations that the creators of "poisonous weeds" were acting in an "antiparty, antisocialist thought" manner had been unjust. Qu Liuyi, who in 1957 had argued that if anything, ghosts were of more utility on stages than mythological characters, echoed the old debates in a January 1979 piece in *Literature & Art Studies*, although the terms had shifted slightly. "Good ghost plays," he stated, should be categorized with mythology plays; "bad ghost plays" should be classed as "religious play" (*zongjiao xi*) (e.g., *Mulian Rescues His Mother*).[16] Over a quarter of a century after the first socialist debates on "mythology" and "superstition" on stages, critics still felt the need to defend ghost literature (or some of it) from being miscategorized.

There were more residual traces of the old debates, even for those not quite so interested in neat definitions. Wang Chunyuan, writing in *People's Daily* in June 1979, used Meng Chao's "skillful" adaptation as a launching point for a passionate defense of ghost operas and supernatural literature—but one laced with the same kind of rhetoric that harkened back to the arguments made by Zhang Zhen, Yang Xianyi, and many others in the 1950s and 1960s. "The apparition of Li Huiniang," Wang wrote, "is of course not the kind of 'ghost' found in superstitious drivel; rather, at the present, [it] is an artistic reflection of the people's resisting spirit, aspirations, and life's willpower," and a natural part of human society.[17] And now, ghost opera could be deployed as yet another avenue to attack disgraced former leaders: "We must continue to criticize Lin Biao, 'the Gang of Four,' the gang that forced upon this kind of play every type of slanderous, false word."[18] Harsh words for Jiang Qing et al. aside, Wang closes with the hope that such classical treasures will encourage younger generations to love justice and socialism. Even after finding herself in a new social and political context, Li Huiniang was still unable to escape the need to offer greater lessons, and she was still a political tool.

All this indicates that, even in the 1980s, ghost plays were still being defended and partially defined on their didactic merits, though perhaps not with as much force as in years past. However, even in such popular products as *lianhuanhua* ("linked picture books," similar to Western comic books) a focus on ghosts needed to be justified. The preface to one beautiful version of *Li Huiniang* from 1982, illustrated by Xu Hengyu, explicitly states in the short introduction: "Although *Li Huiniang* is a ghost opera, it doesn't concern in the least the flavor of superstitious 'ghosts,' and instead is full of the joy and sorrow, love and hate of the human world, as well as a fighting spirit of opposing persecution."[19] The language is similar to the oft-repeated phrase from the high socialist era that theatrical ghosts "encouraged a resisting spirit"; one wonders if the selection of "opposing persecution" (*fanpohai*) in this case is not a conscious reference to the cultural workers who had indeed been terribly persecuted for their activities, including writing and performing ghosts. Although the text of the *lianhuanhua* is not Meng Chao's, it is often extremely lyrical, and there are echoes of Li Huiniang's Kun arias—one panel features Li Huiniang looking just as she described herself in Meng Chao's version, a "ghost bodhisattva"—as well as Meng Chao's own postscript. When Li Huiniang returns from the underworld, for instance, the text sets the scene: "An autumn night, collected fragrances within a garden, in the faint light of the moon, crickets cry desolately."[20] Compare this to Meng Chao's description of Li Huiniang's reappearance: "In 1959, I was harassed by illness; on my sickbed on a cool evening, [I listened] to the rustling of fallen leaves, insects wailed desolately, the cold moon peeped through the window. . . ." Although perhaps simply a literary coincidence—after all, cold moons, rustling leaves, fragrant gardens, and insects chirping on cool autumn nights are hardly unique, especially in describing the appearance of ghosts—considering the outpouring of grief and anger in the early 1980s, it does not seem to be a large leap to suggest a connection.

Even as ghost plays were being defended on didactic merits, the old thread charging that ghosts were representative of fearsome things to be resisted, not characters that could *teach* resistance, reappeared again. *Stories about Not Being Afraid of Ghosts*, which was first published in the early 1960s, reappeared (and in fact, is still in print to the present), complete with its Mao-approved introduction that claimed ghosts were analogous to any manner of real-world terrors. In addition to the standard editions, including translations, a number of handsomely illustrated *lianhuanhua* versions of *Stories* began appearing in April and May of 1979, at the same time Northern Kun Opera was reviving *Li Huiniang* and classical ghosts were returning to the pages of opera journals and newspapers.

Now, however, just as *Li Huiniang* was being used to castigate the Gang of Four and others, so too was *Stories*, an interesting inversion of the decades previous. One 1979 version from Sichuan, for instance, which includes illustrated version of two stories of Pu Songling's and one from Ai

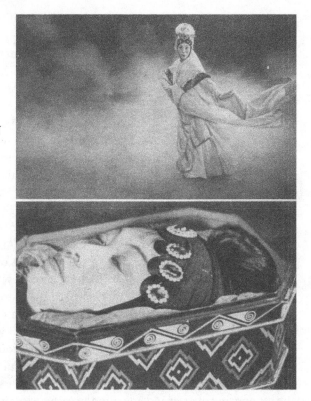

Fig. 11. Two pages from the *Li Huinaing lianhuanhua*, using stills from the 1981 film. On the top, Hu Zhifeng's entrance as Li Huiniang; on the bottom, the slain Li Huiniang's head in a box. In the next frame, the head has disappeared— signaling Li Huiniang's "rebirth" as a ghost (Sha Jie, ed. *Li Huiniang* (Beijing: Zhongguo dianying chubanshe, 1982).

Mei, notes in the brief introduction: "There are no ghosts in the world, this is common scientific knowledge. However, in the world there are many [ghost-like things]. For example: great hegemons, little tyrants, and Lin Biao, 'The Gang of Four,' these ghosts of every shade and description, all of which destroy our revolutionary undertaking."[21] A 1979 *lianhuanhua* edition from a Shanghai press, nearly 200 pages in length, begins with a similar introduction. "The socialist imperialism of the Soviet Union and Lin Biao, 'the Gang of Four' are one type of ox ghost–snake spirits," it declares. "They all look just as the ghosts in legends."[22] The supposed didactic utility of ghost stories and plays was still being used to justify their consumption. But a prominent version of *Li Huiniang*, staged by a troupe from Suzhou, would (at least in part) refocus the discussion away from politics and criticism of Cultural Revolution–era excesses, and back to the artistic and emotional power of ghost opera—this old story of a slain concubine in particular.

Other Echoes in the Garden: Hu Zhifeng's Li Huiniang

If Ma Jianling's *Wandering West Lake* had been the most important revision of *Red Plums* to appear in the 1950s, and Meng Chao's *Li Huiniang* the most important in the 1960s, Hu Zhifeng's *Li Huiniang* was likely the most important and widely discussed version of the 1980s. Hu, leading actress of the Suzhou Peking Opera Troupe, would reimagine Li Huiniang yet again—this time in a very different context than those in which either Ma Jianling or Meng Chao's heroines came to life. The stage and film versions, as well as their reception, underscore the radically different context for some forms of cultural production in the late 1970s and 1980s. The Suzhou Peking Opera's *Li Huiniang* was replete with precisely the sorts of representations that critics in the high socialist period agreed needed to be banned from the stage, and moreover, it was for the most part unencumbered by the ideological discussions that continued to follow Meng Chao's Kun variation, even after the Cultural Revolution. Critics and audiences alike enthused about the artistic and commercial achievement presented to them and praised them for elegant staging and dancing, and novel technique. While discussions of the "ghost play problem" or the Northern Kun Opera version could not escape references to the Gang of Four, Lin Biao, or Kang Sheng, this new *Li Huiniang* seemed almost completely unfettered by political concerns.

Hu Zhifeng had a slightly unorthodox, and rather unexpected, path to becoming an opera star; while she had studied music and opera from age eleven, she decided to set her feet on the path to a performing career while a student at Tsinghua University in the department of engineering physics.[23] However, she studied with some of the great Peking and Kun opera stars of the day (including Mei Lanfang, Xiao Cuihua, and Zhu Chuanming) and furthered her studies with piano and ballet.[24] Indeed, reviewers often commented on her novel and daring techniques, which seem largely to be a product of blending traditional study and slightly less orthodox disciplines. Many photographs of Hu on the stage show her in highly balletic poses not often seen in other pictures of prominent actors. Unsurprisingly, what often comes to the fore in discussions of her version of *Li Huiniang* is both her respect for a variety of operatic traditions *and* her success in "invigorating" Peking opera with her experimentation. Partially on the basis of her technique, then, was the discussion of this *Li Huiniang* refocused from the didactic and political qualities Meng Chao's version still found itself saddled with toward a consideration of aesthetics.

Certainly, political goals were still discussed in reference to the production. A 1980 interview with Hu Zhifeng sheds light on some of her own ideas about the play and its utility. Much of the language she uses to describe the revisions—"stressing [the play's] modern qualities and ideological content," for instance, or "developing [Li Huiniang's] resisting spirit"[25]—mirrors the ways in which ghost plays had been discussed for decades. And yet it seems to be the novelty of Hu's portrayal that kept audiences flocking to theatres. In a number of cities, she notes, "many young people wrote us notes, and said originally, they had no interest in Peking opera, [but] after seeing *Li Huiniang*, they had unexpectedly come to like Peking opera."[26] The import of Hu's revisions was less ideological education than it was the continuing development of an audience for "one of the country's precious artistic riches" through creative adaptation.[27] In many respects, Hu Zhifeng seems to have hit on the combination that writers, artists, and critics had been desperately searching for in the 1950s and 1960s: refashioning an important, traditional play to make it more appealing to contemporary audiences, while still being able to claim some sort of edifying content and authenticity. She did so, it should be noted, under what appear to be significantly fewer restrictions on cultural production that under the frequently rigid ideological and bureaucratic demands of the 1950s and 1960s.

So, despite Hu Zhifeng's words regarding ideology and a didactic purpose, an exceedingly enthusiastic review in *People's Daily*, over a year after the premiere of the Suzhou troupe's *Li Huiniang*, illustrates the new context this version of the Song dynasty concubine found herself in. Unlike the Northern Kun Opera version, which, even in the midst of discussion admiring the artistic content, could never quite escape its history of the preceding two decades, the freshness of Hu Zhifeng's *Li Huiniang* was emphasized, and especially that of Hu's portrayal. Describing the sold-out performances everywhere from Shanghai to Liaoning, including some audience members who apparently went to ten successive performances, Pei Zhen asks what was it about this *Li Huiniang* that attracted people so?[28] Was it the lessons imparted—brave Huiniang opposing a feudal tyrant, or reflecting the "spirit of patriotism"? Neither seems to be the case: Pei placed importance on the high production values for attracting audiences, but emphasized Hu Zhifeng's daring portrayal as the main draw. The review is practically ecstatic as it describes how Hu had managed to synthesize various female operatic roles, drawn from several operatic traditions, and even to incorporate ballet, all while displaying the quintessential features of Peking opera techniques and specialties. Yet, as Pei enthused, Hu Zhi-feng managed "not to be a stickler for old formulas, but [had] the courage to explore."[29] It is worth questioning whether or not Hu Zhifeng would have had the "courage" to explore two decades before. Ma Jianling, Meng Chao, and the artists associated with their productions, to say nothing of many others, were *also* exploring. But now, in the seemingly liberated environment of the 1980s, there was room for real "daring," for true exploration, without the fear of another bureaucratic "gust of wind."

The reception of the Suzhou *Li Huiniang* also speaks to the declining prominence of opera, which was actually one reason why Hu Zhifeng and her compatriots had so much room to maneuver and create something that seemed new, fresh, and interesting. The critic Lan Ling pondered the production a few weeks after Pei Zhen's enthusiastic review. Speaking of the "crisis" facing traditional theatre such as declining audiences and theatre's seeming irrelevance, which Lan found little evidence of (probably somewhat naïvely), he found a useful approach in the example of Hu Zhifeng and the Suzhou troupe. Not very large in size, lacking famous actors, they nevertheless managed to cause a stir in cities all over through new approaches and exceptional beauty.[30] Perhaps this *Li Huiniang* was the intended outcome of the sometimes exuberant experimentation of the high socialist period: a new version of a very old play, being celebrated for artistic daring, while at the same time not having to take wild chances with the core of the material.

Hu Zhifeng's take on *Li Huiniang* also echoes several trends of the late imperial and early Republican periods. The "new style" hybrid plays of the early twentieth century, for instance, provided a visual feast for audiences: "spectacular, bursting with electric lights, colorful sets, and fabulous props."[31] However, the didacticism of those plays, and the socialist-era forerunners of Hu's *Li Huiniang*, seems almost totally absent. The didactic functions and ideological correctness of theatre were de-emphasized, and increasing importance was placed on the artistic and entertainment qualities of plays. A June 1980 review in *Theatre Art* used an old phrase, "pushing out the old to bring in the new," to heap praise upon the Suzhou production. Hu's portrayal was described as a sublime mixture of the best of the old and the freshest of the new, and thus saw audiences drawn to it. "To be sure," Shi Xin wrote, "blazing new trails in art depends on liberating [one's] thoughts."[32] But was it individuals' thoughts that needed to be liberated? Or those of a bureaucracy and an entire cultural apparatus? For the most part, the Suzhou edition of *Li Huiniang* was free of the frighten-

ing burdens placed on opera artists in the 1950s and 1960s, however critics and artists might have gestured toward ideology. What heights might
Meng Chao, Ma Jianling, and even Yang Shaoxuan have reached, without
the fetters of often unreasonable and conflicting expectations placed upon
them? This is an issue that 1980s critics, unsurprisingly, did not explore.

The humble Suzhou Peking Opera troupe's vision of Li Huiniang was
compelling enough, and sold enough tickets, to lead to a cinematic version. Opera films had long been popular with audiences, even in the high
socialist period. As Judith Zeitlin notes, between 1953 and 1966, "at least
115 opera films were released—an extraordinarily high number by any
measure."[33] With the success of the Suzhou troupe's stage production, it
seems little surprise that a film version was planned for this *Li Huiniang*.
And so, in 1981, the concubine fluttered her way across Chinese movie
screens to great acclaim.[34] Just like its theatrical predecessor, this adaptation was a world away from its Mao-era counterparts, and it was obvious
from the start: the film begins with Li Huiniang's descent into Hell and
meeting with Yama. Starring Hu Zhifeng and the Suzhou troupe, the film
was no minor production, and was directed by Liu Qiong—whose résumé
as both an actor and director was lengthy, including starring roles in the
1957 blockbuster *Girl Basketball Player No. 5* (*Nülan wu hao*) and directing
a number of films after 1949.[35]

Just as artistic considerations had been a prime point of discussion for
critics in the high socialist period, so too were they in the 1980s. Now,
however, there was less necessity for considering the political and ideological ramifications of performance decisions. Furthermore, there was
great excitement over scenes that previously would have landed cultural
workers in hot water. One article from *Film Review* discussed how special
effects were created for the film—both the "ghostly" scenes, featuring relative transparency, and, more intriguingly, a key scene immediately after
Li Huiniang's murder which features her head (having been severed from
her body) in a box (see figure 11).[36] An image from the *lianhuanhua* version of the film, featuring movie stills alongside the text, shows clearly the
bloodless, yet still vaguely disturbing, scene. It is not a stretch to suggest
that this sort of effect would be precisely the kind of thing that would
have been described as "fearsome" in the 1950s and 1960s. Furthermore, a
number of key scenes, particularly those taking place in the underworld,
were exactly the type of deletions dramatists in the high socialist period
made as a matter of course. And yet this *Li Huiniang* was not just beloved
by audiences, but was bestowed with honors by the Ministry of Culture,

being named best movie drama of 1981.[37] What better sign that theatrical ghosts had been rehabilitated, only a few short years after the end of the Cultural Revolution? Ma Jianling's visions of Li Huiniang had apparently been quite popular with audiences and later playwrights, while Meng Chao's won the acclaim of the cultural and political elite of the day, but none of them had been awarded prizes by the Ministry of Culture. Here *was* proof that Li Huiniang had outlasted her critics. It is also indicative of the very different environment Hu Zhifeng's version operated in: with the most modest of ideological justifications, the play was received well on multiple levels thanks to both the actress's daring and the relaxation of bureaucratic demands upon artists.

Hu Zhifeng's *Li Huiniang* was certainly not the last gasp of ghost opera, despite the decline in opera's prominence as a vehicle for education and entertainment. As Judith Zeitlin has noted, the classical ghost tale still "exerts a strong grip on the contemporary imagination," and can be seen in a variety of media—including, of course, theatre.[38] However, compared to the political emphasis on theatre and the threat, and potential, that it formerly constituted in the high socialist period, the contemporary climate reflects a relative tempering of theatre as cultural critique. Traditional opera as a form seems much safer today than it was in the 1950s and 1960s: it is difficult to imagine contemporary critics of the CCP turning to revisions of Ming originals in order to criticize the regime. Indeed, the traditional arts have been declared national or international treasures. Kun opera, for instance, was the first Chinese entrant on the United Nations Educational, Scientific, and Cultural Organization (UNESCO) Lists of Intangible Cultural Heritage.[39] Nevertheless, there are new, if subtler, battles to be waged over who controls their presentation and legacy. Thus, opera—including celebrated ghost operas, particularly the *Peony Pavilion*, which has received several high-profile adaptations over the past two decades—is as politicized as it ever was, though with a different inflection than seen in the decades before.

Consider the 1999 production of the *Peony Pavilion*, staged by American-based director Chen Shi-Zheng at New York City's Lincoln Center. Catherine C. Swatek has traced a number of tensions inherent in Chen's production: he aimed to "break out of a mold" that emphasized "overrefinement" and "beautiful forms" of Kun opera, to the exclusion of the richness he believed was found in the Ming original.[40] There are ripples here of the old mythology play debates. Just as Yang Shaoxuan had been castigated for taking liberties with a classic tale, contemporary Chi-

nese reviewers were critical toward Chen's revisions, designed to popular-
ize the high-brow art form and return some of the "leisured atmosphere"
in which such operas would have been viewed during the Ming dynasty.[41]
The question was now not one of ideological correctness, per se, but how
to present a "canonical" Chinese drama on a world stage. Billed as possibly
the first time *Peony* had been performed in its entirety, Chen's production
was to star the Shanghai Kunju Opera Troupe. But Shanghai bureaucrats
impounded the sets, declared the play "feudal, superstitious and porno-
graphic," and refused to let the troupe leave the country. The rhetoric was
straight from 1963, but the real issue was one of control and presentation.
Chen and Lincoln Center were forced to put together a new troupe, having only two members of the original cast. They eventually staged the play
to excellent reviews in the West, even though, as Zeitlin described, staging
the full play required audiences to sit through "a grueling six hours a day
for three days straight."[42]

As a "rebuttal" to Chen's *Peony*, the Shanghai government funded and
managed its own production with the Shanghai Kunju Opera Troupe. It
was also billed as part of celebrations marking the fiftieth anniversary of
the establishment of the PRC, something that would have been unimagi-
nable a mere fifteen years after the country's founding.[43] Still, the continuing furor over at least one ghost opera indicates something of the cultural
power these products held and still hold, as well as the continuing fas-
cination of the public and cultural workers with the form. It is no wonder, then, that they were such objects of heated interest and debate, and
enchanted writers and artists who were firmly entrenched in the state cultural apparatus, even during the heights of the socialist period. Theatrical
ghosts did not "creep" back to stages after 1949; rather, they continued to
hold prominent positions there, up to and including the outright banning
of ghost operas in 1963.[44] And even after they had been forced off stages
due to the 1963 ban, they lingered in the cultural memory, as evidenced by
their speedy return in 1979.

Perry Link has noted the strangeness of Red Guards chanting "We
want to see Chairman Mao," using a rhythmic pattern common to classical Chinese. "Were they aware," he asks, "that they were using an example
of the 'four olds' in order to praise the leading opponent of the 'four olds'?
. . . It seemed that no one noticed the irony, even as everyone was intui-
tively enjoying the lilt and rightness of the phrases."[45] This is a subtler version of the linguistic turns that were never expunged, even in the most
radical periods: Wei Wenbo's late 1963 deployment of a Tang dynasty lyric

to praise drama on contemporary themes, for instance, or the continued use of the old Buddhist phrase "ox ghost–snake spirit" to describe supposed enemies of the CCP. To exterminate a tradition that was not only deeply embedded in Chinese culture, but actively promoted throughout much of the socialist period, was all but impossible. Still, as the early 1950s rash of wide-ranging bans on local and regional levels show, if the state and its cultural apparatus had truly been bent on complete destruction, they would have been capable of achieving it. And, as the example of Xiao Cuihua highlights, some parts of the canon and their interpreters were forced off stages, never to return, with lasting impacts on both careers and repertoires.

All That Is Left Unsaid: The Allure of Ghosts

With the benefit of hindsight, it seems obvious that the high socialist experiments in ghost opera would probably not end well: there were simply too many conflicting demands being placed on writers and artists from the start, and an ill-timed misstep could have dire consequences. Meng Chao and Ma Jianling had multiple other avenues for creativity, oblique criticism, and production; why take the chance, then, on this ghost? Historical plays, including Meng Chao's *Li Huiniang,* have often been thought of in terms of remonstrance, an opportunity for writers to criticize party policies in the wake of the Great Leap Forward. But *Li Huiniang,* and other products like it, ought to be read in a broader context than subtle rebukes. What else drove these cultural workers to write—and write about—"traditional" culture? Meng Chao was a well-known writer of *zawen,* and just like Wu Han, Deng Tuo, Liao Mosha, and many others, he turned to that familiar form in the early 1960s. Thus, Meng Chao did not *need* to write a Kun opera to express his dissatisfaction, and the form seems an odd selection for a writer who was, at the very least, not experienced in *writing* a Kun libretto. Why the ghost, then? Why this form in particular? Likewise, Ma Jianling had risen to prominence writing revolutionary dramas in a contemporary setting. He was talented with the form, and had no particular *need* to turn to a play that had been popular since the Ming dynasty, especially considering the emphasis placed on the creation of contemporary-themed dramas in the 1950s. Returning to Zeitlin's observation that the ghost tale is still appealing for contemporary audiences, they were certainly no less appealing in the high socialist period.

And certainly, for some writers, the opportunity for remonstrance must have been part of the allure.

But we might ask what other attractions ghosts and historical subjects held for socialist writers. Link, referencing literary theorist Li Tuo, writes of the "power engineering of political language in Communist, and especially Maoist, China," and wonders whether writers acculturated to the system "can extricate themselves from its worldview," or even become aware that they are inside of it.[46] The play that Meng Chao chose to write was so obviously different from much of his other literary production, in form and content, he and his audience could not have helped but to have recognized those differences. I must wonder if this aspect—not the potential to criticize the actions of the CCP during a time of national crisis, or even the desire to maintain a truly "national" literary product—was not the most appealing. Even for cultural workers closer to the grassroots, such as Ma Jianling, the opportunity to highlight some of the very best the Chinese literary canon had to offer surely reminded them of the great traditions they were heirs to. Despite sometimes wildly experimental attempts to bring those traditions into the high socialist period, they were all ultimately aimed at *preserving* these traditions, not at destroying them. But this also helps explain, I think, why such experiments proved so controversial in the first fourteen years of the PRC. Ghosts, and subjects like them, represented, at least in part, fantasy and escapism, whatever arguments about their representations of "reality" were put forth. One imagines being confronted with the results of an experiment in ghost opera gone wrong would be frustrating indeed, should such experiments not align with one's own opinion on how to correctly handle such treasures.

I take seriously the idea that these cultural workers and critics were fundamentally—and in many cases, primarily—interested in the very things they discussed so hotly. Debates on ghosts and mythological characters were not simply smokescreens for ideological arguments or a chance to debate the finer points of historical materialism. Yet, although I have largely focused on the surface of the debates on supernatural subjects, there is of course much that these writers left unsaid. There is an amusing scene in Han Shaogong's 1996 novel *A Dictionary of Maqiao* that has always reminded me of the repartee examined in this study, and in particular the enthusiasm with which many cultural workers undertook debates over supernatural literature, as well as the production of such. Han's narrator, an educated youth sent down to a Hunan village during the Cultural Revolution, recalls the problems of staging a model work in a rural area.[47] A peasant who, in former years, used to act in plays and who was proud of his singing voice, reacts in an unfathomable way when pressed into service for an opera celebrating plowing and field work:

> Having studied [the script] a while, he suddenly seized me by the arm.
>   "Sing this? Hoes and rakes and carrying poles filling manure pits watering rice seedlings?"
> I wasn't sure what he meant.
> "Comrade, I have to put up with all this stuff every day in the fields, and now you want me to get on stage and sing about it?" (49–50)

Although a fictional account, the story rings true. Perhaps we can read a parallel to the peasant's outrage in the fierce discussions over *The Cowherd and the Weaving Maid*, *Wandering West Lake*, and even Meng Chao's *Li Huiniang*. One can imagine the things left unsaid to those critical of traditional literature, *this* type of literature in particular, buried under acceptable critiques of ideology and form, as writers filled pages of journals and newspapers with arguments about plays whose histories stretched back hundreds of years: "Comrade, we have to write appropriately Marxist works all day, every day—and now you want our historical tales, our ancient ghosts, too?" The disconnect between present reality and plays that told stories of a distant past, mixed with fantastical imaginings of what might be possible—places where the powerless could become powerful, love could overcome death, and the supernatural could offer a fix for a traumatic present—was (and is), perhaps, the very reason for their appeal. It is little wonder that audiences, artists, and writers cherished these vehicles to express hopes and fears—and no less surprising that they were fervently debated.

Six centuries before Li Huiniang stepped out onto Chinese stages after her Cultural Revolution–era exile, Qu You—his dreams of a bureaucratic career in ruins due to the upheaval of the Yuan-Ming transition—finally completed work on his collection of strange tales. *New Tales Told by Lamplight* would prove one of his most lasting contributions to the Chinese literary canon, and provided inspiration for generations of writers—including those who would write the tale of Li Huiniang.[48] It seems fitting that she would make her first major, if nameless, literary appearance in another time of crisis. The story, "The Woman in Green," was just one of many, and it is not particularly remarkable. Indeed, it treads rather standard ground: a beautiful, mysterious woman, romance, and of course a fantastical, supernatural twist.

In the story, a man named Zhao Yuan one day meets a girl of fifteen or sixteen, an uncommon beauty unadorned by makeup or jewelry. Working up his courage, he asks where she lives, and she laughingly replies that they are in fact neighbors: he simply hasn't noticed. The flirtation develops into a full-fledged romance, and after a month he finally asks for her name. Was it really necessary, she says, to know her name or learn her family origins—wasn't having a beautiful woman enough? After he presses her further, she says only "I often wear green, so you may call me 'the woman in green.'"

The "woman in green" was no ordinary person, as she later explains, but neither was she a malevolent spirit. No, she was a long-dead servant of Jia Sidao; Zhao, the reincarnation of the ghost's soulmate of a lifetime ago. The two had been forced to commit suicide at West Lake in the waning years of the Song dynasty. But, true to fantastical tales, the apparition and the reincarnation are able to move on from this century-old trauma, living together as husband and wife. Was it not fate, she asks him, to meet again like this? After several years of marital bliss, the woman dies a second death. Declaring that the time she spent with her soulmate's reincarnation satisfied her mortal desires, she closes her eyes for the last time (or does she?). After bearing her coffin to its final resting place, her lover finds it curiously light. Opening it, he discovers only clothing, a hairpin, and other jewelry.

It's an appropriate end, or beginning, for a ghost that will live many more lives in many different contexts. Clothing and jewelry: she puts on the same gown, the same glittering headdress again and again, always the same and yet different. Qu You provided the empty vessel, into which generations of artists could—and would—pour their fantasies and fears. She is malleable and ever changing, using her past to offer commentary on whatever present she finds herself in. One trusts she will outlast her critics in any era, just as she has done for generations.

Is it not fate to meet again like this?[49]

Coda

Haunted by Beautiful Ghosts

In March 2011, the Chinese State Administration of Radio, Film, and Television issued guidelines that discouraged content including "fantasy, time-travel, random compilations of mythical stories, bizarre plots, [and] absurd techniques" in television shows. The justification was that such stories were "propagating feudal superstitions, fatalism and reincarnation, ambiguous moral lessons, and a lack of positive thinking."[1] Living in Shanghai at the time, I was struck by rhetoric that could have come straight from the high socialist documents I was trawling through at the municipal archives. "Superstitious" subjects had been criticized throughout the 1950s for spreading "feudal" ideas. In 1956, the Ministry of Culture had castigated troupes for hiding parts of banned plays in "safe" librettos, creating strange, confused plots that found Han dynasty heroes in Qing dynasty settings. Throughout the Mao years, critics constantly questioned *what* lessons were being imparted by plays. And in 1965, Meng Chao, his *Li Huiniang*, and their supporters were explicitly attacked for encouraging "fatalism" and displaying "a lack of positive thinking." Their critics were, in essence, doing the same thing as the directive: criticizing people for wanting to escape the present. For who wishes to escape a present moment they find positive?

One afternoon, taking a break from staring at a computer monitor, I stood at a window in the archive, which is located at a far end of the Bund—one of the most iconic parts of the city, not entirely unlike Chicago's Magnificent Mile. Looking across to the fantastical, modern skyscrapers of Pudong, I wondered what the cultural workers in my study would think of the view and the contemporary PRC. Certainly, there would be much that was unfamiliar, just like the tall buildings across the river. But surely, they would also hear echoes of their own experiences, the pieces they had written, the things that had been written about them, just as I did and still do today. Their lives and writings continue to haunt my understandings of modern China.

This study is ultimately a small slice of the cultural and political story of the People's Republic of China, but it is a history that offers insights far beyond the world of elite drama journals and newspapers. Supernatural literature has proven to be a useful way of connecting socialist cultural production with a much broader sweep of Chinese cultural history, and not simply in terms of literary "remonstrance." Ghosts tend to reassert themselves in times of trouble or imbalance, at least in Chinese literary history, so it seems no accident that they came to the fore in the 1950s and 1960s. Traditional theatre may no longer enjoy the widespread popularity it once did, but perhaps we can see spiritual descendants of Li Huiniang in other media. The time-traveling protagonists of television dramas—often young women out of step with their own worlds—echo the resisting spirits of earlier revolutions.

The cultural products of the high socialist period and the debates that surrounded them illustrate just how connected many cultural workers remained to classical and literary traditions. These underscore, too, the enduring power of language. The party remains preoccupied with control over cultural production, deploying rhetoric that has a long history to shape and define what people can and should be consuming. Such concerns are not simply the domain of twentieth- or twenty-first-century China, of course. I still hear the anxieties of Qing moralists, concerned about girls reading the *Peony Pavilion* and falling hopelessly, fatally under a ghost story's spell, in contemporary discourses on video games, television, and film.

In focusing on the debates over supernatural literature and the various retellings of Li Huiniang, I underscore the dynamic, experimental nature of cultural production in the high socialist period. Not all experiments were successful, but they show the lengths to which artists went in order to balance competing, conflicting demands. Furthermore, a dichotomy between "grassroots" culture on the one hand, and "official," state-sponsored culture on the other falls apart in considering the whole of the theatre world. These two parts were mutually constitutive, as the relationship between the *Guangming Daily* debates and discussions among Shanghai theatre troupes shows. Nor was "official" culture contested only at the grassroots; as the passionate discussions on supernatural literature illustrate, it was just as contentious at the highest echelons of the cultural apparatus.

This study illustrates the utility of bringing a variety of sources to bear even on subjects that are well-represented in the historiography. Combining archival sources with published discussions allowed me to gain a much greater understanding of how cultural policy and regulation impacted both elite writers and critics, as well as artists tasked with carrying out directives on a day-to-day basis. The 1963 Shanghainese troupe discussions add a rich complexity to the *Guangming Daily* debates of that year, revealing tensions and opinions that are rarely, if ever, seen in published sources. Purchasing original sources allowed me to access materials that simply do not exist in most archives or libraries, since they are, I assume, considered unimportant debris of the high socialist period. In many cases, they have proved to be priceless. Ma Jianling's ill-fated ghostless adaptation of *Wandering West Lake*, for instance, has not been passed down in his collected works, and it was only by buying an original 1953 edition that I got to see his first script. Although the focus on source collecting for PRC historians has been on "subarchival" documents, such as personnel records that have been tossed out by work units, I have found much inspiration in neglected 1950s and 1960s publications. What other topics might be enhanced by looking beyond the obvious periodicals, newspapers, archival documents, and books available in libraries?

On a methodological level, taking seriously the debates over ghost opera *as* debates over ghost opera—not simply conduits for other types of political or ideological discussion—underscores Sharon Marcus's observation that "surface reading" is complementary to "symptomatic reading." I have never denied that Meng Chao and other writers used historical subjects as methods of political criticism; to the contrary, I am sympathetic to such readings of these plays. At the same time, it is quite difficult to reconcile essays extolling the virtues of more romance, more literary language, and more lyricism with the image of intellectuals largely preoccupied with criticizing party policy. The overwhelming historiographical emphasis on what they *might have been implying* with their plays and writings, versus what was said on the surface—and how—has wound up obscuring many other interesting features of the ghost play debates and the plays themselves.

Marcus's alternative term for "surface reading" is "just reading." I put the inflection on *just*, as in, simply reading. In my first tentative explorations of this project as a graduate student, I hewed closely to approaches taken by earlier scholars and treated my examination of Meng Chao and his *Li Huiniang* as a focused study of an understudied play and author within the traditional approach. How did this play reflect coded political criticism of the Leap? What were the consequences? But when I began to "just read" Meng Chao's play and his postscript, as one often only does when one has read a piece over and over and over, I found myself enthralled by how different it was from other high socialist sources (or so I thought). It resembled all the beautiful writing that I thought was simply the domain of literary scholars of the imperial period that I so admired, not something in which a historian of the PRC would find herself utterly caught up. Simply reading opened other avenues of inquiry: How did *Li Huiniang* relate to earlier debates on ghosts, beyond the context of the Great Leap Forward? In what ways did socialist cultural production connect to earlier Chinese literary traditions? What could the impassioned discussions on theatrical ghosts tell us about other aspects of culture and politics in the high socialist period, beyond issues of "remonstrance?"

When I turned to other pieces in this fashion—*just* reading—I began to realize how witty, how learned, how elegant many of them were, even only in seemingly straightforward essays published in *Theatre Report* or *People's Daily*. I had read studies that seemed most eager to prove a connection between pre-1949 literature and modes of thought with the post-Mao milieu, glossing over the years between 1949 and 1976. In so doing they seemed to flatten the cultural production of the Maoist period, and more alarmingly, the people producing that culture. But in simply reading, I found many of these socialist writers to be the heirs to cultural traditions that they valued, even within an extremely complicated, politically fraught context. Meng Chao may have been criticizing the Leap, and those who reviewed his play might have been in on the implication, but they were also all enjoying exquisitely poetic language and reminders of China's literary riches. *Just reading* gave another perspective to symptomatic readings, and they enriched each other. What else might we discover by "just" reading other sources?

I eventually began to consider what the appeal of these products was. Did Meng Chao really write a Kun opera only to offer "remonstrance?" Did Ma Jianling pick up a Ming dynasty play only to update it slightly for a socialist present? Did scores of people write hundreds of thousands of characters to the *Guangming Daily* on the "ghost play problem" simply to have an avenue to express dissatisfaction with their present? Why have these fantastical stories proved so popular across generations and cultures?

The answer may be as simple as "escapism"—the desire to abscond into a time and place that bears no resemblance to the present. The more I consider the question, the more I think about how and why the party-state and many other governments like it decide to regulate escapism in its various forms. A ghost play, a time travel story—these lift the veil between a current moment and what might be possible, somewhere, at some time. A ghost is the agency of the struggling person projected into a future denied to them in life. Yet to write or view a ghost play is in part to travel in time, to turn away from the hopeless present and affirm the past as an arena of genuine agency.

Writing from the safer vantage point of the post-Mao years, Lou Shiyi recalled the terror of late 1965 and 1966, when everyone was afraid and saw "ghosts" everywhere. But if undertaking a study centered on debates over literary ghosts in the high socialist period taught me anything, it is that ghosts are not always fearsome. For many of the cultural workers I examine, these phantasms represented undying bravery, love, and righteousness. Many who argued for the importance of ghostly literature paid a terrible price for their defense of such beauty. So it is fitting, I think, that I feel the ghosts of this work—the lives of these talented individuals, as well as the literary ghosts they discussed with such passion—in my approaches to everything else I study, no matter the subject.

I am haunted—and inspired—by their beautiful ghosts.

Glossary

Ai Qing	艾青
Baimao nü	白毛女
Baishe zhuan	白蛇传
bangzi	梆子
Beifang kunqu juyuan	北方昆曲剧院
Bishang Liangshan	逼上梁山
Bu pa gui de gushi	不怕鬼的故事
caomang shijia	草莽史家
Chalutiao	查路条
chuanshuo	传说
chufeng qing yu laofeng sheng	雏凤清于老凤声
Duanqiao	断桥
fankang de jingshen	反抗的精神
fanpohai	反迫害
geju	歌剧
geming	革命
Guangming ribao	光明日报
Guibian	鬼辩
guibu	鬼步
gui pusa	鬼菩萨
guixi	鬼戏
Guohun	国魂
Hai Rui baguan	海瑞罢官
haoxi	好戏
Hongdeng ji	红灯记
Hongmei ge	红梅阁
Hongmei ji	红梅记
Hu Zhifeng	胡芝风
huaixi	坏戏

huaju	话剧
huidaomen	会道门
Jiandeng xinhua	剪灯新话
jingju	京剧
jiu shehui shiren bian gui, xin shehui shigui bian ren	旧社会使人变鬼，新社会使
Juben	剧本
kunqu	昆曲
Li Huiniang	李慧娘
Liao Mosha	廖沫沙
Liaozhai zhiyi	聊斋志异
lilun quanwei	理论权威
Lou Shiyi	楼适夷
lüyiren	绿衣人
Ma Jianling	马健翎
Ma Shaobo	马少波
Meng Chao	孟超
Meng Jian	孟健
Minzhong jutuan	民众剧团
mixin	迷信
Mu Xin	穆欣
Mudan ting	牡丹亭
niugui-sheshen	牛鬼蛇神
Niulang zhinü	牛郎织女
niupeng	牛棚
Nülan wuhao	女篮五号
pailianben	排练本
Renmin wenxue	人民文学
renminxing	人民性
qinqiang	秦腔
qiqiao	乞巧
Qixi	七夕
Qiyuan bao	奇冤报
Qu You	瞿佑
san nian kunnan	三年困难
shenhua	神话
Shiwu guan	十五贯
su	俗
Taiyang she	太阳社
Tan yinshan	探阴山

Tianhe pei	天河配
tuichen buchuxin, tuichen chujiu	推陈不出新, 推陈出旧
Wenyi bao	文艺报
wenyi gongzuozhe	文艺工作者
Wupen ji	乌盆记
wuqiao bucheng shu, wugui bucheng xi	无巧不成书，无鬼不成戏
xiandai	现代
Xiangtu jutuan	乡土剧团
Xie shouyin	血手印
Xie Yaohuan	谢瑶环
Xiju bao	戏剧报
xinbian lishiju	新编历史剧
xiqu	戏曲
Xixiang ji	西厢记
Xiyou ji	西游记
ya	雅
Ya, meizai yi shaonian ye	呀，美哉一少年也
Yang Shaoxuan	杨绍萱
yangxi	洋戏
Ye cao	野草
yizhen feng	一阵风
yougui wuhai lun	有鬼无害论
Youhen	幽恨
you shen shuohua	有神说话
You xihu	游西湖
Youyuan jingmeng	游园惊梦
yuan de hen na	冤得很哪
yuanna	冤哪
yuanwang	冤枉
yuanyu	冤狱
zawen	杂文
Zhang Zhen	张真
zhe shi yige haoxi	这是一个好戏
Zhi qu weihu shan	智取威虎山
Zhongguo hun	中国魂
Zhongguo xiqu	中国戏曲
Zhou Chaojun	周朝俊
zhuang zai shaonian, mei zai shaonian	壮哉少年，美哉少年
Zhumulangma	珠穆朗玛
zongjiao xi	宗教戏

Notes

Introduction

1. *Li Huiniang*, dir. Liu Qiong (Shanghai: Shanghai dianying zhipianchang, 1981); *Li Huiniang* (dianying wancheng taiben) [*Li Huiniang* (complete film script and stage instructions)] (Shanghai: Shanghai dianying zhipianchang, n.d.).

2. Meng Jian, "Xie zai *Li Huiniang* zaiban de shihou" [Writings at the time of the republication of *Li Huiniang*], in Meng Chao, *Li Huiniang* (Shanghai: Shanghai wenyi chubanshe, 1980), 125–28, 125.

3. Qin Si, "Yi Meng Chao" [Remembering Meng Chao], *Xin wenxue shike* 4 (April 1984): 128–33, 132.

4. Meng, "Xie zai," 127.

5. Qu You, *Jiandeng xinhua* [New tales told by lamplight] (Shanghai: Shanghai guxiang chubanshe, 1981), 104–7.

6. Zhou Chaojun, *Hongmei ji* [*Story of Red Plums*] (Shanghai: Shanghai guxiang chubanshe, 1985).

7. The canon here refers not to the "Confucian canon," but to the "flexible, more contemporary 'literary' canon" that developed over the centuries; both parts formed the core of literati education in the imperial period. By the twentieth century, the great novels and plays of the Ming and Qing periods were "fully admitted into the canon of traditional Chinese literature" (William H. Nienhauser, ed., *The Indiana Companion to Traditional Chinese Literature, Part Two* [Bloomington: Indiana University Press, 1998], 95).

8. For an examination of the development of "anomaly accounts" (*zhiguai*), the origins of these fantastical literary tales, see Robert Ford Campany, *Strange Writing: Anomaly Accounts in Early Medieval China* (Albany: State University of New York Press, 1996).

9. These dramas were also known, as it happens, as *chuanqi*, just like the Tang stories. See Judith T. Zeitlin, *The Phantom Heroine: Ghosts and Gender in Seventeenth-Century Chinese Literature* (Honolulu: University of Hawai'i Press, 2007), 5–6; see also her *Historian of the Strange: Pu Songling and the Chinese Classical Tale* (Stanford: Stanford Uni-

versity Press, 1993). As Zeitlin notes, the full complement of *guixi* "would include the Buddhist Mulian plays performed at the annual 'Ghost Festival' and masked exorcist drama" (*Phantom Heroine*, 9). My focus here is not the entire range of "ghost opera," but debates surrounding the production and performance of plays descending largely from the dramas of the Ming and Qing periods.

10. Jeremy Brown and Matthew D. Johnson, eds., *Maoism at the Grassroots: Everyday Life in China's Era of High Socialism* (Cambridge: Harvard University Press, 2015), 6. The critics and artists who debated ghost opera in the 1950s and 1960s were themselves mostly concerned with productions and adaptations of classical drama, particularly Ming *chuanqi*.

11. Liao Mosha, "Yougui wuhai lun" [Some ghosts are harmless], in *Liao Mosha wenji, di er juan: Zawen* [Collected writings of Liao Mosha, vol. 2: Zawen], 109–11. Beijing: Beijing chubanshe, 1986.

12. See Liang Qichao, "On the Relationship between Fiction and the Government of the People," trans. Gek Nai Cheng, in Kirk Denton, ed., *Modern Chinese Literary Thought: Writings on Literature, 1893–1945* (Stanford: Stanford University Press, 1996), 74–81, 79.

13. Chen Duxiu, "On Literary Revolution," trans. Timothy Wong, in Kirk Denton, ed., *Modern Chinese Literary Thought: Writings on Literature, 1893–1945* (Stanford: Stanford University Press, 1996), 140–45, 145.

14. See Shuk-Wah Poon, *Negotiating Religion in Modern China: State and Common People in Guangzhou, 1900–1937* (Hong Kong: Chinese University Press, 2011).

15. Rebecca Nedostup, *Superstitious Regimes: Religions and the Politics of Chinese Modernity* (Cambridge: Harvard University Press, 2009), 18.

16. "Guanyu tingyan 'guixi' de qingshi baogao" [Instructions regarding ceasing performances of "ghost plays"], in *Jianguo yilai zhongyao wenxian xuanbian, di shiliu ce* [Selected important party documents from after the founding of the country, volume 16], ed. Zhonggong zhongyang wenxian yanjiushi (Beijing: Zhongyang wenxian chubanshe, 1997), 248.

17. Cai Xiang, *Revolution and Its Narratives: China's Socialist Literary and Cultural Imaginaries, 1949–1966*, ed. and trans. Rebecca E. Karl and Zueping Zhong (Durham: Duke University Press, 2016), 13–17.

18. I follow Nancy Guy and many other scholars in the usage of "Peking opera," rather than "Beijing opera" or *jingju*. As she has argued, Peking opera is "*the* English-language name for the genre," up to the point that articles published in the *Beijing Review*, the national English-language weekly in the PRC, use the term "Peking opera," illustrating "that although the place-name is 'Beijing,' 'Peking opera' stands as the genre name" ("Peking Opera as 'National Opera' in Taiwan: What's in a Name?," *Asian Theatre Journal* 12.1 [Spring 1995]: 85–103, 96).

19. Joshua Goldstein, *Drama Kings: Players and Publics in the Re-Creation of Peking Opera, 1870–1937* (Berkeley: University of California Press, 2007) (see especially chapter 3, "The Experimental Stage").

20. Franz Schurmann, *Ideology and Organization in Communist China*, 2nd ed. (Berkeley: University of California Press, 1971), 59.

21. This is in contrast to an older reading of this period, which emphasizes the flatness and dullness of cultural production. As Rebecca Karl and Xueping Zhong have also noted, cultural movements of the late 1970s and 1980s in the PRC had the effect of "casting doubt upon, if not completely delegitimizing, many of the socialist premises, practices, and accomplishments of the 1930s through the 1970s" (*Revolution and Its Narratives*, xx). Of course, the object here is "socialist literature," not imperial throwbacks, but even those Song dynasty concubines were, in the 1950s and 1960s, produced *in* the socialist literary system by socialist writers, even if they were not wholly *of* it.

22. Goldstein, *Drama Kings*; Jin Jiang, *Women Playing Men: Yue Opera and Social Change in Twentieth-Century Shanghai* (Seattle: University of Washington Press, 2009); Andrea S. Goldman, *Opera and the City: The Politics of Culture in Beijing, 1770–1900* (Stanford: Stanford University Press, 2012).

23. Catherine C. Swatek, Peony Pavilion *Onstage: Four Centuries in the Career of a Chinese Drama* (Ann Arbor: Center for Chinese Studies, University of Michigan, 2002).

24. Fu Jin, ed. *Ershi shiji zhongguo xiju de xiandaixing yu bentuhua* [Modernity and localization of Chinese theatre in the twentieth century] (Taipei: Guojia chubanshe, 2005); Fu Jin, *20 shiji Zhongguo xijushi* [Twentieth-century Chinese theatre history], 2 vols. (Beijing: Zhongguo shehui kexue chubanshe, 2017).

25. Anne E. Rebull, "Theatres of Reform and Remediation: *Xiqu* (Chinese Opera) in the Mid-Twentieth Century" (PhD diss., University of Chicago, 2017).

26. Emily Wilcox, *Revolutionary Bodies: Chinese Dance and the Socialist Legacy* (Berkeley: University of California Press, 2018), 5.

27. Brian J. DeMare, *Mao's Cultural Army: Drama Troupes in China's Rural Revolution* (Cambridge: Cambridge University Press, 2015); Wilt L. Idema, *The Metamorphosis of Tianxian Pei: Local Opera under the Revolution (1949–1956)* (Hong Kong: Chinese University Press, 2015).

28. Max L. Bohnenkamp, "Turning Ghosts into People: *The White-Haired Girl*, Revolutionary Folklorism, and the Politics of Aesthetics in Modern China" (PhD diss., University of Chicago, 2014).

29. Yang Qiuhong, *Zhongguo gudai guixi yanjiu* [Research on China's premodern ghost plays] (Beijing: Zhongguo chuanmei daxue chubanshe, 2009); Xu Xianglin, *Zhongguo guixi* [Chinese ghost plays] (Tianjin: Tianjin jiaoyu chubanshe, 1997). However, as Yang noted in 2009, in Chinese-language scholarship there are only two monographs and perhaps thirty essays addressing the subject—from any period.

30. Christina Ezrahi, *Swans of the Kremlin: Ballet and Power in Soviet Russia* (Pittsburgh: University of Pittsburgh Press, 2012).

31. Michael Dylan Foster, *Pandemonium and Parade: Japanese Monsters and the Culture of Yōkai* (Berkeley: University of California Press, 2009); Gerald Figal, *Civilization and Monsters: Spirits of Modernity in Meiji Japan* (Durham: Duke University Press, 2000).

32. Roderick MacFarquhar, *The Coming of the Cataclysm: 1961–1966*, vol. 3, *The Origins of the Cultural Revolution* (New York: Columbia University Press, 1997), 384.

33. Gail Hershatter, *The Gender of Memory: Rural Women and China's Collective Past* (Berkeley: University of California Press, 2011), 4.

34. Rudolf G. Wagner, *The Contemporary Chinese Historical Drama: Four Studies* (Berkeley: University of California Press, 1990), xi.

35. For more on the Leap and the resulting famine, see Yang Jisheng, *Tombstone: The Great Chinese Famine, 1958–1962*, ed. Edward Friedman, Guo Jian, and Stacy Mosher, trans. Stacy Mosher and Guo Jian (New York: Farrar, Straus and Giroux, 2012); Roderick MacFarquhar, *The Great Leap Forward 1958–1960*, vol. 2, *The Origins of the Cultural Revolution* (New York: Columbia University Press, 1983); Edward Friedman, Paul G. Pickowicz, and Mark Selden, *Chinese Village, Socialist State* (New Haven: Yale University Press, 1991); Jasper Becker, *Hungry Ghosts: Mao's Secret Famine* (New York: Holt Paperbacks, 1998); Frank Dikötter, *Mao's Great Famine: The History of China's Most Devastating Catastrophe, 1958–1962* (London: Bloomsbury, 2010).

36. Merle Goldman, *China's Intellectuals: Advise and Dissent* (Cambridge: Harvard University Press, 1981), 43

37. Maggie Greene, "A Ghostly Bodhisattva and the Price of Vengeance: Meng Chao, *Li Huiniang*, and the Politics of Drama, 1959–1979," *Modern Chinese Literature and Culture* 24.1 (Spring 2012): 149–99.

38. Brown and Johnson, "Introduction," in *Maoism at the Grassroots*, 1–15, 4.

39. See, for instance, Hershatter, *Gender of Memory*; Jeremy Brown and Paul Pickowicz, eds., *Dilemmas of Victory: The Early Years of the People's Republic of China* (Cambridge: Harvard University Press, 2007).

40. Matthew D. Johnson, "Beneath the Propaganda State: Official and Unofficial Cultural Landscapes in Shanghai, 1949–1965," in *Maoism at the Grassroots*, ed. Brown and Johnson, 199–229, 199.

41. E.g., see Swatek, *Peony Pavilion Onstage*; Sheila Melvin, "China's Homegrown *Peony Pavilion*," *Wall Street Journal*, November 24, 1999; Judith T. Zeitlin, "My Year of Peonies," *Asian Theatre Journal* 19.1 (Spring 2002): 124–33, 126.

42. *Zhongguo xiju nianjian 1982* [1982 Chinese theatre yearbook] (Beijing: Zhongguo xiqu chubanshe, 1982), 532.

43. Wagner, *Historical Drama*, 80. Meng Chao does appear with more regularity in Chinese language scholarship, especially for his pre-1949 literary activities. For example, Zhao Xinshun, *Taiyang she yanjiu* [Research on the Sun Society] (Beijing: Zhongguo shehui kexue chubanshe, 2010); Zhai Guangshun, "Meng Chao zai Qingdao de jiaoyu ji geming wenyi huodong" [Meng Chao's teaching and revolutionary art and literature activities in Qingdao], *Zhonggong Qingdao shiwei dangxiao—Qingdao xingzheng xueyuan xuebao* 4 (2013): 115–23; He Baomin, "Meng Chao he *Yicong*" [Meng Chao and *Yicong*], *Wenhua xuekan* 1 (January 2014): 183–86.

44. E.g., in two splendid studies of traditional arts in the PRC: Richard C. Kraus, *Brushes with Power: Modern Politics and the Chinese Art of Calligraphy* (Berkeley: Uni-

versity of California Press, 1991), and Julia F. Andrews, *Painters and Politics in the People's Republic of China, 1949–1979* (Berkeley: University of California Press, 1994).

45. Meng Chao, "*Li Huiniang*," *Juben* (July–August 1961): 78–91, 78.

46. Jiang, *Women Playing Men*, 7.

47. Goldstein, *Drama Kings*, 11.

48. Goldstein, *Drama Kings*, 11.

49. Colin Mackerras, *Chinese Drama: A Historical Survey* (Beijing: New World Press, 1990), 27–34.

50. "Shanghai shi wenhuaju yijiusijiu nian dao yijiuliuernian linian shangyan jumu (haoxi, huaixi) bijiaobiao" [Shanghai Culture Bureau comparison table of the performed repertoire (good plays, bad plays) over the years from 1949 to 1962], SMA B172-5-530; "Shanghai shi wenhuaju guanyu yijiu e liusan nian quannian shanyan jumu tongji, jingjuyuan jumu paidui, guojia juyuantuan baoliu jumu gelin biao" [Shanghai Culture Bureau statistics on annual performed repertoire for previous years, Peking opera theatre repertoire list, list of every type of national theatre repertoire], SMA B172-5-682.

51. Wagner, *Historical Drama*, x.

52. See Wagner, who focuses on the remonstrative qualities of many of these works; Goldman, *China's Intellectuals*, 43.

53. This flattening of socialist cultural production is not confined to studies of the PRC. As Christina Ezrahi has described in her study of ballet in the Soviet Union, the traditional narrative emphasizes "ideological control as a force that crushed artistic creativity" (*Swans of the Kremlin*, 3).

54. See, for instance, the Yang Shaoxuan–Ai Qing–Ma Shaobo debate over *The Cowherd and the Weaving Maid* in *People's Daily*, discussed in chapter 1 of this book.

55. Sharon Marcus, *Between Women: Friendship, Desire, and Marriage in Victorian England* (Princeton: Princeton University Press, 2007), 75–76; see also Stephen Best and Sharon Marcus, "Surface Reading: An Introduction," *Representations* 108.1 (Fall 2009): 1–21.

56. Marcus, *Between Women*, 75.

57. The publication and premiere of *Li Huiniang* is, for instance, described as leading "to a spurt of interest in ghost plays" in the early 1960s (see MacFarquhar, *Cataclysm*, 384), an appraisal of the situation that glosses over the more than ten years of discussion that occurred prior to the premiere of Meng Chao's play.

58. Goldman, *China's Intellectuals*, 140, 150.

Chapter 1

1. William Dolby, "Early Chinese Plays and Theatre," in *Chinese Theater: From Its Origins to the Present Day*, ed. Colin Mackerras (Honolulu: University of Hawai'i Press, 1983), 7–30, 7.

2. Guy, *Peking Opera*, 8.

3. Dorothy Ko, *Teachers of the Inner Chambers: Women and Culture in Seventeenth-Century China* (Stanford: Stanford University Press, 1994), 68–69.

4. Goldman, *Opera and the City*, 87.

5. Goldstein, *Drama Kings*, 98–100.

6. Nedostup, *Superstitious Regimes*.

7. Mao Zedong, "Talks at the Yan'an Forum on Literature and Art," in *Modern Chinese Literary Thought: Writings on Literature, 1893–1945*, ed. Kirk Denton (Stanford: Stanford University Press, 1996), 458–84, 481.

8. Mao, "Talks at the Yan'an Forum," 469–70.

9. See Goldman, *China's Intellectuals*; Wagner, *Chinese Historical Drama*; Kun Qian, *Imperial-Time-Order: Literature, Intellectual History, and China's Road to Empire* (Leiden: Brill, 2016).

10. Siyuan Liu, "Theatre Reform as Censorship: Censoring Traditional Theatre in China in the Early 1950s," *Theatre Journal* 61.3 (October 2009): 387–406, 390–91.

11. Liu, "Theatre Reform," 390.

12. Liu, "Theatre Reform," 390–91.

13. The early 1950s bans have been explored in depth by scholars Li Desheng, Liu Siyuan, and Fu Jin. Li's work is particularly useful, and includes short historical overviews as well as more in-depth explanations of plays that had been banned at various points from the Qing dynasty onwards. See Li Desheng, *Jinxi* [Banned plays] (Tianjin: Baihua wenyi chubanshe, 2009); Liu, "Theatre Reform"; Fu Jin, *20 Shiji*, also *Ershi shiji*.

14. See Fu Jin, *Ershi shiji*, 218.

15. This bureau was made up of a who's who of the theatre world. Headed by Zhou Yang, members included Tian Han, Ouyang Yuqian, Hong Shen, A Ying, Lao She, Mei Lanfang, Zhou Xinfang, Ma Jianling, Yang Shaoxuan, Ai Qing, Mao Shaobo, and a number of other important intellectuals and artists. Ma Shaobo, "Mixin yu shenhua de benzhi qubie" [The essential difference between superstition and mythology], in Ma Shaobo, *Xiqu yishu lunji* [Collected essays on theatre and art] (Beijing: Zhongguo xiju chubanshe, 1982), 24–27, 27.

16. Li, *Jinxi*, 12.

17. Liu, "Theatre Reform," 391.

18. Li, *Jinxi*, 12.

19. Liu, "Theatre Reform," 391.

20. Fu Jin, *Ershi Shiji*, 212–13.

21. Paola Iovene, "Chinese Operas on Stage and Screen: An Introduction," *Opera Quarterly* 26.2–3 (Spring–Summer 2010): 181–99, 185.

22. Fu Jin, *Ershi shiji*, 202.

23. "Quanguo xiqu gongzuozhe dahuishi xianyou xiqu gongzuozhe sanshiwuwan ren guanzhong sanbaiwan huiyi jiang taolun yu jiejue xigai fangzhen zhengce deng wenti" [All-China theatre workers assembly; currently, theatre workers number 350,000 people, audiences number three million; conference will discuss and settle general and

specific policies and other problems related to drama reform], *People's Daily*, December 1, 1950.

24. "Quanguo xiqu."

25. Yue opera was consistently one of the most popular genres in Shanghai and the surrounding regions between the 1930s and 1960s; it is a southern Chinese form, and troupes are composed entirely of women. See Jiang, *Women Playing Men*.

26. "Shanghai shi wenhuaju guanyu Shanghai shi 1949 nian–1958 nian yanchu jumu de fennian tongji biao, mulu biao" [Shanghai Culture Bureau, regarding repertoire performed in Shanghai from 1949 to 1958—tables of statistics and catalogue, divided by year], SMA B172-1-326. One exception was Hu opera (*huju*), a local Shanghainese form, where contemporary-themed dramas comprised nearly 80 percent of the repertoire of the 1950s.

27. Fu Jin, *Ershi shiji*, 210.

28. For instance, see the description of his revised version of the legend of Mulan in Shiamin Kwa and Wilt L. Idema, *Mulan: Five Versions of a Classic Chinese Legend, with Related Texts* (Indianapolis: Hackett, 2010), 112. Ma had participated in the literary scene of Shandong in the 1930s. He joined the CCP in 1939 and continued to participate in a variety of cultural work, from writing plays to editing journals. After 1949, he held important posts related to theatre reform in the Ministry of Culture and served as the associate dean of the Chinese Theatre Research Institute. See Shi Ai, "Ma Shaobo xiaozhuan" [Biographical sketch of Ma Shaobo], *Shanxi shiyuan xuebao (shehui kexue ban)* 1 (1982): 96–97.

29. Ma, "Mixin yu," 24.

30. Ma, "Mixin yu," 24.

31. See Qitao Guo's enlightening study of the Buddhist Mulian dramas in *Ritual Opera and Mercantile Lineage: The Confucian Transformation of Popular Culture in Late Imperial Huizhou* (Stanford: Stanford University Press, 2005).

32. Susan Mann, *Precious Records: Women in China's Long Eighteenth Century* (Stanford: Stanford University Press, 1997), 170–71, 177.

33. Ma, "Mixin yu," 26.

34. Liu Ching-chi, *A Critical History of New Music in China*, trans. Caroline Mason (Hong Kong: Chinese University Press, 2010), 173, 311. See also Yuwu Song, ed., *Biographical Dictionary of the People's Republic of China* (Jefferson, NC: McFarland & Co., 2013), 423–24.

35. Zhou Weizhi, "Fazhan aiguozhuyi de renmin xin xiqu—zhu quanguo xiqu gongzuo huiyi" [Developing the patriotism of the people's new opera—celebrating the All-China opera work conference], *People's Daily*, December 10, 1950.

36. Hong Zicheng, *A History of Contemporary Chinese Literature*, trans. Michael M. Day (Leiden: Brill, 2007), 197–98. Idema has given an excellent overview of the debates over *The Cowherd and the Weaving Maid* in *Tianxian Pei*, including the Yang Shaoxuan incident.

37. Song, *Biographical Dictionary*, 4.

38. Goldman, *China's Intellectuals*, 39.

39. Quoted in Derek Jones, ed., *Censorship: A World Encyclopedia* (London: Routledge, 2001), 22. Ai Qing would, of course, be one of the most prominent people labeled a "rightist" in the wake of the Anti-Rightist Campaign. He was essentially exiled for twenty years. See Jones, *Censorship*, 22; Song, *Biographical Dictionary*, 4; Hong, *Chinese Literature*, 71.

40. Ai Qing, "Tan 'Niulang zhinü'" [Discussing *The Cowherd and the Weaving Maid*], *People's Daily*, August 31, 1951.

41. Ai, "Tan 'Niulang.'"

42. Ai, "Tan 'Niulang.'"

43. Ai, "Tan 'Niulang.'"

44. Ai, "Tan 'Niulang.'"

45. Yang Shaoxuan, "Lun 'wei wenxue er wenxue, wei yishu er yishu' de weixianxing—ping Ai Qing de 'Tan niulang zhinü" [Discussing the harmfulness of "literature for the sake of literature, art for the sake of art"—criticizing Ai Qing's "Discussing *The Cowherd and the Weaving Maid*"], *People's Daily*, November 3, 1951.

46. Yang, "Lun 'wei.'"

47. Yang, "Lun 'wei.'"

48. Yang, "Lun 'wei.'"

49. Yang, "Lun 'wei.'"

50. Hong, *Chinese Literature*, 197n18.

51. Hong, *Chinese Literature*, 453. The letter reads in part: "[I] have seen your play, you have done very good work—I extend my thanks to you. . . . Guo Moruo has done excellent work on historical plays; you have done this sort of work in regards to old plays. . . . I am extremely pleased, [and] hope that you adapt more and perform more [dramas]." Mao Zedong, "Mao Zedong gei Yang Shaoxuan, Qi Yanming de xin" [The letter sent from Mao Zedong to Yang Shaoxuan and Qi Yanming], in *Jiandang yilai zhongyao wenxian xuanbian: Yijiueryi–yijiusijiu* [Selection of important documents since the founding of the Party: 1921–1949], vol. 21, ed. Zhonggong zhongyan wenxian yanjiu shi, Zhongyang dang'anguan (Beijing: Zhongyang wenxian chuban she, 2011), 5.

52. Idema, *Tianxian Pei*, 36.

53. Idema, *Tianxian Pei*, 36.

54. Yang, "Lun 'wei.'"

55. Ma Shaobo, "Yansu duidai zhengli shenhuaju de gongzuo—cong *Tianhe pei* de gaibian tanqi" [A serious treatment of the work of putting mythology plays in order—speaking from the adaptation of *Tianhe pei*], *People's Daily*, November 4, 1951.

56. Ma, "Yansu duidai."

57. Ma, "Yansu duidai." Wu Zuguang (who was not a member of the party) was a playwright who continued to run afoul of the establishment for more serious violations than apparently distasteful revisions of classic myths. During the Hundred Flowers Movement, he was a vocal critic of party policy concerning cultural production. Tian

Han "led the attack" against Wu during the Anti-Rightist Campaign (Wagner, *Historical Drama*, 4)—though Tian Han had in fact similarly argued against nonprofessional (i.e., party) control of the drama world. After 1976, Wu and his acid tongue—sharpened after decades of marginalization and oppression—harshly criticized party policy in the years after Mao's death. See Merle Goldman, *Sowing the Seeds of Democracy in China: Political Reform in the Deng Xiaoping Era* (Cambridge: Harvard University Press, 1994).

58. Like *The Cowherd and the Weaving Maid*, this has been an exceedingly popular story in a variety of times, places, and mediums.

59. Ma, "Yansu duidai."

60. Ma, "Yansu duidai."

61. Ai Qing, "Da Yang Shaoxuan tongzhi" [An answer to Comrade Yang Shaoxuan], *People's Daily*, November 12, 1951.

62. Ai, "Da Yang."

63. Ai, "Da Yang."

64. Johnson, "Propaganda State," 206.

65. Fu Jin, *Ershi shiji*, 206.

66. Liu, "Theatre Reform," 402.

67. Although the documents do not detail methods of collecting statistics, it is clear based on the numbers that they must have counted the same play multiple times. That is, one script performed by two troupes would be counted twice.

68. "Shanghai shi wenhuaju 1949–1958 nian shangyan jumu tongjibiao" [Shanghai Culture Bureau statistics of repertoire performed, 1949–1958], SMA B172-4-917.

Chapter 2

1. Sigrid Schmalzer defines "mass science" as "the production of scientific knowledge wholly or in part by nonscientists": *The People's Peking Man: Popular Science and Human Identity in Twentieth-Century China* (Chicago: University of Chicago Press, 2008), xviii.

2. Schmalzer, *People's Peking Man*, 75–77.

3. As S. A. Smith has argued, there was often a political dimension to the dissemination of "superstitious" rumors. See "Talking Toads and Chinless Ghosts: The Politics of 'Superstitious' Rumors in the People's Republic of China," *American Historical Review* 111.2 (April 2006): 405–27. Smith's object is rumors in the wake of the Great Leap Forward. For another example of the connection between rumors and politics, see Luise White, *Speaking with Vampires: Rumor and History in Colonial Africa* (Berkeley: University of California Press, 2000).

4. Chen Cisheng, *You meiyou gui?* [Are there ghosts or not?] (Nanjing: Jiangsu renmin chubanshe, 1956). Many similar small pamphlets were published throughout the 1950s and 1960s, and they are almost exclusively concerned with popular practice and belief; see *Daodi youmeiyou guishen* [Are there supernatural beings or not] (Beijing:

Jiefangjun bao chubanshe, 1959); Guangdong sheng kexuezhishu puji xiehui, ed., *Tan "shen" jiang "gui"* [Talking of "spirits" and speaking of "ghosts"] (Guangdong: Guandong renmin chubanshe, 1958); Dai Jinsheng, *Shijie shang you guishen ma?* [Does the world have ghosts and spirits?] (Shanghai: Shanghai renmin chubanshe, 1962); Jilin sheng kexuezhishu puji, ed., *Zhen you shengui ma?* [Are there really gods and ghosts?] (Changchun: Jilin renmin chubanshe, 1956).

5. Chen, *You meiyou gui?*, 14.

6. Steven A. Smith, "Local Cadres Confront the Supernatural: The Politics of Holy Water (*Shenshui*) in the PRC, 1949–1966," *China Quarterly* 188 (December 2006): 999–1022, 1012.

7. Smith, "Local Cadres," 1012–13.

8. Smith, "Local Cadres," 1013; Vincent Goossaert and David A. Palmer, *The Religious Question in Modern China* (Chicago: University of Chicago Press, 2011), 148–50.

9. Chen Yan, "Ma Jianling zhe ge ren" [This person Ma Jianling], *Meiwen* (April 2007): 75–79, 76. Ma's father was a teacher, a profession his sons would also take up.

10. Chen Yan, "Ma Jianling zhe ge ren," 76.

11. Zhang Chengping, ed, *Babaoshan geming gogmu beiwen lu* [Collection of epitaphs from Babaoshan revolutionary cemetery] (Beijing: Gaige chubanshe, 1990), 55.

12. Bonnie S. McDougall and Kam Louie, *The Literature of China in the Twentieth Century* (New York: Columbia University Press, 1997), 268–69.

13. Ke, unlike Ma, had a more prominent literary career prior to his move to Yan'an in 1938. But Ke spent three years in prison and four years in Japan after his 1920s involvement in the Creation Society, an absence that possibly influenced his move away from the urbane literary cliques of Republican Shanghai (McDougall and Louie, *Literature of China in the Twentieth Century*, 268).

14. Ellen Judd, "Prelude to the 'Yan'an Talks': Problems in Transforming a Literary Intelligentsia," *Modern China* 11.3 (July 1985): 377–408, 388.

15. D. L. Holm, "Local Color and Popularization in the Literature of the Wartime Border Regions," *Modern Chinese Literature and Culture* 2.1 (Spring 1986): 7–20, 11.

16. Judd, "Prelude to the 'Yan'an Talks,'" 386.

17. Yang Bujun, "Minyishujia Ma Jianling" [People's artist Ma Jianling], *Jinqiu* 1 (2012): 41–42, 42.

18. See, for example, Dong Dingcheng, "Ma Jianling juzuo de pingjie wenti" [The problems with evaluations of Ma Jianling's dramas], *Dangdai xiju* 4 (1988): 10–12.

19. Yi-Tsi Mei Feuerwerker, *Ding Ling's Fiction: Ideology and Narrative in Modern Chinese Literature* (Cambridge: Harvard University Press, 1992), 121.

20. Ma Jianling, "Xiugai *You xihu* de shuoming" [Explaining the alterations to *Wandering West Lake*], in Ma Jianling, *You xihu (qinqiang juben)* [*Wandering West Lake* (qinqiang script)] (Xi'an: Xibei renmin chubanshe, 1953), 1. In some ways, this has intriguing symmetry with Qu You's original tale, "The Woman in Green," found in his early Ming collection *New Tales Told by Lamplight*. In that story, the character that provided the model for Li Huiniang meets her soulmate for the second time, decades after they

parted—having been forced to commit suicide in the late Song—she as a ghost, he as a reincarnated being.

21. See Zhou, *Hongmei ji*. Act four is "Killing the Concubine" [*Sha qie*].

22. Ma Jianling, *You xihu (qinqiang juben)* [*Wandering West Lake (qinqiang* script)] (Xi'an: Xibei renmin chubanshe, 1953).

23. See Zeitlin's description of one such story from Pu Songling's *Liaozhai*, in *Phantom Heroine*, 24–25.

24. Jianfu Chen, *Chinese Law: Context and Transformation* (Leiden: Martinus Nijhoff, 2008), 399.

25. Chen, *Chinese Law*, 401.

26. Neil J. Diamant, *Revolutionizing the Family: Politics, Love, and Divorce in Urban and Rural China, 1949–1968* (Berkeley: University of California Press, 2000), ix. For examination of unintended contemporary social consequences of Maoist reform, see Yunxiang Yan, *Private Life under Socialism: Love, Intimacy, and Family Change in a Chinese Village, 1949–1999* (Stanford: Stanford University Press, 2003).

27. Hershatter, *Gender of Memory*, 4–5, 105.

28. Hershatter, *Gender of Memory*, 109.

29. Hershatter's study includes several hair-raising accounts of just how badly the new law was received in some cases, and reveals the extent to which provincial-level cadres were concerned with winning over the masses.

30. Antonia Finnane, "What Should Chinese Women Wear? A National Problem," *Modern China* 22.2 (April 1996): 99–131, 112–13.

31. As Finnane aptly quips, "Progressive male intellectuals, sympathetic with the oppressed Nora [of Ibsen's *The Doll's House*], sympathized even more with their oppressed selves and not untypically deserted their unfortunate, bound-footed, traditional wives" (112).

32. See Bohnencamp, "Turning Ghosts into People," especially chapter 1.

33. Hershatter, *Gender of Memory*, 102–3.

34. Ma, "Xiugai *You xihu*."

35. Ma, "Xiugai *You xihu*."

36. Hershatter, *Gender of Memory*, 103.

37. Li, *Jinxi*, 13.

38. Liu Naichong, "Duzhe dui Ma Jianling gaibian *You xihu* juben de yijian" [Readers' opinions on Ma Jianling's revised *Wandering West Lake* script], *Play Monthly* 6 (1955): 162–66, 162.

39. "Gaibian *You xihu* de taolun" [Discussion of the adaptation of *Wandering West Lake*], *Wenyi bao* 5 (1954): 40–41, 40.

40. "Gaibian *You xihu*," 40.

41. "Gaibian *You xihu*," 41.

42. See Liu Naichong, "Yi Zhang Zhen de jijian shi" [Recalling some works of Zhang Zhen], *Zhongguo xiju* 12 (2008): 48–49, 48. In this essay—written after Zhang Zhen's death—Liu refers specifically to the *Wandering West Lake* essays, noting that they were quite persuasive, having an impact far beyond Ma's revisions (49).

43. Zhang Zhen, "Tan *You xihu* de gaibian" [Discussing *Wandering West Lake's* revisions], *Wenyi bao* 21 (1954): 41–43, 42. Realism and the uses of literature were under debate throughout the 1950s; see Rudolf G. Wagner, "The Cog and the Scout—Functional Concepts of Literature in Socialist Political Culture: The Chinese Debate in the Mid-Fifties," in *Essays in Modern Chinese Literature and Literary Criticism*, ed.Wolfgang Kubin and Rudolf G. Wagner (Bochum: Studienverlag Brockmeyer, 1982).

44. Zhang, "Tan *You xihu*," 42.

45. Liu, "Duzhe dui," 162.

46. Liu, "Duzhe dui," 163.

47. Liu, "Duzhe dui," 163.

48. Liu, "Duzhe dui," 164.

49. Liu, "Duzhe dui," 165.

50. Zhou, *Hongmei ji*, 4.

51. Ma, *You xihu*, 10.

52. Ma, *You xihu*, 13.

53. Liu, "Duzhe dui," 166.

54. Liang Qichao, for instance, claimed in 1902 that "[t]he superstitious belief in geomancy has driven people to oppose the construction of railroads and the opening of mines. . . . Processions and festivals intended to welcome the spirits or offer thanksgiving to the gods annually cause people to squander millions of dollars, waste their time, stir up trouble, and drain the national economy." See Liang, "On the Relationship," 79. This concern over the combination of popular belief, science, and rationality was hardly confined to East Asia; see, for example, Allison P. Coudert, *Religion, Magic, and Science in Early Modern Europe and America* (Santa Barbara, CA: Praeger, 2011); Richard Godbeer, *The Devil's Dominion: Magic and Religion in Early New England* (Cambridge: Cambridge University Press, 1994).

55. Roderick MacFarquhar, *Contradictions among the People 1956–1957*, vol. 1, *The Origins of the Cultural Revolution* (New York: Columbia University Press, 1974), 34.

56. MacFarquhar, *Contradictions*, 52.

57. MacFarquhar, *Contradictions*, 52.

58. Andrews, *Painters and Politics*, 180.

59. "Ji quanguo xiqu jumu gongzuo huiyi" [Remembering the all-China theatre repertoire work conference], *Theatre Report* (July 1956): 25.

60. See Fu Jin, *Ershi shiji*, 218.

61. "Fajue zhengli yichan, fengfu shangyan jumu" [Excavate and put in order our heritage, enrich performed repertoire], *Theatre Report* (July 1956): 4–5, 4.

62. "Fajue zhengli," 5.

63. "Fajue zhengli," 5.

64. "Zhonghua renmin gongheguo wenhua bu duiyu Shenyang shi wenhuaju fengfu quyi shangyan jiemu de pifu yijian" [Reply from the Ministry of Culture regarding the Shenyang Culture Bureau's enrichment of performed operatic arts programs], October 18, 1956, SMA B172-1-196-23.

65. SMA B172-1-196-23.

66. SMA B172-1-196-23. One of the great challenges facing performers was the tension between what the government (at several levels—not always in agreement) desired on an ideological level and what audiences simply wanted to watch.

67. Wagner, *Chinese Historical Drama*, 3–4.

68. "Xiao Cuihua shuo: 'Wo yao changxi!' Beijing wenhuaju jing zhizhibuli" [Xiao Cuihua says: "I want to sing opera!" The Beijing Culture Bureau brushes [him] aside], *People's Daily*, May 14, 1957.

69. "Xiao Cuihua shuo."

70. Liu, "Theatre Reform," 401. Liu here is interested in the deleterious effects the early 1950s had on performance techniques in the opera repertoire. Since opera relies on person-to-person transmission and teaching, forcing masters like Xiao off the stage essentially killed certain parts of his repertoire. Despite efforts to recover elements of Xiao Cuihua's style, "there is," Liu says, "an unfortunate lack of actors capable of performing Xiao's plays, some of which have not been revived" (401).

71. Wagner, *Chinese Historical Drama*, 4.

72. Mao Zedong, "Speech at Conference of Members and Cadres of Provincial-Level Organizations of CPC in Shandong (March 18, 1957)," in *The Writings of Mao Zedong, 1949–1976, vol. 2, January 1956-December 1957*, ed. Michael Y. M Kau and John K. Leung (Armonk, NY: M. E. Sharpe, 1986), 411–32, 415.

73. Li, *Jinxi*, 13.

74. MacFarquhar, *Contradictions*, 262–64. For definitions, see discussion in Henry Yuhuai He, *Dictionary of the Political Thought of the People's Republic of China* (Armonk, NY: M. E. Sharpe, 2001), 617–20.

75. Jones, *Censorship*, 22; Song, *Biographical Dictionary*, 4; Hong, *History of Contemporary Chinese Literature*, 71; Liang Luo, *The Avant-Garde and the Popular: Tian Han and the Intersection of Performance and Politics* (Ann Arbor: University of Michigan Press, 2014), 222.

76. Qu Liuyi, "Mantan guixi" [Discussing ghost plays], *Theatre Report* (July 1957): 4–7.

77. Qu, "Mantan," 4.

78. Ma Jianling, Huang Junyao, Jiang Bingtai, and Zhang Digeng, *You xihu* [*Wandering West Lake*] (Xi'an: Shaanxi renmin chubanshe, 1958).

79. "Guanyu baihua qifang, tuichen chuxin wenti de xuexi" [Regarding the study of the "let a hundred flowers bloom, pushing out the old to bring in the new" issue], SMA B172-5-664, 72.

80. E.g., Ma Jianling, Huang Junyao, Jiang Bingtai, and Zhang Digeng, *You xihu* [*Wandering West Lake*] (Xi'an: Dongfeng wenyi chubanshe, 1961). It is of course possible that there were even more reprints and other editions, though I have only found copies of the 1953 Xibei renmin, 1958 Shaanxi renmin, and 1961 Dongfeng wenyi chubanshe runs.

81. Liu Naichong, "Ping qinqiang *You xihu* gaibianben" [A review of the revised edition of the *qinqiang Wandering West Lake*], *Xiju yanjiu* (January 1959): 43–45.

82. Liu, "Ping qinqiang," 43. He specifically picks out examples like Liu Lanzhi from "The Peacock Southeast Flew" [Kongque dongnan fei], a long narrative poem from the fifth century AD. In the course of the poem, Liu Lanzhi and her lover-husband commit suicide to circumvent familial pressures and arranged marriages. Lanzhi shows herself to be a stronger character in many respects than her husband, who vacillates under pressure from his mother; his wife, on the other hand, never wavers from her commitment— even to the point of death. See the poem in Victor H. Mair, ed., *The Columbia Anthology of Traditional Chinese Literature* (New York: Columbia University Press, 1994), 462–72.

83. Liu, "Ping qinqiang," 44.

84. Liu, "Ping qinqiang," 45.

85. Liu, "Ping qinqiang," 45

86. Furthermore, it is the 1958 revision that is included in contemporary collections of Ma's work or published independently.

87. David Der-Wei Wang, *The Monster That Is History: History, Violence, and Fictional Writing in Twentieth-Century China* (Berkeley: University of California Press, 2004), 265–66.

Chapter 3

1. "Bright moonlight before the bed / Appearing as if frost. / I lift my head, gazing at the moon; / I lower my head, thinking of my old home." See Lin Jing, ed., *Gudai huaixiang shici sanbaishou* [Three hundred classical poems and lyrics of being homesick] (Beijing: Zhongguo guoji guangbo chubanshe, 2014), 115–16.

2. Meng Chao, "Shi fa danqing tu guixiong—kunqu *Li Huiniang* chuban daiba" [An attempt to portray a ghost hero—the postscript to the publication of the Kun opera *Li Huiniang*], in Meng Chao, *Kunju Li Huiniang* [Kun opera *Li Huiniang*] (Shanghai: Shanghai wenyi chubanshe, 1980), 108–19, 109.

3. Tom Fisher and others have forced us to question Wu Han's motivation in writing *Hai Rui*. See "'The Play's the Thing': Wu Han and Hai Rui Revisited," *Australian Journal of Chinese Affairs* 7 (January 1982): 1–35. While I generally think a reading that favors a critical angle is correct—or, at the very least, quite understandable—Fisher's point that there was more to the creation of these plays than a criticism of party leadership is worth keeping in mind.

4. Merle Goldman has written that "the Leap had produced the chill and that [Meng Chao], like his traditional forebears, sought to alleviate the distress of the peasants was revealed later [in the play]" (Goldman, *China's Intellectuals*, 43).

5. Richard Kraus notes that the "delight in traditional elite culture among the senior leaders of a radical army of peasant recruits may seem surreal, but it is amply documented. Indeed, had intelligent and ambitious men like Mao and Chen Yi completely cast aside all that they had learned in their traditional education, their history would have been odder still" (*Brushes with Power*, 61).

6. Zhongguo kexueyuan wenxue yanjiusuo, ed., *Bu pa gui de gushi* [Stories about not being afraid of ghosts] (Beijing: Renmin wenxue, 1961). There were multiple publications of *Stories* over the course of 1961.

7. Chen Jin, "Mao Zedong yuanhe yao bian *Bu pa gui de gushi*" [Why Mao Zedong wished to compile *Stories about Not Being Afraid of Ghosts*], *Dangshi zonglan* 12 (2013): 52; Christopher Marsh, *Religion and the State in Russia and China: Suppression, Survival, and Revival* (New York: Continuum, 2011), 174.

8. The Institute of Literature of the Chinese Academy of Social Sciences, ed., *Stories about Not Being Afraid of Ghosts* (Beijing: Foreign Language Press, 1961), 1.

9. *Stories* (English), 1.

10. Zhongguo kexueyuan, *Bu pa gui de gushi*.

11. *Bu pa gui de gushi (tongsu ben)* [Stories about not being afraid of ghosts (popular edition)] (Beijing: Qunzhong chubanshe, 1961).

12. *Stories* (English edition).

13. Wu Nanxing [Liao Mosha], "Pa gui de 'yaxue'" [The "elegant joke" of fearing ghosts], *Frontline* 22 (1961): 22.

14. Goldman, *China's Intellectuals*, 2. Goldman's focus is on the liberal-radical split after the Great Leap Forward, which culminated in the Cultural Revolution. Although she pays little attention to Meng Chao specifically, he is noted as part of the liberal group of prominent intellectuals.

15. MacFarquhar, *Cataclysm*, 290.

16. MacFarquhar, *Cataclysm*, 290–92.

17. MacFarquhar, *Cataclysm*, 291.

18. MacFarquhar, *Cataclysm*, 382–83.

19. MacFarquhar, *Cataclysm*, 382–84.

20. Wang Xinrong and Lu Zhengyan, "Huodong zai zhengzhi yu wenxue zhijian de Meng Chao" [Meng Chao's activities between politics and literature], *Shanghai shifan daxue xuebao* 4 (1988): 63–69, 63.

21. For more on the atmosphere of Shanghai University in this period, see Wen-hsin Yeh, *The Alienated Academy: Culture and Politics in Republican China, 1919–1937* (Cambridge: Harvard University Asia Center, 1990), 138. In the 1920s, Shanghai University was full of important, left-leaning writers—including Qu Qiubai, Yu Pingbo, Tian Han, and Guo Morou, among others—and this clearly influenced his thinking and writing (Wang and Lu, "Huodong zai," 63).

22. Wang-chi Wong, *Politics and Literature in Shanghai: The Chinese League of Left-Wing Writers, 1930–1936* (Manchester: Manchester University Press, 1991), 49. Meng Chao makes a small cameo in writer Xie Bingying's autobiography; when Xie is arrested in Shanghai in 1928 or 1929 and thrown into jail on account of living in the house of robbers, she recalls: "The gendarme slashed at us with his leather whip, whipping each of us twice. And now suddenly Meng Chao, a poet, stumbled into the cell with us, and when he saw me he groaned, 'Are you a ghost? I was looking for you at your apartment, to deliver your royalties, and suddenly . . . this!' The gendarme whipped him. At that point we decided to

talk as loudly as we pleased. This so enraged the jailer that he put us into separate cells" (*A Woman Soldier's Own Story: The Autobiography of Xie Bingying*, trans. Lily Chia Brissman and Barry Brissman [New York: Columbia University Press, 2001], 181.

23. Kirk Denton, ed., *Modern Chinese Literary Thought: Writings on Literature, 1893–1945* (Stanford: Stanford University Press, 1996), 259. Along with other radical intellectuals, Sun Society members engaged in attacks on the literary giants of the May Fourth period, particularly luminaries like Lu Xun, and argued about the course literature was to take.

24. Denton, *Literary Thought*, 260. The group published seven issues of the *Sun Monthly* [*Taiyang yuekan*] between January and July 1928; Meng Chao contributed a play and four short stories to the effort. The magazine was reprinted in April 1961 as a seven-volume set by the Shanghai Art and Literature Press. See *Taiyang yuekan* (*yingyin ben*) [*Sun Monthly* (facsimile)], 7 vols. (Shanghai: Shanghai wenyi chubanshe, 1961). Meng Chao's short stories appear in the January, February, May, and July issues, while his play *Under the Iron Heel* (*Tieti xia*) appeared in March.

25. His drama on the subject of the workers' movement entitled *Under the Iron Heel* was published in *Sun Monthly*, and his *The Story of Tanzi Island* (*Tanzi wan de gushi*) was the earliest depiction of the May 30th events in fictional form. Wang and Lu, "Huodong zai," 64. The May 30th Movement was an important anti-imperialist and labor movement in 1925. On May 30th, police in the International Settlement of Shanghai arrested demonstrators and later opened fire on the large crowd that gathered. The following day, further antiforeign protests broke out. It proved a popular subject for Communist writers, with two especially famous examples: Mao Dun's *Rainbow* and Ye Shengtao's *Ni Huanzhi*. See Jeffrey N. Wasserstrom, *Global Shanghai, 1850–2010: A History in Fragments* (New York: Routledge, 2009), particularly "A City in the Streets"; also Richard W. Rigby, *The May 30 Movement: Events and Themes* (Canberra: Australian National University Press, 1980).

26. Lou Shiyi, "Wo huai Meng Chao" [I think of Meng Chao], *People's Daily*, October 10, 1979.

27. "Meng Chao tongzhi zhuidaohui daoci" [The eulogy at the memorial meeting for comrade Meng Chao], *Xin wenxue shiliao* 1 (1980): 282.

28. Meng Chao, *Shuibo Liangshan yingxiong pu* [Guide to the heroes of the Liangshan marsh] (Beijing: Sanlian shudian, 1985); Meng Chao, *Jinping mei renwu* [Characters of Plum in the Golden Vase] (Beijing: Beijing chubanshe, Beijing chuban jituan gongsi, 2011).

29. Owing to the large number of pen names he used, tracing the small details of his career trajectory can be somewhat difficult, though the broad sweep is relatively easy to follow. The earliest use of the pen name Meng Chao seems to have been in 1924, when he published a poem and short story in a Shanghai literary magazine, but he continued, even after 1949, to use a variety of others, often for a single essay. Lu Zhengyan, "Meng Chao minghao biming huilu" [A record of the titles and pen names of Meng Chao], *Shanghai shifan daxue xuebao* 2 (1986): 151–52, 151.

30. "Meng Chao tongzhi."

31. "Meng Chao tongzhi."

32. Mackerras, *Chinese Drama*, 27–34. For an in-depth analysis of Kun opera in Beijing during the late Qing dynasty, as well as its relationship to more popular forms such as *qinqiang*, see Goldman, *Opera and the City*.

33. "Shanghai shi wenhuaju guanyu jumu gongzuoshi de gongzuo zhidu, fengong yijian ji Shanghai jingju guanzhong qingkuang chubu diaocha" [Shanghai municipal Culture Bureau, regarding the repertoire office work system and separation of work and suggesting a preliminary investigation of the situation concerning Shanghai's Peking opera audiences], SMA B172-5-680.

34. Beifang kunqu juyuan, ed., *Jicheng yu fazhan kunqu yishu* [Inherit and develop the art of Kun opera] ([Beijing?]: Dongdan yinshuachang, n.d.).

35. Meng Chao, "Shifa," 110.

36. "Guowuyuan Chen Yi fuzongli zai chengli dahui shang de jianghua" [The speech of the state council's vice-premier Chen Yi at the establishment meeting], in Beifang kunqu juyuan, *Jicheng yu fazhan kunqu yishu*, 10–11, 10.

37. "Zhonggong zhongyang xuanchanbu Zhou Yang fubuzhang zai chengli dahui shang de jianghua" [The speech of the central committee's vice minister of propaganda Zhou Yang at the establishment meeting], in Beifang kunqu juyuan, *Jicheng yu fazhan kunqu yishu*, 12–14, 14.

38. Mu Xin, *Ban Guangming ribao shinian zishu* [My thoughts on ten years of publishing the *Guangming Daily*] (Beijing: Zhonggongdang shi chubanshe, 1994), 197. Ma Lianliang was the actor who brought Wu Han's Hai Rui to life on stage—and suffered greatly in the Cultural Revolution on account of it. He died in 1966 (see Mackerras, *Chinese Drama*, 169).

39. Beifang kunqu juyuan, *Jicheng yu fazhan kunqu yishu*, 1–3.

40. Beifang kunqu juyuan, *Jicheng yu fazhan kunqu yishu*, 7. Li Shujun, who would bring Li Huiniang to life, is on the far left of the frame, standing next to Mao Dun.

41. Mu Xin, "Guixi Li Huiniang" [The ghost play *Li Huiniang*], *Yanhuang chunqiu* (October 1994): 34–43, 36.

42. Mu Xin, "Meng Chao Li Huinaing yuan'an shimo" [The whole unjust case of Meng Chao's *Li Huinaing*], *Xin wenxue shiliao* 2 (1995): 156–203, 158–59.

43. Mu Xin, "Guixi," 34–43, 36.

44. Only Mu Xin refers to Kang Sheng directly by name; Lou Shiyi (writing in 1979) and Meng Jian (writing in 1981) speak of "an authority on theory" [*lilun quanwei*], the standard euphemism applied to Kang Sheng in this period. See Perry Link, *An Anatomy of Chinese: Rhythm, Metaphor, Politics* (Cambridge: Harvard University Press, 2013), 311.

45. Mu Xin, "Guixi," 34–43, 37.

46. Cong Zhaohuan and Chen Jun, "Wo suo qinli de *Li Huiniang* shijian" [My personal experience of *Li Huiniang*], *Xin wenxue shiliao* 2 (2007): 54–62, 55.

47. Meng Chao, *Li Huiniang* (Beifang kunqu juyuan pailianben, May 12, 1961). In author's personal collection.

48. Alexandra B. Bonds, *Beijing Opera Costumes: The Visual Communication of Character and Culture* (Honolulu: University of Hawai'i Press, 2008), 223–24.

49. Cong and Chen, "Wo suo," 55. For more on *Fifteen Strings of Cash*, see chapter 3 of Rebull, "Theaters of Reform and Remediation."

50. The 1980 reprint of *Li Huiniang* added a further 17,000 copies to the run; still, this is not even a quarter of the total number that Ma Jianling's two versions saw between 1953 and 1961.

51. Goldman, *China's Intellectuals*, 27–28.

52. Like *Evening Chats at Yanshan* (Deng Tuo), *Notes from a Three Family Village* (Deng Tuo, Wu Han, and Liao Mosha), *The Long and the Short* was a series of *zawen* (written under pennames) that appeared over several months in major publications: the *Beijing Evening News*, *Frontline*, and *People's Daily*, respectively. Xia Yan, Wu Han, Liao Mosha, Meng Chao, and Tang Tao contributed, though Liao became "the major personality," according to Timothy Cheek, *Propaganda and Culture in Mao's China: Deng Tuo and the Intelligentsia* (Oxford: Oxford University Press, 1997), 235; see further 229–237; Xia Yan, Wu Han, Liao Mosha, Meng Chao, and Tang Tao, *Changduan lu* [The long and the short] (Beijing: Renmin ribao chubanshe, 1980). Meng Chao published twelve essays in all.

53. Zhang Zhen, "Kan kunqu xinfan *Li Huiniang*," 47–49, 47.

54. Zhang, "Kan kunqu," 49.

55. Cong's account also makes it clear that the actors had to go to some effort to improve their performance of these "traditional" skills, in the case of the ghost step, integral to performing the role "well." Zhang's review is very positive, but the comments that specifically pick out the *preparation* of these stage skills are curious. The implication is, I think, that younger performers are not receiving training critical to carrying on theatrical tradition in the course of daily study.

56. Song, *Biographical Dictionary*, 367.

57. Yang Xianyi, "Hongmei jiuqu xi xifan," 90–92, 90.

58. Yang, "Hongmei," 90.

59. Yang, "Hongmei," 91.

60. Yang, "Hongmei," 91–92.

61. Li Liming, *Zhongguo xiandai liubai zuojia xiaozhuan* [Biographical profiles of six hundred contemporary Chinese authors] (Hong Kong: Bowen shuju, 1977), 413.

62. Meng Chao, *Li Huiniang* (1962), 1.

63. Modern-day Hangzhou.

64. See Alfreda Murck, *Poetry and Painting in Song China: The Subtle Art of Dissent* (Cambridge: Harvard University Press, 2000); Allen J. Berkowitz, "The Moral Hero: A Pattern of Reclusion in Traditional China," *Monumenta Serica* 40 (1992): 1–32.

65. Wagner, *Historical Drama*, 307.

66. Tao Junqi and Li Dake, "Yi duo xianyan de 'hongmei'—cong *Hongmei ji* de gaibian, tandao kunqu *Li Huiniang*" [A brightly colored "red plum"—using the adaptations of the *Story of Red Plums* to discuss the Kun opera *Li Huiniang*], *People's Daily*, December 28, 1961.

67. "Jingshantianhua—*Li Huiniang, Zhong Li jian* zuotanhui jiyao" [Making perfection even more perfect—a summary of the symposiums on Li Huiniang and Zhong Li's sword], *Beijing wenyi* 10 (1961): 54–55.

68. Meng, "Shi fa," 115.

69. Haiyan Lee, *Revolution of the Heart: A Genealogy of Love in China, 1900–1950* (Stanford: Stanford University Press, 2007), 286.

70. Goldman, *China's Intellectuals*, 27.

71. Liao Mosha, "Wo xie 'yougui wuhai lun' de qianhou" [Surrounding my writing of the "some ghosts are harmless theory'], in *Liao Mosha wenji, di er juan: Zawen* [The collected works of Liao Mosha, volume 2: Zawen] (Beijing: Beijing chubanshe, 1986), 492–95, 493. As it stands, Liao's essays on the subject of his famous pieces of theatre criticism were written years after the fact, and in somewhat suspect conditions. An essay penned in 1969 on the creation of "History" reads very similarly to his essay on writing "Ghosts," which was written in 1978.

72. Fisher, "Wu Han," 7.

73. Liao Mosha, "'Shi' he 'xi'—he Wu Han de *Hai Rui baguan* yanchu" ["History" and "theatre"—congratulating Wu Han's production of *Hai Rui Dismissed from Office*], in *Liao Mosha wenji, di er juan: Zawen* [The collected works of Liao Mosha, volume 2: Zawen] (Beijing: Beijing chubanshe, 1986): 80–82.

74. Liao, "Wo xie," 493–94

75. Mao Zedong, *Selected Works of Mao Tse-Tung, Volume V* (Beijing: Foreign Languages Press, 1977), 434.

76. Goldman, *China's Intellectuals*, 44.

77. Liao, "Yougui," 109.

78. Liao, "Yougui," 109.

79. Liao, "Yougui," 111.

80. Meng Chao, *Li Huiniang* (1962).

81. Meng Chao, *Li Huiniang, Juben* (1961), 89.

82. Meng Chao, "Shi fa," 114.

83. Li Qingyun, "Tantan *Li Huiniang* de 'tigao'" [Discussing *Li Huiniang*'s "improvement"], *Theatre Report* (May 1962): 47–50, 47.

84. Meng Chao, *Li Huiniang* (Beifang kunqu juyuan pailianben, 1961).

85. Li, "Tantan," 49.

86. Li, "Tantan," 49.

87. Li, "Tantan," 50.

88. Feng Qiyong, "Cong 'Lüyiren chuan' dao *Li Huiniang*" [From "The Woman in Green" to *Li Huiniang*], *Beijing wenyi* (November 1962): 51–56.

Chapter 4

1. "Guanyu tingyan," 248.

2. McDougall and Louie, *Literature of China in the Twentieth Century*, 296.

3. Goldman, *China's Intellectuals*, 63–64.

4. McDougall and Louie, *Literature of China in the Twentieth Century*, 296.

5. As Ross Terrill describes in his biography of Jiang Qing, Kang Sheng moved to make even greater matches—including that between Jiang Qing and Mao (*The White-Boned Demon: A Biography of Madame Mao Zedong* [New York: William Marrow & Co., 1984], 152.). While this may have been his greatest coup politically, at least in terms of matchmaking, setting up Meng Chao and Ling Junqi probably had a good dose of self-serving interests at its core: it was Ling Junqi's father who supported Kang Sheng during his tenure in Shanghai and later in Jinan (Mu Xin, "Meng Chao *Li Huiniang*," 158–59).

6. Mu, "Guixi *Li Huiniang*," 38.

7. Mu, *Ban* Guangming, 197–98. The purpose of the trip was for "rest and recreation"—and, taking advantage of their political positions, the opportunity to see many "bawdy and erotic" plays not staged for many years. However, several years later when the Propaganda Bureau, spurred on by reports that "two 'central leaders' had watched 'old plays' in Hangzhou," Jiang Qing claimed they had "merely watched the 'intolerable' plays advertised in the local paper." Considering they apparently ordered Hangzhou troupes to make trips to Shanghai to gather necessary materials to stage the plays, this seems a somewhat suspect explanation. John Byron and Robert Pack, *The Claws of the Dragon: Kang Sheng, the Evil Genius behind Mao—and His Legacy of Terror in People's China* (New York: Simon & Schuster, 1992), 265–67.

8. MacFarquhar, *Cataclysm*, 283.

9. MacFarquhar, *Cataclysm*, 384.

10. Mu, "Guixi *Li Huiniang*," 37; Li Zhisui, *The Private Life of Chairman Mao*, trans. Tai Hung-chao (New York: Random House, 1994), 402.

11. Li, *Private Life*, 403–4.

12. "Guanyu tingyan."

13. "Guanyu tingyan," 248.

14. "Guanyu tingyan," 248.

15. "Guanyu tingyan," 248.

16. "Guanyu tingyan," 249.

17. "Guanyu tingyan," 250.

18. As Rudolf Wagner has noted, the importance of *Journey to the West* in Communist narratives may explain why many mythological subjects escaped being banned. As he notes, *Journey to the West* was one of the few familiar, popular plots able to resonate with the Marxist narrative of "revolutionary transformation" (*Historical Drama*, 140). Connecting Wagner's argument to theatrical ghosts, we can say that *Journey to the West* was useful in a way that ghosts simply were not. Even cultural radicals were not ready to throw out so useful a plot structure as the Monkey King's adventure.

19. Zhao Xun, "Yan 'guixi' meiyou haichu ma?" [Does staging "ghost plays" do no harm?], *Wenyi bao* 4 (1963): 16–18, 18.

20. Liang Bihui [Yu Minghuang], "'Yougui wuhai' lun" [On "some ghosts are harmless"], *Wenhui bao*, May 6–7, 1963.

21. Wagner, *Historical Drama*, 312.

22. Li Song, ed., *"Yangbanxi" biannian yu shishi* [Annals and historical facts of "yangbanxi"] (Beijing: Zhongyang bianyi chubanshe, 2012), 56n2.

23. Liang, "'Yougui.'"

24. Wagner, *Historical Drama*, 312. The publication of this essay, and its attendant warning, is likely why, in August of that year, Zhou Yang informed Kang Sheng that Meng Chao had written another self-criticism—one that the minister of culture apparently felt was unwarranted. Mu Xin, "Guixi *Li Huiniang*," 38.

25. Jing Guxie, "Guixi zhi hai" [The harmfulness of ghost plays], *Guangming Daily*, May 21, 23, 25, 1963.

26. Jing, "Guixi zhi," May 23.

27. Mu, *Ban* Guangming, 189. As discussed in the introduction, Mu Xin certainly had an agenda with his memoirs, and had the luxury of decades of reflection on the issues discussed, with all that it implies. However, while he may be passionate about the injustice done to Meng Chao, there seems to be little reason to distrust his rather dispassionate telling of the events that took place in the fall of 1963.

28. Mu Xin, *Ban* Guangming, 189.

29. Mu Xin, *Ban* Guangming, 190.

30. Mu Xin, *Ban* Guangming, 191.

31. Mu Xin, *Ban* Guangming, 191–92.

32. Li Xifan, "Feichang youhai de 'yougui wuhai' lun" [Extremely harmful "some ghosts are harmless" theory], *Guangming Daily*, September 10, 1963.

33. Ruo He [Chen Gongdeng], "Yan 'guixi' youhai ma?—'Yan 'guixi' meiyou haichu ma?' duhou" [Staging "ghost plays" is harmful?—on reading "Staging 'ghost plays' doesn't have any harmful points?"], *Guangming Daily*, September 10, 1963. Mu Xin provides the identification of "Ruo He," see *Ban* Guangming, 202.

34. Ruo He, "Yan 'guixi.'" For more on the origins of *The White-Haired Girl*, see Bohnenkamp, "Turning Ghosts into People."

35. Ruo He, "Yan 'guixi.'"

36. Chen Ying, "Tingyan guixi shi yinye feishi" [Stopping performances of ghost plays is giving up at the slightest obstacle], *Guangming Daily*, September 23, 1963.

37. Kong Xiang, "Guixi he shenxi ying yilü kandai" [Ghost plays and mythology plays ought to be treated the same with one law], *Guangming Daily*, October 4, 1963.

38. Shen Yao, "Shenhuaxi yu guixi bixu yange qubie kailai—jianping Ruo He, Tan Peng tongzhi de yixie lundian" [Mythology plays and ghost plays must have a strict separation—a simultaneous critique of a few of Comrades Rou He and Tan Peng's points], *Guangming Daily*, November 17, 1963.

39. Tan Peng, "Youxie 'guixi' yinggai jiayi kending" [Some "ghost plays" ought to be treated positively], *Guangming Daily*, September 20, 1963.

40. Mu Xin, *Jiehou changyi—shinian dongluan jishi* [Long reminiscences after the disaster—chronicle of the decade of disturbances] (Hong Kong: Xintian chubanshe, 1997).

41. SMA B172-5-664.

42. MacFarquhar, *Cataclysm*, 382.

43. SMA B172-5-664, 72.

44. SMA B172-5-664, 73.

45. SMA B172-5-664, 148–49.

46. SMA B172-5-664, 72.

47. SMA B172-5-664, 74.

48. SMA B172-5-664, 147.

49. SMA B172-5-664, 74.

50. SMA B172-5-664, 72.

51. Bo Yibo, *Ruogan zhongda juece yu shijian de huigu, xia* [A review of certain major decisions and incidents, volume 2] (Beijing: Zhonggong zhongyang dangxiao chubanshe, 1993), 1226.

52. See "Shi 'wenhua dageming de xumu' haishi cuandang de xumu?—benkan bianjibu juxing zuotanhui pipan Yao Wenyuan de 'ping xinbian lishiju *Hai Rui baguan*' [Was it "the prologue to the Great Cultural Revolution," or the prologue to seizing the party by force?—the editorial board holds a meeting to criticize Yao Wenyuan's "Criticizing the new historical play *Hai Rui Dismissed from Office*"], *People's Theatre* (January 1979): 4–9.

53. See Greene, "Ghostly Bodhisattva."

Chapter 5

1. Lou Shiyi, "Wo huai."

2. MacFarquhar, *Cataclysm*, 381.

3. Goldman, *China's Intellectuals*, 90. Mao was remarking positively on an article written by Ke Qingshi, mayor of Shanghai and an important supporter of Jiang Qing prior to his death in 1965.

4. Goldman, *China's Intellectuals*, 92.

5. Mao Zedong, "Talks at the Yan'an Forum on Literature and Art," 461.

6. "Shanghai shi wenhuaju guanyu canjia wenhubu juban de jingju xiandaixi guanmo yanchu de mingdan, zongjie baogao" [Name list and final report of the Shanghai Culture Bureau regarding attending the Ministry of Culture–sponsored festival on contemporary themes in Peking opera] (August 29, 1964), SMA B172-1-527.

7. Goldman, *China's Intellectuals*, 77.

8. "Guanche Mao zhuxi wenyi fangxiang dali tichang xiandaiju—Ke Qingshi tongzhi zai Huadongqu huaju guanmo yanchu kamushi shang jianghua" [Implement Chairman Mao's artistic trends, energetically advocate for drama on contemporary themes—Comrade Ke Qingshi's speech at the opening ceremonies of the East China

Spoken Language Drama Festival], *Shanghai Theatre* 1 (January 1964): 2–5, 2–3. He further critiqued the decadent cultural world of Shanghai in the Republican period, something that later chroniclers have argued was an attack on senior dramatist (and one of Jiang Qing's bêtes noires) Tian Han. Dai Zhixian, *Shanyu yulai feng manlou—60 niandai qianqi de 'dapipan'* [Mountain rains about to come, wind fills the building—the early days of mass criticism in the 1960s] (Henan: Henan renmin chubanshe, 1990), 88.

9. Wei Wenbo, "Zai yijiuliusan nian Huadongqu huaju guanmo yanchu bimu shishang Wei Wenbo tongzhi de bimuci" [Comrade Wei Wenbo's closing remarks at the closing ceremonies of the 1963 East China Spoken Language Drama Festival], *Shanghai Theatre* 2 (February 1963): 2–3, 2.

10. See Yan Chunguang, ed., *Lingdao ganbu bidu de zuimei gushici* [The most beautiful ancient poetry and lyrics leading cadres must read] (Beijing: Renmin chubanshe, 2014), 120.

11. MacFarquhar, *Cataclysm*, 387.

12. Peng Zhen, "Zai jingju xiandaixi guanmo yanchu dahuishang de jianghua" [Speech at the festival on contemporary themes in Peking opera], *Theatre Report* (July 1964): 4–9, 5.

13. Peng Zhen, "Zai jingju," 5.

14. SMA B172-5-680, 1–2.

15. SMA B172-5-680, 3.

16. SMA B172-5-680, 3.

17. Terrill, *White-Boned Demon*, 248; MacFarquhar, *Cataclysm*, 388–89. It was not, unlike the remarks of Peng Zhen and others, published at the time, only being published as a pamphlet in 1967 (a Foreign Languages Press translation followed in 1968). Jiang Qing, *On the Revolution of Peking Opera* (Beijing: Foreign Languages Press, 1968).

18. Jiang Qing, *On the Revolution*.

19. Zhong Kan, *Kang Sheng pingzhuan* [A critical biography of Kang Sheng] (Beijing: Hongqi chubanshe, 1982), 93.

20. Terrill, *White-Boned Demon*, 248–49. B172-1-527, 1.

21. SMA B172-1-527, 6.

22. SMA B172-5-682, 2.

23. SMA B172-5-682, 5.

24. Mackerras, *Chinese Theatre*, 168. The *Far Eastern Economic Review* article Mackerras cites here must not have been including spoken drama. However, the Shanghai statistics still illustrate that troupes of all genres, with the exception of Kun opera (which itself was not often performed), were performing at least a few plays on contemporary themes.

25. SMA B172-1-527, 13.

26. SMA B172-1-527, 22.

27. SMA B172-5-682.

28. Liu, *Critical History*, 388.

29. "Shanghai shi yijiuliuwu nian shangyan jumu tongjibiao" [Statistics of repertoire performed in Shanghai, 1965], SMA B172-5-934.

30. MacFarquhar, *Cataclysm*, 385.

31. Terrill, *White-Boned Demon*, 249. One of the problems of establishing what was going on in elite literary and cultural circles, particularly where the leaders are concerned, has to do with the sources available to us; Terrill's citations for Peng's and Deng's disapproving comments derive from 1967 sources, hardly an unbiased period. The Chinese and English-language biographies of Jiang Qing and Kang Sheng almost read like scandal sheets, and Terrill is no exception.

32. MacFarquhar, *Cataclysm*, 385; Dai Zhixian, *Shanyu*, 87.

33. Dai, *Shanyu*, 88.

34. Cheng Yun, "Deng Shaoji," in *Mingshi huicui: Zhongguo shehui kexue yuan yanjiushengyuan boshisheng daoshi jianjie (yi)* [A distinguished assembly of famous teachers: A brief introduction to doctoral supervisors of the graduate school of the Chinese academy of social sciences] (Beijing: Zhongguo jingji chubanshe, 1998), 478-79. As Merle Goldman has pointed out in *China's Intellectuals*, there was often an obvious generational divide among "liberal" and "radical" intellectuals. At the time this criticism was launched, Meng Chao was in his early sixties.

35. Deng Shaoji, "*Li Huiniang*—yizhu ducao" [*Li Huiniang* —a poisonous weed], *Wenxue pinglun* 6 (1964): 10-20.

36. Deng, "Li Huiniang," 14.

37. Nie Gannu, "Huai Meng Chao—zuowei *Shuibo liangshan yingxiong pu* de xu" [Thinking of Meng Chao—written as a preface to *A Guide to the Heroes of the Marsh*], in Meng Chao, *Shuibo liangshan yingxiong pu* [*A Guide to the Heroes of the Marsh*] (Beijing: Sanlian shudian, 1985), 1-4, 4.

38. Deng Shaoji, "Li Huiniang," 15. Deng explains how *he* reads Meng Chao's use of *caomang*: "it often refers to a person 'out of power,' such as a 'minister out of power' . . . or a person of low social status, such as a '*caomang* hero' [e.g., Robin Hood]."

39. Qi Xiangqun, "Chongping Meng Chao xinbian *Li Huiniang*" [A serious criticism of Meng Chao's adaptation *Li Huiniang*], *Theatre Report* (January 1965): 2-8. The piece, like most criticisms of this period, was republished widely in regional publications, as well as in the March 1, 1965 edition of *People's Daily*.

40. Qi, "Chongping," 4.

41. Qi, "Chongping," 4.

42. Meng Chao, "Shi fa," 113.

43. Qi, "Chongping," 6.

44. Meng Chao, *Li Huiniang* (1962).

45. Modern-day Hangzhou.

46. Qi, "Chongping," 7.

47. Bu Linfei, "Fan shehuizhuyi de sixiang he yishu—pipan Meng Chao tongzhi de kunju *Li Huiniang* daiba" [Antisocialist thought and art—criticizing comrade Meng Chao's postscript to the Kun opera *Li Huiniang*], *Theatre Report* (February 1965): 44-45.

48. Bu, "Fan," 45.

49. Fan Xing [Liao Mosha], "Wo de 'yougui wuhai lun' shi cuowu de" [My "some ghosts are harmless theory" was a mistake], *Beijing wenyi* (March 1965): 59–64, 62.

50. Fan, "Cuowu," 62.

51. Lou, "Wo huai."

52. Lou, "Wo huai."

53. MacFarquhar, *Cataclysm*, 453.

54. MacFarquhar, *Cataclysm*, 454–55.

55. MacFarquhar, *Cataclysm*, 456–67.

56. Wagner notes that Tian Han was the last to be attacked, largely because of his connections to Zhou Enlai. Wagner, *Historical Drama*, 137.

57. Yun Song, "Tian Han de *Xie Yaohuan* shi yike daducao" [Tian Han's *Xie Yaohuan* is a big poisonous weed], *People's Daily*, February 1, 1966.

58. Zhongguo yuyan wenxuexi ziliaoshi, eds., *Guanyu* Li Huiniang *wenti ziliao xuanbian* [A selection of materials relating to the *Li Huiniang* problem] (Changchun: Jilin Normal University, 1966). In author's personal collection.

59. See, for instance, Hanyuyuan wenxue jiaoyanshi, ed., "Hai Rui Baguan, Xie Yaohuan, Li Huiniang *zilao xuanji*" [Selected materials of *Hai Rui Dismissed from Office, Xie Yaohuan, Li Huiniang*] (N.p.: Hubei sheng hanshou xueyuan, 1966), published in February of that year.

60. Liu Housheng, "Fandang fanshehuizhuyi gongtongti—*Li Huiniang, Hai Rui baguan, Xie Yaohuan* zonglun" [The antiparty, antisocialist thought community—a discussion of *Li Huiniang, Hai Rui Dismissed from Office, Xie Yaohuan*], *Theatre Report* 3 (March 1966): 7–13.

61. Zhou Yang described revolutionary romanticism as "the manifestation of revolutionary idealism in artistic methods," and a key component of the new drama on contemporary themes. Lan Yang, *Chinese Fiction of the Cultural Revolution* (Hong Kong: Hong Kong University Press, 1998), 19.

62. Joshua Mostow, ed., *The Columbia Companion to Modern East Asian Literature* (New York: Columbia University Press, 2003), 471–72.

63. Liu, "Fandang," 11. Here, he is quoting the Russian writer Maxim Gorky.

64. Liu, "Fandang," 9.

65. Liu, "Fandang," 9–10.

66. Liu, "Fandang," 12.

67. Roderick MacFarquhar and Michael Schoenhals, *Mao's Last Revolution* (Cambridge: Harvard University Press, 2006), 40. There are of course many studies of various facets of the Cultural Revolution, as well as memoirs. See, for instance, Ji Xianlin, *The Cowshed: Memories of the Chinese Cultural Revolution*, trans. Chenxin Jiang (New York: New York Review of Books, 2016); Joseph W. Esherick, Paul G. Pickowicz, and Andrew G. Walder, eds., *The Chinese Cultural Revolution as History* (Stanford: Stanford University Press, 2006); Paul Clark, *The Chinese Cultural Revolution: A History* (Cambridge: Cambridge University Press, 2008); Edward Friedman, Paul G. Pickowicz, and Mark

Selden, *Revolution, Resistance, and Reform in Village China* (New Haven: Yale University Press, 2005); Feng Jicai, *Voices from the Whirlwind: An Oral History of the Chinese Cultural Revolution* (New York: Pantheon, 1991).

68. MacFarquhar and Schoenhals, *Revolution*, 54–61.

69. MacFarquhar and Shoenhals, *Revolution*, 123–24. Liao Mosha was attacked—along with Wu Han and Deng Tuo, who committed suicide in May 1966—not for his "some ghosts are harmless" theory, but for his participation in the *Three Family Village* series of essays.

70. Yang, "Minyishujia," 42.

71. Lou, "Wo huai."

72. "1949–1963 Shanghai yanchu de guixi" [Ghost plays performed in Shanghai between 1949 and 1963], *Wenyi zhanbao*, July 5, 1967.

73. Wagner, *Historical Drama*, 201.

74. "1949–1963 Shanghai"

75. Wagner, *Historical Drama*, 137

76. Chen Xiaomei, "Tian Han and the Southern Society Phenomenon: Networking the Personal, Communal, and Cultural," in *Literary Societies of Republican China*, ed. Kirk A. Denton and Michael Hockx (Lanham, MD: Lexington Books, 2008), 245.

77. Mary G. Mazur, *Wu Han, Historian: Son of China's Times* (Lanham, MD: Lexington Books, 2009), 429.

78. Mu, *Jiehou changyi*, 449.

79. Lou, "Wo huai."

80. Mu, *Jiehou changyi*, 448–49.

81. Lou, "Wo huai."

82. Lou, "Wo huai.

83. Meng Jian, "Xie zai," 125.

Chapter 6

1. "Shi 'wenhua.'"

2. "Shi 'wenhua,'" 5.

3. Lou, "Wo huai."

4. Lou, "Wo huai."

5. Meng, "Xie zai," 125.

6. Lou, "Wo huai."

7. Meng Chao, *Li Huiniang*. Beifang kunqu juyuan pailianben [practice edition], December 1978. In author's personal collection.

8. Hui Min, "Beifang kunqu juyuan huifu *Li Huiniang* chongxin shangyan" [The Northern Kun Opera Theatre's important new staging of the revived *Li Huiniang*], *Renmin xiju* (May 1979): 47.

9. "Beifang kunqu juyuan huifu bing shangyan *Li Huiniang*" [The Northern Kun Opera Theatre is restored and staging *Li Huiniang*], *People's Daily*, June 14, 1979.

10. MacFarquhar, *Cataclysm*, 113.

11. It wasn't simply plays being (re)premiered and republished, but also other cultural products that had come under attack during the Cultural Revolution. For instance, the early 1960s *People's Daily zawen* series that Meng Chao participated in—*The Long and the Short*—was collected and published again in 1980. See Xia Yan et al., *Changduan lu.*

12. *Zhongguo xiju nianjian 1982*, 532.

13. Hunan sheng xiqu gongzuoshi, Hunan sheng xiangjuyuan, eds., *Xiangju gaoqiang: Li Huiniang* (N.p.: Hunan sheng xiangjutuan, January 1979), 22. In author's personal collection.

14. *Chuju: Li Huiniang, genju qinqiang yizhi* (N.p.: [Hubei sheng chujutuan?], 1979). My copy of the practice edition, rather oddly, has the troupe name blacked out (see figure 8); however, comparison of an undated publication (though likely produced around the same time, based on printing, binding, and paper quality) of the musical score from the Hubei Chu Opera confirms it is the same script: see Yi Youzhuang, composer, *Chuju: Li Huiniang* (N.p.: Hubei sheng chujutuan, n.d.). In author's personal collection.

15. Possibly the Kunming Dian Opera troupe? Wang Zhichi, *Li Huiniang (canzhao qinqiang, chuanju, kunqu, yuju deng yanchuben zhengli)* (N.p: N.p., December 24, 1979). In author's personal collection.

16. Qu Liuyi, "Guihunxi guankui—jianji jianguo yilai guihunxi de lunzheng" [A restricted view of ghost opera—and the controversy over ghost opera from the founding of the country], *Wenyi yanjiu* 1 (January 1979): 78–86, 80–81. Qu, like Liao Mosha and Meng Jian, declines to name Kang Sheng outright, referring instead to the "master of theory" who encouraged Meng Chao's efforts at revising *Red Plums.*

17. Wang Chunyuan, "Cong *Li Huiniang* de chongyan tandao guihunxi" [Talking about ghost opera from the re-premiere of *Li Huiniang*], *People's Daily*, June 25, 1979.

18. Wang, "Cong *Li Huiniang*."

19. Wang Zhaoqi and Xu Hengyu (illustrator), *Li Huiniang* (Shanghai: Shanghai renmin yishu chubanshe, 1982).

20. Wang and Xu, *Li Huiniang*, 71.

21. *Bu pa gui de gushi* [Stories about not being afraid of ghosts] (Chengdu: Sichuan renmin chubanshe, 1979).

22. Xie Baogeng, ed., *Bu pa gui de gushi* [Stories about not being afraid of ghosts] (Shanghai: Shanghai renmin yishu chubanshe, 1979).

23. Gong Yijiang, "Hu Zhifeng he ta de *Li Huiniang*" [Hu Zhifeng and her *Li Huiniang*], *Renmin xiju* (June 1980): 33–34, 34.

24. Even, according to one article, the art of *qiaogong*, the wearing of special stilts (*qiao*) that simulate the gait of a woman with bound feet; the author does not explain how she accomplished this, since this was one of the performance practices ushered off stages in the high socialist period (see Liu, "Theatre Reform," 400–401).

25. Zhou Heping and Xu Ming, "Hu Zhifeng tan *Li Huiniang*" [Hu Zhifeng talks about *Li Huiniang*], *Dianying pingjie* (November 1981): 36–37, 36.

26. Zhou and Xu, "Hu Zhifeng tan *Li Huiniang*," 37.

27. Zhou and Xu, "Hu Zhifeng tan *Li Huiniang*," 37.

28. Pei Zhen, "Xinying biezhi de *Li Huiniang*" [The novel and unique *Li Huiniang*], *People's Daily*, October 25, 1980.

29. Pei, "Xinying."

30. Lan Ling, "Kan jingju *Li Huiniang* de zagan" [Scattered thoughts on seeing the Peking opera *Li Huiniang*], *People's Daily*, November 8, 1980.

31. Goldstein, *Drama Kings*, 104.

32. Shi Xin, "Ruiyi chuangxin, hongmei canran—cong Hu Zhifeng biaoyan de *Li Huiniang* tan tuichen chuxin" [Brilliantly blazing new trails, a dazzling red plum—observing Hu Zhifeng's production of *Li Huiniang* to discuss pushing out the old to uncover the new], *Xiqu yishu* 4 (1980): 54–55, 55.

33. Judith T. Zeitlin, "Operatic Ghosts on Screen: The Case of *A Test of Love* (1958)," *Opera Quarterly* 26.2–3 (Spring–Summer 2010): 220–55, 220.

34. *Li Huiniang*, dir. Liu Qiong; *Li Huiniang* (dianying wancheng taiben).

35. Zhang Ruipeng, "Jingyan—tansuo—chuangxin—ji *Li Huiniang* daoyan Liu Qiong" [Experience—explore—blaze new trails—remembering *Li Huiniang*'s director Liu Qiong], *Dianying pingjie* (November 1981): 36–37.

36. Chen Jizhang and Jiang Suzhen, "*Li Huiniang* zhong 'rentou' yu 'guihun' de teji sheying" [The "human head" and "ghost" special effects of *Li Huiniang*'s filming], *Dianying pingjie* (October 1981): 7.

37. See "Hu Zhifeng," *Hong Kong Academy of the Performing Arts*, https://www.hkapa.edu/honorary-awardees/hu-zhifeng

38. Zeitlin, *Phantom*, 1.

39. See Li Xiao, *Chinese Kunqu Opera*, trans. Li Li and Zhang Liping (San Francisco: Long River Press, 2005), 7.

40. Swatek, Peony Pavilion *Onstage*, 234.

41. Swatek, Peony Pavilion *Onstage*, 236–37.

42. Swatek, Peony Pavilion *Onstage*, 232; Melvin, "China's Homegrown"; Zeitlin, "My Year of Peonies," 126.

43. Zeitlin, "My Year," 126. Zeitlin gives a hilarious—and brutal—review of the Shang Kun production; 129–32.

44. Wang, *Monster*, 265.

45. Link, *Anatomy*, 3, 5.

46. Link, *Anatomy*, 13.

47. Han Shaogong, *A Dictionary of Maqiao*, trans. Julia Lovell (New York: Columbia University Press, 2003).

48. There are interesting parallels with the political trouble Meng Chao and others would run into for rewriting Qu You's ghost. Qu proved anxious about the contents of *New Tales*—which, despite the form, were very contemporary in setting and rather critical of the Ming regime—and it was not published until 1400, perhaps to avoid persecution. As it turned out, Qu You ran afoul of the Yongle emperor for political (not literary) reasons, was arrested, and spent seventeen years in a labor camp, only being

released when he was nearly eighty. However, this collection of tales proved so popular that it, too, was banned for around twenty years, proving that it was not just Communist censors who found such miraculous subjects problematic. See Kang-i Sun Chang and Stephen Owen, eds., *Cambridge History of Chinese Literature, Volume II, From 1375* *(Cambridge: Cambridge University Press, 2010)*, 8–10.

49. Adapted from Maggie Greene, "The Woman in Green: A Chinese Ghost Tale from Mao to Ming, 1981–1381," *Appendix* 1.2 (2013): 124–32, http://theappendix.net/issues/2013/4/the-woman-in-green-a-chinese-ghost-tale-from-mao-to-ming-1981–1381

Coda

1. "China Bans Time Travel for Television," *China Digital Times* (April 13, 2011). Accessed October 21, 2018, http://chinadigitaltimes.net/2011/04/china-bans-time-travel-for-television/

Bibliography

"1949–1963 Shanghai yanchu de guixi" [Ghost plays performed in Shanghai between 1949 and 1963]. *Wenyi zhanbao*, July 5, 1967.

Ai Qing. "Da Yang Shaoxuan tongzhi" [An answer to Comrade Yang Shaoxuan]. *People's Daily*, November 12, 1951.

Ai Qing. "Tan 'Niulang zhinü'" [Discussing *The Cowherd and the Weaving Maid*]. *People's Daily*, August 31, 1951.

Andrews, Julia F. *Painters and Politics in the People's Republic of China, 1949–1979*. Berkeley: University of California Press, 1994.

Becker, Jasper. *Hungry Ghosts: Mao's Secret Famine*. New York: Holt Paperbacks, 1998.

Beifang kunqu juyuan, ed. *Jicheng yu fazhan kunqu yishu* [Inherit and develop the art of Kun opera]. [Beijing ?]: Dongdan yinshuachang, n.d.

"Beifang kunqu juyuan huifu bing shangyan *Li Huiniang*" [The Northern Kun Opera Theatre is restored and staging *Li Huiniang*]. *People's Daily*, June 14, 1979.

Berkowitz, Allen J. "The Moral Hero: A Pattern of Reclusion in Traditional China." *Monumenta Serica* 40 (1992): 1–32.

Best, Stephen, and Sharon Marcus. "Surface Reading: An Introduction." *Representations* 108.1 (Fall 2009): 1–21.

Bo Yibo. *Ruogan zhongda juece yu shijian de huigu, xia* [A review of certain major decisions and incidents, volume 2]. Beijing: Zhonggong zhongyang dangxiao chubanshe, 1993.

Bohnenkamp, Max L. "Turning Ghosts into People: *The White-Haired Girl*, Revolutionary Folklorism, and the Politics of Aesthetics in Modern China." PhD diss., University of Chicago, 2014.

Bonds, Alexandra B. *Beijing Opera Costumes: The Visual Communication of Character and Culture*. Honolulu: University of Hawai'i Press, 2008.

Brown, Jeremy, and Matthew D. Johnson, eds. *Maoism at the Grassroots: Everyday Life in China's Era of High Socialism*. Cambridge: Harvard University Press, 2015.

Brown, Jeremy, and Paul Pickowicz, eds. *Dilemmas of Victory: The Early Years of the People's Republic of China*. Cambridge: Harvard University Press, 2007.

Bu Linfei. "Fan shehuizhuyi de sixiang he yishu—pipan Meng Chao tongzhi de kunju *Li*

Huiniang daiba" [Antisocialist thought and art—criticizing comrade Meng Chao's postscript to the Kun opera *Li Huiniang*]. *Theatre Report* (February 1965): 44–45.

Bu pa gui de gushi [Stories about not being afraid of ghosts]. Chengdu: Sichuan renmin chubanshe, 1979.

Bu pa gui de gushi (tongsu ben) [Stories about not being afraid of ghosts (popular edition)]. Beijing: Qunzhong chubanshe, 1961.

Byron, John, and Robert Pack. *The Claws of the Dragon: Kang Sheng, the Evil Genius behind Mao—and His Legacy of Terror in People's China*. New York: Simon & Schuster, 1992.

Cai Xiang. *Revolution and Its Narratives: China's Socialist Literary and Cultural Imaginaries, 1949–1966*. Edited and translated by Rebecca E. Karl and Zueping Zhong. Durham: Duke University Press, 2016.

Campany, Robert Ford. *Strange Writing: Anomaly Accounts in Early Medieval China*. Albany: State University of New York Press, 1996.

Chang, Kang-i Sun and Stephen Owen, eds. *Cambridge History of Chinese Literature: Volume II, From 1375*. Cambridge: Cambridge University Press, 2010.

Cheek, Timothy. *Propaganda and Culture in Mao's China: Deng Tuo and the Intelligentsia*. Oxford: Oxford University Press, 1997.

Chen Cisheng. *You meiyou gui?* [Are there ghosts or not?]. Nanjing: Jiangsu renmin chubanshe, 1956.

Chen Duxiu. "On Literary Revolution." In *Modern Chinese Literary Thought: Writings on Literature, 1893–1945*, edited by Kirk Denton and translated by Timothy Wong, 140–45. Stanford: Stanford University Press, 1996.

Chen, Jianfu. *Chinese Law: Context and Transformation*. Leiden: Martinus Nijhoff, 2008.

Chen Jin. "Mao Zedong yuanhe yao bian *Bu pa gui de gushi*" [Why Mao Zedong wished to compile *Stories about Not Being Afraid of Ghosts*]. *Dangshi zonglan* 12 (2013): 52.

Chen Jizhang and Jiang Suzhen. "*Li Huiniang* zhong 'rentou' yu 'guihun' de teji sheying" [The "human head" and "ghost" special effects of *Li Huiniang*'s filming]. *Dianying pingjie* 1981 (October): 7.

Chen, Xiaomei. "Tian Han and the Southern Society Phenomenon: Networking the Personal, Communal, and Cultural." In *Literary Societies of Republican China*, edited by Kirk A. Denton and Michael Hockx. Lanham, MD: Lexington Books, 2008.

Chen Yan. "Ma Jianling zhe ge ren" [This person Ma Jianling]. *Meiwen* (April 2007): 75–79.

Chen Ying. "Tingyan guixi shi yinye feishi" [Stopping performances of ghost plays is giving up at the slightest obstacle]. *Guangming Daily*, September 23, 1963.

Cheng Yun. "Deng Shaoji." In *Mingshi huicui: Zhongguo shehui kexue yuan yanjiushengyuan boshisheng daoshi jianjie (yi)* [A distinguished assembly of famous teachers: A brief introduction to doctoral supervisors of the graduate school of the Chinese academy of social sciences], 478–79. Beijing: Zhongguo jingji chubanshe, 1998.

"China Bans Time Travel for Television." *China Digital Times*, April 13, 2011. http://chinadigitaltimes.net/2011/04/china-bans-time-travel-for-television/

Chuju: Li Huiniang, genju qinqiang yizhi. N.p.: [Hubei sheng chujutuan?], 1979.

Clark, Paul. *The Chinese Cultural Revolution: A History*. Cambridge: Cambridge University Press, 2008.

Cong Zhaohuan and Chen Jun. "Wo suo qinli de *Li Huiniang* shijian" [My personal experience of *Li Huiniang*]. *Xin wenxue shiliao* 2 (2007): 54–62.

Coudert, Allison P. *Religion, Magic, and Science in Early Modern Europe and America*. Santa Barbara, CA: Praeger, 2011.

Dai Jinsheng. *Shijie shang you guishen ma?* [Does the world have ghosts and spirits?]. Shanghai: Shanghai renmin chubanshe, 1962.

Dai Zhixian. *Shanyu yulai feng manlou—60 niandai qianqi de 'dapipan'* [Mountain rains about to come, wind fills the building—the early days of mass criticism in the 1960s]. Henan: Henan renmin chubanshe, 1990.

Daodi youmeiyou guishen [Are there supernatural beings or not]. Beijing: Jiefangjun bao chubanshe, 1959.

DeMare, Brian J. *Mao's Cultural Army: Drama Troupes in China's Rural Revolution*. Cambridge: Cambridge University Press, 2015.

Deng Shaoji. "*Li Huiniang*—yizhu ducao" [Li Huiniang—a poisonous weed]. *Wenxue pinglun* 6 (1964): 10–20.

Denton, Kirk, ed. *Modern Chinese Literary Thought: Writings on Literature, 1893–1945*. Stanford: Stanford University Press, 1996.

Diamant, Neil J. *Revolutionizing the Family: Politics, Love, and Divorce in Urban and Rural China, 1949–1968*. Berkeley: University of California Press, 2000.

Dikötter, Frank. *Mao's Great Famine: The History of China's Most Devastating Catastrophe, 1958–1962*. London: Bloomsbury, 2010.

Dolby, William. "Early Chinese Plays and Theatre." In *Chinese Theater: From Its Origins to the Present Day*, edited by Colin Mackerras, 7–30. Honolulu: University of Hawai'i Press, 1983.

Dong Dingcheng. "Ma Jianling juzuo de pingjie wenti" [The problems with evaluations of Ma Jianling's dramas]. *Dangdai xiju* 4 (1988): 10–12.

Esherick, Joseph W., Paul G. Pickowicz, and Andrew G. Walder, eds. *The Chinese Cultural Revolution as History*. Stanford: Stanford University Press, 2006.

"Fajue zhengli yichan, fengfu shangyan jumu" [Excavate and put in order our heritage, enrich performed repertoire]. *Theatre Report* (July 1956): 4–5.

Fan Xing [Liao Mosha]. "Wo de 'yougui wuhai lun' shi cuowu de" [My "some ghosts are harmless theory" was a mistake]. *Beijing wenyi* (March 1965): 59–64.

Feng Jicai. *Voices from the Whirlwind: An Oral History of the Chinese Cultural Revolution*. New York: Pantheon, 1991.

Feng Qiyong. "Cong 'Lüyiren chuan' dao *Li Huiniang*" [From "The Woman in Green" to *Li Huiniang*]. *Beijing wenyi* (November 1962): 51–56.

Feuerwerker, Yi-Tsi Mei. *Ding Ling's Fiction: Ideology and Narrative in Modern Chinese Literature*. Cambridge: Harvard University Press, 1992.

Figal, Gerald. *Civilization and Monsters: Spirits of Modernity in Meiji Japan*. Durham: Duke University Press, 2000.

Finnane, Antonia. "What Should Chinese Women Wear? A National Problem." *Modern China* 22.2 (April 1996): 99–131.

Fisher, Tom. "'The Play's the Thing': Wu Han and Hai Rui Revisited." *Australian Journal of Chinese Affairs* 7 (January 1982): 1–35.

Foster, Michael Dylan. *Pandemonium and Parade: Japanese Monsters and the Culture of Yōkai*. Berkeley: University of California Press, 2009.

Friedman, Edward, Paul G. Pickowicz, and Mark Selden. *Chinese Village, Socialist State*. New Haven: Yale University Press, 1991.

Friedman, Edward, Paul G. Pickowicz, and Mark Selden. *Revolution, Resistance, and Reform in Village China*. New Haven: Yale University Press, 2005.

Fu Jin. *20 shiji Zhongguo xijushi* [Twentieth century Chinese theatre history]. 2 vols. Beijing: Zhongguo shehui kexue chubanshe, 2017.

Fu Jin, ed. *Ershi shiji zhongguo xiju de xiandaixing yu bentuhua* [Modernity and localization of Chinese theatre in the twentieth century]. Taipei: Guojia chubanshe, 2005.

"Gaibian *You xihu* de taolun" [Discussion of the adaptation of *Wandering West Lake*]. *Wenyi bao* 5 (1954): 40–41.

Godbeer, Richard. *The Devil's Dominion: Magic and Religion in Early New England*. Cambridge: Cambridge University Press, 1994.

Goldman, Andrea S. *Opera and the City: The Politics of Culture in Beijing, 1770–1900*. Stanford: Stanford University Press, 2012.

Goldman, Merle. *China's Intellectuals: Advise and Dissent*. Cambridge: Harvard University Press, 1981.

Goldman, Merle. *Sowing the Seeds of Democracy in China: Political Reform in the Deng Xiaoping Era*. Cambridge: Harvard University Press, 1994.

Goldstein, Joshua. *Drama Kings: Players and Publics in the Re-Creation of Peking Opera, 1870–1937*. Berkeley: University of California Press, 2007.

Gong Yijiang. "Hu Zhifeng he ta de *Li Huiniang*" [Hu Zhifeng and her *Li Huiniang*]. *Renmin xiju* (June 1980): 33–34.

Goossaert, Vincent, and David A. Palmer. *The Religious Question in Modern China*. Chicago: University of Chicago Press, 2011.

Greene, Maggie. "A Ghostly Bodhisattva and the Price of Vengeance: Meng Chao, *Li Huiniang*, and the Politics of Drama, 1959–1979." *Modern Chinese Literature and Culture* 24.1 (Spring 2012): 149–99.

Greene, Maggie. "The Woman in Green: A Chinese Ghost Tale from Mao to Ming, 1981–1381." *Appendix* 1.2 (2013): 124–32. http://theappendix.net/issues/2013/4/the-woman-in-green-a-chinese-ghost-tale-from-mao-to-ming-1981-1381

"Guanche Mao zhuxi wenyi fangxiang dali tichang xiandaiju—Ke Qingshi tongzhi zai Huadongqu huaju guanmo yanchu kamushi shang jianghua" [Implement Chairman Mao's artistic trends, energetically advocate for drama on contemporary themes—Comrade Ke Qingshi's speech at the opening ceremonies of the East China Spoken Language Drama Festival]. *Shanghai Theatre* 1 (January 1964): 2–5.

Guangdong sheng kexuezhishu puji xiehui, ed. *Tan "shen" jiang "gui"* [Talking of "spirits" and speaking of "ghosts"]. Guangdong: Guandong renmin chubanshe, 1958.

"Guanyu tingyan 'guixi' de qingshi baogao" [Instructions regarding ceasing performances of "ghost plays"]. In *Jianguo yilai zhongyao wenxian xuanbian, di shiliu ce* [Selected important party documents from after the founding of the country, volume 16], edited by Zhonggong zhongyang wenxian yanjiushi, 248. Beijing: Zhongyang wenxian chubanshe, 1997.

Guo, Qitao. *Ritual Opera and Mercantile Lineage: The Confucian Transformation of Popular Culture in Late Imperial Huizhou.* Stanford: Stanford University Press, 2005.

"Guowuyuan Chen Yi fuzongli zai chengli dahui shang de jianghua" [The speech of the state council's vice-premier Chen Yi at the establishment meeting]. In *Jicheng yu fazhan kunqu yishu* [Inherit and develop the art of Kun opera], edited by Beifang kunqu juyuan, 10–11. [Beijing?]: Dongdan yinshuachang, n.d.

Guy, Nancy. "Peking Opera as 'National Opera' in Taiwan: What's in a Name?" *Asian Theatre Journal* 12.1 (Spring 1995): 85–103.

Han Shaogong. *A Dictionary of Maqiao.* Translated by Julia Lovell. New York: Columbia University Press, 2003.

Hanyuyuan wenxue jiaoyanshi, eds. Hai Rui Baguan, Xie Yaohuan, Li Huiniang *zilao xuanji* [Selected materials of *Hai Rui Dismissed from Office, Xie Yaohuan, Li Huiniang*]. N.p.: Hubei sheng hanshou xueyuan, 1966.

He Baomin. "Meng Chao he *Yicong*" [Meng Chao and *Yicong*]. *Wenhua xuekan* 1 (January 2014): 183–86.

He, Henry Yuhuai. *Dictionary of the Political Thought of the People's Republic of China.* Armonk, NY: M. E. Sharpe, 2001.

Hershatter, Gail. *The Gender of Memory: Rural Women and China's Collective Past.* Berkeley: University of California Press, 2011.

Holm, D. L. "Local Color and Popularization in the Literature of the Wartime Border Regions." *Modern Chinese Literature and Culture* 2.1 (Spring 1986): 7–20.

Hong Zicheng. *A History of Contemporary Chinese Literature.* Translated by Michael M. Day. Leiden: Brill, 2007.

"Hu Zhifeng." Hong Kong Academy of the Performing Arts, https://www.hkapa.edu/honorary-awardees/hu-zhifeng

Hui Min. "Beifang kunqu juyuan huifu *Li Huiniang* chongxin shangyan" [The Northern Kun Opera Theatre's important new staging of the revived *Li Huiniang*]. *Renmin xiju* (May 1979): 47.

Hunan sheng xiqu gongzuoshi, Hunan sheng xiangjuyuan, eds. *Xiangju gaoqiang: Li Huiniang.* N.p.: Hunan sheng xiangjutuan, January 1979.

Idema, Wilt L. *The Metamorphosis of Tianxian Pei: Local Opera under the Revolution (1949–1956).* Hong Kong: Chinese University Press, 2015.

Institute of Literature of the Chinese Academy of Social Sciences, eds. *Stories about Not Being Afraid of Ghosts.* Beijing: Foreign Language Press, 1961.

Iovene, Paola. "Chinese Operas on Stage and Screen: An Introduction." *Opera Quarterly* 26.2–3 (Spring–Summer 2010): 181–99.

"Ji quanguo xiqu jumu gongzuo huiyi" [Remembering the all-China theatre repertoire work conference]. *Theatre Report* (July 1956): 25.

Ji Xianlin. *The Cowshed: Memories of the Chinese Cultural Revolution.* Translated by Chenxin Jiang. New York: New York Review of Books, 2016.

Jiang, Jin. *Women Playing Men: Yue Opera and Social Change in Twentieth-Century Shanghai.* Seattle: University of Washington Press, 2009.

Jiang Qing. *On the Revolution of Peking Opera.* Beijing: Foreign Languages Press, 1968.

Jilin sheng kexuezhishu puji, eds. *Zhen you shengui ma?* [Are there really gods and ghosts?]. Changchun: Jilin renmin chubanshe, 1956.

Jing Guxie. "Guixi zhi hai" [The harmfulness of ghost plays]. *Guangming Daily,* May 21, 23, 25, 1963.

"Jingshantianhua—*Li Huiniang, Zhong Li jian* zuotanhui jiyao" [Making perfection even more perfect—a summary of the symposiums on Li Huiniang and Zhong Li's sword]. *Beijing wenyi* 10 (1961): 54–55.

Johnson, Matthew D. "Beneath the Propaganda State: Official and Unofficial Cultural Landscapes in Shanghai, 1949–1965." In *Maoism at the Grassroots: Everyday Life in China's Era of High Socialism,* edited by Jeremy Brown and Matthew D. Johnson, 199–229. Cambridge: Harvard University Press, 2015.

Jones, Derek, ed. *Censorship: A World Encyclopedia.* London: Routledge, 2001.

Judd, Ellen. "Prelude to the 'Yan'an Talks': Problems in Transforming a Literary Intelligentsia." *Modern China* 11.3 (July 1985): 377–408.

Ko, Dorothy. *Teachers of the Inner Chambers: Women and Culture in Seventeenth-Century China.* Stanford: Stanford University Press, 1994.

Kong Xiang. "Guixi he shenxi ying yilü kandai" [Ghost plays and mythology plays ought to be treated the same with one law]. *Guangming Daily,* October 4, 1963.

Kraus, Richard C. *Brushes with Power: Modern Politics and the Chinese Art of Calligraphy.* Berkeley: University of California Press, 1991.

Kwa, Shiamin, and Wilt L. Idema. *Mulan: Five Versions of a Classic Chinese Legend, with Related Texts.* Indianapolis: Hackett Publishing, 2010.

Lan Ling. "Kan jingju *Li Huiniang* de zagan" [Scattered thoughts on seeing the Peking opera *Li Huiniang*]. *People's Daily,* November 8, 1980.

Lee, Haiyan. *Revolution of the Heart: A Genealogy of Love in China, 1900–1950.* Stanford: Stanford University Press, 2007.

Li Desheng. *Jinxi* [Banned plays]. Tianjin: Baihua wenyi chubanshe, 2009.

Li Huiniang. Directed by Liu Qiong. Shanghai: Shanghai dianying zhipianchang, 1981.

Li Huiniang (dianying wancheng taiben) [*Li Huiniang* (complete film script and stage instructions)]. Shanghai: Shanghai dianying zhipianchang, n.d.

Li Liming. *Zhongguo xiandai liubai zuojia xiaozhuan* [Biographical profiles of six hundred contemporary Chinese authors]. Hong Kong: Bowen shuju, 1977.

Li Qingyun. "Tantan *Li Huiniang* de 'tigao'" [Discussing *Li Huiniang*'s "improvement"]. *Theatre Report* (May 1962): 47–50.

Li Song, editor. *"Yangbanxi" biannian yu shishi* " [Annals and historical facts of "yangbanxi"]. Beijing: Zhongyang bianyi chubanshe, 2012.

Li Xiao. *Chinese Kunqu Opera*. Translated by Li Li and Zhang Liping. San Francisco: Long River Press, 2005.

Li Xifan. "Feichang youhai de 'yougui wuhai' lun" [Extremely harmful "some ghosts are harmless" theory]. *Guangming Daily*, September 10, 1963.

Li Zhisui. *The Private Life of Chairman Mao*. Translated by Tai Hung-chao. New York: Random House, 1994.

Liang Bihui [Yu Minghuang]. "'Yougui wuhai' lun" [On "some ghosts are harmless"]. *Wenhui bao*, May 6–7, 1963.

Liang Qichao. "On the Relationship between Fiction and the Government of the People." In *Modern Chinese Literary Thought: Writings on Literature, 1893–1945*, edited by Kirk Denton and translated by Gek Nai Cheng, 74–81. Stanford: Stanford University Press, 1996.

Liao Mosha. "'Shi' he 'xi'—he Wu Han de *Hai Rui baguan* yanchu" ["History" and "theatre"—congratulating Wu Han's production of *Hai Rui Dismissed from Office*]. In *Liao Mosha wenji, di er juan: Zawen* [The collected works of Liao Mosha, volume 2: Zawen], 80–82. Beijing: Beijing chubanshe, 1986.

Liao Mosha. "Wo xie 'yougui wuhai lun' de qianhou" [Surrounding my writing of the "some ghosts are harmless theory"]. In *Liao Mosha wenji, di er juan: Zawen* [The collected works of Liao Mosha, volume 2: Zawen], 492–95. Beijing: Beijing chubanshe, 1986.

Liao Mosha. "Yougui wuhai lun" [Some ghosts are harmless]. In *Liao Mosha wenji, di er juan: Zawen* [Collected writings of Liao Mosha, vol. 2: Zawen], 109–11. Beijing: Beijing chubanshe, 1986.

Lin Jing, ed. *Gudai huaixiang shici sanbaishou* [Three hundred classical poems and lyrics of being homesick]. Beijing: Zhongguo guoji guangbo chubanshe, 2014.

Link, Perry. *An Anatomy of Chinese: Rhythm, Metaphor, Politics*. Cambridge: Harvard University Press, 2013.

Liu Ching-chi. *A Critical History of New Music in China*. Translated by Caroline Mason. Hong Kong: Chinese University Press, 2010.

Liu Housheng. "Fandang fanshehuizhuyi gongtongti—*Li Huiniang, Hai Rui baguan, Xie Yaohuan* zonglun" [The antiparty, antisocialist thought community—a discussion of *Li Huiniang, Hai Rui Dismissed from Office, Xie Yaohuan*]. *Theatre Report* 3 (March 1966): 7–13.

Liu Naichong. "Duzhe dui Ma Jianling gaibian *You xihu* juben de yijian" [Readers' opinions on Ma Jianling's revised *Wandering West Lake* script]. *Play Monthly* 6 (1955): 162–66.

Liu Naichong. "Ping qinqiang *You xihu* gaibianben" [A review of the revised edition of the qinqiang *Wandering West Lake*]. *Xiju yanjiu* (January 1959): 43–45.

Liu Naichong. "Yi Zhang Zhen de jijian shi" [Recalling some works of Zhang Zhen]. *Zhongguo xiju* 12 (2008): 48–49.

Liu, Siyuan. "Theatre Reform as Censorship: Censoring Traditional Theatre in China in the Early 1950s." *Theatre Journal* 61.3 (October 2009): 387–406.

Lou Shiyi. "Wo huai Meng Chao" [I think of Meng Chao]. *People's Daily*, October 10, 1979.

Luo, Liang. *The Avant-Garde and the Popular: Tian Han and the Intersection of Performance and Politics*. Ann Arbor: University of Michigan Press, 2014.

Lu Zhengyan. "Meng Chao minghao biming huilu" [A record of the titles and pen names of Meng Chao]. *Shanghai shifan daxue xuebao* 2 (1986): 151–52.

Ma Jianling. "Xiugai *You xihu* de shuoming" [Explaining the alterations to *Wandering West Lake*]. In Ma Jianling. *You xihu (qinqiang juben)* [*Wandering West Lake (qinqiang* script)]. Xi'an: Xibei renmin chubanshe, 1953.

Ma Shaobo. "Mixin yu shenhua de benzhi qubie" [The essential difference between superstition and mythology]. In Ma Shaobo, *Xiqu yishu lunji* [Collected essays on theatre and art], 24–27. Beijing: Zhongguo xiju chubanshe, 1982.

Ma Shaobo. "Yansu duidai zhengli shenhuaju de gongzuo—cong *Tianhe pei* de gaibian tanqi" [A serious treatment of the work of putting mythology plays in order—speaking from the adaptation of *Tianhe pei*]. *People's Daily*, November 4, 1951.

Ma Jianling, Huang Junyao, Jiang Bingtai, and Zhang Digeng. *You xihu* [*Wandering West Lake*]. Xi'an: Shaanxi renmin chubanshe, 1958.

Ma Jianling, Huang Junyao, Jiang Bingtai, and Zhang Digeng. *You xihu* [*Wandering West Lake*]. Xi'an: Dongfeng wenyi chubanshe, 1961.

MacFarquhar, Roderick. *The Coming of the Cataclysm: 1961–1966*, vol.3, *The Origins of the Cultural Revolution*. New York: Columbia University Press, 1997.

MacFarquhar, Roderick. *Contradictions among the People 1956–1957*, vol. 1, *The Origins of the Cultural Revolution*. New York: Columbia University Press, 1974.

MacFarquhar, Roderick. *The Great Leap Forward 1958–1960*, vol. 2, *The Origins of the Cultural Revolution*. New York: Columbia University Press, 1983.

MacFarquhar, Roderick, and Michael Schoenhals. *Mao's Last Revolution*. Cambridge: Harvard University Press, 2006.

Mackerras, Colin. *Chinese Drama: A Historical Survey*. Beijing: New World Press, 1990.

Mair, Victor H., ed. *The Columbia Anthology of Traditional Chinese Literature*. New York: Columbia University Press, 1994.

Mann, Susan. *Precious Records: Women in China's Long Eighteenth Century*. Stanford: Stanford University Press, 1997.

Marsh, Christopher. *Religion and the State in Russia and China: Suppression, Survival, and Revival*. New York: Continuum, 2011.

Mao Zedong. "Mao Zedong gei Yang Shaoxuan, Qi Yanming de xin" [The letter sent from Mao Zedong to Yang Shaoxuan and Qi Yanming]. In *Jiandang yilai zhongyao wenxian xuanbian: Yijiueryi–yijiusijiu* [Selection of important documents since the founding of the Party—1921–1949], vol.21, edited by Zhonggong zhongyan wenxian yanjiu shi, Zhongyang dang'anguan, 5. Beijing: Zhongyang wenxian chuban she, 2011.

Mao Zedong. *Selected Works of Mao Tse-Tung, Volume V*. Beijing: Foreign Languages Press, 1977.

Mao Zedong. "Speech at Conference of Members and Cadres of Provincial-Level Organizations of CPC in Shandong (March 18, 1957)." In *The Writings of Mao Zedong*,

1949–1976, vol. 2, January 1956-December 1957, edited by Michael Y. M Kau and John K. Leung, 411–32. Armonk, NY: M. E. Sharpe, 1986.

Mao Zedong. "Talks at the Yan'an Forum on Literature and Art." In *Modern Chinese Literary Thought: Writings on Literature, 1893–1945*, edited by Kirk Denton, 458–84. Stanford: Stanford University Press, 1996.

Marcus, Sharon. *Between Women: Friendship, Desire, and Marriage in Victorian England*. Princeton: Princeton University Press, 2007.

Mazur, Mary G. *Wu Han, Historian: Son of China's Times*. Lanham, MD: Lexington Books, 2009.

McDougall, Bonnie S., and Kam Louie. *The Literature of China in the Twentieth Century*. New York: Columbia University Press, 1997.

Melvin, Sheila. "China's Homegrown *Peony Pavilion*." *Wall Street Journal*, November 24, 1999.

Meng Chao. *Jinping mei renwu* [Characters of *Plum in the Golden Vase*]. Beijing: Beijing chubanshe, Beijing chuban jituan gongsi, 2011.

Meng Chao. *Li Huiniang*. Beifang kunqu juyuan pailianben [practice edition]. May 12, 1961.

Meng Chao. *Li Huiniang*. Beifang kunqu juyuan pailianben [practice edition]. December 1978.

Meng Chao. *Li Huiniang*. *Juben* (July–August 1961): 78–91.

Meng Chao. *Li Huiniang*. Shanghai: Shanghai wenyi chubanshe, 1962.

Meng Chao. *Kunju Li Huiniang* [Kun opera *Li Huiniang*]. Shanghai: Shanghai wenyi chubanshe, 1980.

Meng Chao. "Shi fa danqing tu guixiong—kunqu *Li Huiniang* chuban daiba" [An attempt to portray a ghost hero—the postscript to the publication of the Kun opera Li Huiniang]. In Meng Chao, *Kunju Li Huiniang* [Kun opera *Li Huiniang*], 108–19. Shanghai: Shanghai wenyi chubanshe, 1980.

Meng Chao. *Shuibo Liangshan yingxiong pu* [Guide to the heroes of the Liangshan marsh]. Beijing: Sanlian shudian, 1985.

"Meng Chao tongzhi zhuidaohui daoci" [The eulogy at the memorial meeting for comrade Meng Chao]. *Xin wenxue shiliao* 1 (1980): 282.

Meng Jian. "Xie zai *Li Huiniang* zaiban de shihou" [Writings at the time of the republication of *Li Huiniang*]. In Meng Chao, *Li Huiniang*, 125–28. Shanghai: Shanghai wenyi chubanshe, 1980.

Mostow, Joshua, ed. *The Columbia Companion to Modern East Asian Literature*. New York: Columbia University Press, 2003.

Mu Xin. *Ban Guangming ribao shinian zishu* [My thoughts on ten years of publishing the *Guangming Daily*]. Beijing: Zhonggongdang shi chubanshe, 1994.

Mu Xin. "Guixi *Li Huiniang*" [The ghost play *Li Huiniang*]. *Yanhuang chunqiu* (October 1994): 34–43.

Mu Xin. *Jiehou changyi—shinian dongluan jishi* [Long reminiscences after the disaster—chronicle of the decade of disturbances]. Hong Kong: Xintian chubanshe, 1997.

Mu Xin. "Meng Chao *Li Huiniang* yuan'an shimo" [The whole unjust case of Meng Chao's *Li Huinaing*]. *Xin wenxue shiliao* 2 (1995): 156–203.

Murck, Alfreda. *Poetry and Painting in Song China: The Subtle Art of Dissent*. Cambridge: Harvard University Press, 2000.

Nedostup, Rebecca. *Superstitious Regimes: Religions and the Politics of Chinese Modernity*. Cambridge: Harvard University Press, 2009.

Nie Gannu. "Huai Meng Chao—zuowei *Shuibo liangshan yingxiong pu* de xu" [Thinking of Meng Chao—written as a preface to *A Guide to the Heroes of the Marsh*]. In Meng Chao, *Shuibo liangshan yingxiong pu* [*A Guide to the Heroes of the Marsh*], 1–4. Beijing: Sanlian shudian, 1985.

Nienhauser, William H., ed. *The Indiana Companion to Traditional Chinese Literature, Part Two*. Bloomington: Indiana University Press, 1998.

Pei Zhen. "Xinying biezhi de *Li Huiniang*" [The novel and unique *Li Huiniang*]. *People's Daily*, October 25, 1980.

Peng Zhen. "Zai jingju xiandaixi guanmo yanchu dahuishang de jianghua" [Speech at the festival on contemporary themes in Peking opera]. *Theatre Report* (July 1964): 4–9.

Poon, Shuk-Wah. *Negotiating Religion in Modern China: State and Common People in Guangzhou, 1900–1937*. Hong Kong: Chinese University Press, 2011.

Qi Xiangqun. "Chongping Meng Chao xinbian *Li Huiniang*" [A serious criticism of Meng Chao's adaptation *Li Huiniang*]. *Theatre Report* (January 1965): 2–8.

Qian, Kun. *Imperial-Time-Order: Literature, Intellectual History, and China's Road to Empire*. Leiden: Brill, 2016.

Qin Si. "Yi Meng Chao" [Remembering Meng Chao]. *Xin wenxue shike* 4 (April 1984): 128–33.

Qu Liuyi. "Guihunxi guankui—jianji jianguo yilai guihunxi de lunzheng" [A restricted view of ghost opera—and the controversy over ghost opera from the founding of the country]. *Wenyi yanjiu* 1 (January 1979): 78–86.

Qu Liuyi. "Mantan guixi" [Discussing ghost plays]. *Theatre Report* (July 1957): 4–7.

Qu You. *Jiandeng xinhua* [New tales told by lamplight]. Shanghai: Shanghai guxiang chubanshe, 1981.

"Quanguo xiqu gongzuozhe dahuishi xianyou xiqu gongzuozhe sanshiwuwan ren guanzhong sanbaiwan huiyi jiang taolun yu jiejue xigai fangzhen zhengce deng wenti" [All-China theatre workers assembly; currently, theatre workers number 350,000 people, audiences number three million; conference will discuss and settle general and specific policies and other problems related to drama reform]. *People's Daily*, December 1, 1950.

Rebull, Anne E. "Theatres of Reform and Remediation: *Xiqu* (Chinese Opera) in the Mid-Twentieth Century." PhD diss., University of Chicago, 2017.

Rigby, Richard W. *The May 30 Movement: Events and Themes*. Canberra: Australian National University Press, 1980.

Ruo He [Chen Gongdeng]. "Yan 'guixi' youhai ma?—'Yan 'guixi' meiyou haichu ma?'

duhou" [Staging "ghost plays" is harmful?—on reading "Staging 'ghost plays' doesn't have any harmful points?"]. *Guangming Daily*, September 10, 1963.

Schmalzer, Sigrid. *The People's Peking Man: Popular Science and Human Identity in Twentieth-Century China*. Chicago: University of Chicago Press, 2008.

Schurmann, Franz. *Ideology and Organization in Communist China*. 2nd ed. Berkeley: University of California Press, 1971.

Shen Yao. "Shenhuaxi yu guixi bixu yange qubie kailai—jianping Ruo He, Tan Peng tongzhi de yixie lundian" [Mythology plays and ghost plays must have a strict separation—a simultaneous critique of a few of Comrades Rou He and Tan Peng's points]. *Guangming Daily*, November 17, 1963.

Shi Ai. "Ma Shaobo xiaozhuan" [Biographical sketch of Ma Shaobo]. *Shanxi shiyuan xuebao (shehui kexue ban)* 1 (1982): 96–97.

"Shi 'wenhua dageming de xumu' haishi cuandang de xumu?—benkan bianjibu juxing zuotanhui pipan Yao Wenyuan de 'ping xinbian lishiju *Hai Rui baguan*' [Was it "the prologue to the Great Cultural Revolution," or the prologue to seizing the party by force?—the editorial board holds a meeting to criticize Yao Wenyuan's "Criticizing the new historical play *Hai Rui Dismissed from Office*"]. *People's Theatre* (January 1979): 4–9.

Shi Xin. "Ruiyi chuangxin, hongmei canran—cong Hu Zhifeng biaoyan de *Li Huiniang* tan tuichen chuxin" [Brilliantly blazing new trails, a dazzling red plum—observing Hu Zhifeng's production of *Li Huiniang* to discuss pushing out the old to uncover the new]. *Xiqu yishu* 4 (1980): 54–55.

Smith, Steven A. "Local Cadres Confront the Supernatural: The Politics of Holy Water (*Shenshui*) in the PRC, 1949–1966." *China Quarterly* 188 (December 2006): 999–1022.

Smith, S[teven]. A. "Talking Toads and Chinless Ghosts: The Politics of 'Superstitious' Rumors in the People's Republic of China." *American Historical Review* 111.2 (April 2006): 405–27.

Song, Yuwu, ed. *Biographical Dictionary of the People's Republic of China*. Jefferson, NC: McFarland & Co., 2013.

Swatek, Catherine C. Peony Pavilion *Onstage: Four Centuries in the Career of a Chinese Drama*. Ann Arbor: Center for Chinese Studies, University of Michigan, 2002.

Taiyang yuekan (yingyin ben) [Sun monthly (facsimile)]. 7 vols. Shanghai: Shanghai wenyi chubanshe, 1961.

Tan Peng. "Youxie 'guixi' yinggai jiayi kending" [Some "ghost plays" ought to be treated positively]. *Guangming Daily*, September 20, 1963.

Tao Junqi and Li Dake. "Yi duo xianyan de 'hongmei'—cong *Hongmei ji* de gaibian, tandao kunqu *Li Huiniang*" [A brightly colored "red plum"—using the adaptations of the *Story of Red Plums* to discuss the Kun opera *Li Huiniang*]. *People's Daily*, December 28, 1961.

Terrill, Ross. *The White-Boned Demon: A Biography of Madame Mao Zedong*. New York: William Marrow & Co., 1984.

Wagner, Rudolf G. "The Cog and the Scout—Functional Concepts of Literature in So-cialist Political Culture: The Chinese Debate in the Mid-Fifties." In *Essays in Modern Chinese Literature and Literary Criticism*, edited by Wolfgang Kubin and Rudolf G. Wagner. Bochum: Studienverlag Brockmeyer, 1982.

Wagner, Rudolf G. *The Contemporary Chinese Historical Drama: Four Studies*. Berkeley: University of California Press, 1990.

Wang Chunyuan. "Cong *Li Huiniang* de chongyan tandao guihunxi" [Talking about ghost opera from the re-premiere of *Li Huiniang*]. *People's Daily*, June 25, 1979.

Wang, David Der-Wei. *The Monster That Is History: History, Violence, and Fictional Writing in Twentieth-Century China*. Berkeley: University of California Press, 2004.

Wang Xinrong and Lu Zhengyan. "Huodong zai zhengzhi yu wenxue zhijian de Meng Chao" [Meng Chao's activities between politics and literature]. *Shanghai shifan dax-ue xuebao* 4 (1988): 63–69.

Wang Zhaoqi and Xu Hengyu (illustrator). *Li Huiniang*. Shanghai: Shanghai renmin yishu chubanshe, 1982.

Wang Zhichi. *Li Huiniang (canzhao qinqiang, chuanju, kunqu, yuju deng yanchuben zhengli)* [Li Huiniang (arranged according to *qinqiang, chuanju, kunqu*, and *yuju* scripts)]. N.p.: N.p., December 24, 1979.

Wasserstrom, Jeffrey N. *Global Shanghai, 1850–2010: A History in Fragments*. New York: Routledge, 2009.

Wei Wenbo. "Zai yijiuliusan nian Huadongqu huaju guanmo yanchu bimu shishang Wei Wenbo tongzhi de bimuci" [Comrade Wei Wenbo's closing remarks at the clos-ing ceremonies of the 1963 East China Spoken Language Drama Festival]. *Shanghai Theatre* 2 (February 1963): 2–3.

White, Luise. *Speaking with Vampires: Rumor and History in Colonial Africa*. Berkeley: University of California Press, 2000.

Wilcox, Emily. *Revolutionary Bodies: Chinese Dance and the Socialist Legacy*. Berkeley: University of California Press, 2018.

Wong, Wang-chi. *Politics and Literature in Shanghai: The Chinese League of Left-Wing Writers, 1930–1936*. Manchester: Manchester University Press, 1991.

Wu Nanxing [Liao Mosha]. "Pa gui de 'yaxue'" [The "elegant joke" of fearing ghosts]. *Frontline* 22 (1961): 22.

Xia Yan, Wu Han, Liao Mosha, Meng Chao, and Tang Tao. *Changduan lu* [The long and the short]. Beijing: Renmin ribao chubanshe, 1980.

"Xiao Cuihua shuo: 'Wo yao changxi!' Beijing wenhuaju jing zhizhibuli" [Xiao Cuihua says: "I want to sing opera!" The Beijing Culture Bureau brushes [him] aside]. *Peo-ple's Daily*, May 14, 1957.

Xie Baogeng, editor. *Bu pa gui de gushi* [Stories about not being afraid of ghosts]. Shang-hai: Shanghai renmin yishu chubanshe, 1979.

Xie Bingyin. *A Woman Soldier's Own Story: The Autobiography of Xie Bingying*. Trans-lated by Lily Chia Brissman and Barry Brissman. New York: Columbia University Press, 2001.

Xu Xianglin. *Zhongguo guixi* [Chinese ghost plays]. Tianjin: Tianjin jiaoyu chubanshe, 1997.

Yan Chunguang, editor. *Lingdao ganbu bidu de zuimei gushici* [The most beautiful ancient poetry and lyrics leading cadres must read]. Beijing: Renmin chubanshe, 2014.

Yan, Yunxiang. *Private Life under Socialism: Love, Intimacy, and Family Change in a Chinese Village, 1949–1999.* Stanford: Stanford University Press, 2003.

Yang Bujun. "Minyishujia Ma Jianling" [People's artist Ma Jianling]. *Jinqiu* 1 (2012): 41–42.

Yang Jisheng. *Tombstone: The Great Chinese Famine, 1958–1962.* Edited by Edward Friedman, Guo Jian, and Stacy Mosher, and translated by Stacy Mosher and Guo Jian. New York: Farrar, Straus and Giroux, 2012.

Yang, Lan. *Chinese Fiction of the Cultural Revolution.* Hong Kong: Hong Kong University Press, 1998.

Yang Qiuhong. *Zhongguo gudai guixi yanjiu* [Research on China's premodern ghost plays]. Beijing: Zhongguo chuanmei daxue chubanshe, 2009.

Yang Shaoxuan. "Lun 'wei wenxue er wenxue, wei yishu er yishu' de weixianxing—ping Ai Qing de 'Tan niulang zhinü'" [Discussing the harmfulness of "literature for the sake of literature, art for the sake of art"—criticizing Ai Qing's "Discussing *The Cowherd and the Weaving Maid*"]. *People's Daily*, November 3, 1951.

Yang Xianyi. "Hongmei jiuqu xi xifan—kunqu *Li Huiniang* guanhou gan" [A welcome new turn for an old red plum drama—feelings after seeing the Kun opera *Li Huiniang*]. *Juben* (October 1961): 90–92.

Yeh, Wen-hsin. *The Alienated Academy: Culture and Politics in Republican China, 1919–1937.* Cambridge: Harvard University Asia Center, 1990.

Yi Youzhuang, composer. *Chuju: Li Huiniang.* N.p.: Hubei sheng chujutuan, n.d.

You xihu (qinqiang juben) [*Wandering West Lake (qinqiang script)*]. Xi'an: Xibei renmin chubanshe, 1953.

Yun Song. "Tian Han de *Xie Yaohuan* shi yike daducao" [Tian Han's *Xie Yaohuan* is a big poisonous weed]. *People's Daily*, February 1, 1966.

Zeitlin, Judith T. *Historian of the Strange: Pu Songling and the Chinese Classical Tale.* Stanford: Stanford University Press, 1993.

Zeitlin, Judith T. "My Year of Peonies." *Asian Theatre Journal* 19.1 (Spring 2002): 124–33.

Zeitlin, Judith T. "Operatic Ghosts on Screen: The Case of *A Test of Love* (1958)." *Opera Quarterly* 26.2–3 (Spring–Summer 2010): 220–55.

Zeitlin, Judith T. *The Phantom Heroine: Ghosts and Gender in Seventeenth-Century Chinese Literature.* Honolulu: University of Hawai'i Press, 2007.

Zhai Guangshun. "Meng Chao zai Qingdao de jiaoyu ji geming wenyi huodong" [Meng Chao's teaching and revolutionary art and literature activities in Qingdao]. *Zhonggong Qingdao shiwei dangxiao—Qingdao xingzheng xueyuan xuebao* 4 (2013): 115–23.

Zhang Chengping, ed. *Babaoshan geming gogmu beiwen lu* [Collection of epitaphs from Babaoshan revolutionary cemetery]. Beijing: Gaige chubanshe, 1990.

Zhang Ruipeng. "Jingyan—tansuo—chuangxin—ji *Li Huiniang* daoyan Liu Qiong"

[Experience—explore—blaze new trails—remembering *Li Huiniang*'s director Liu Qiong]. *Dianying pingjie* (November 1981): 36–37.

Zhang Zhen. "Kan kunqu xinfan *Li Huiniang*" [Watching the new Kun opera translation of *Li Huiniang*]. *Theatre Report* 8 (August 1961): 47–49.

Zhang Zhen. "Tan *You xihu* de gaibian" [Discussing *Wandering West Lake*'s revisions]. *Wenyi bao* 21 (1954): 41–43.

Zhao Xinshun. *Taiyang she yanjiu* [Research on the Sun Society]. Beijing: Zhongguo shehui kexue chubanshe, 2010.

Zhao Xun. "Yan 'guixi' meiyou haichu ma?" [Does staging "ghost plays" do no harm?]. *Wenyi bao* 4 (1963): 16–18.

"Zhonggong zhongyang xuanchanbu Zhou Yang fubuzhang zai chengli dahui shang de jianghua" [The speech of the central committee's vice minister of propaganda Zhou Yang at the establishment meeting]. In *Jicheng yu fazhan kunqu yishu* [Inherit and develop the art of Kun opera], edited by Beifang kunqu juyuan, 12–14. [Beijing?]: Dongdan yinshuachang, n.d..

Zhongguo kexueyuan wenxue yanjiusuo, ed. *Bu pa gui de gushi* [Stories about not being afraid of ghosts]. Beijing: Renmin wenxue, 1961.

Zhongguo xiju nianjian 1982 [1982 Chinese theatre yearbook]. Beijing: Zhongguo xiqu chubanshe, 1982.

Zhongguo yuyan wenxuexi ziliaoshi, ed. *Guanyu* Li Huiniang *wenti ziliao xuanbian* [A selection of materials relating to the *Li Huiniang* problem]. Changchun: Jilin Normal University, 1966.

Zhong Kan. *Kang Sheng pingzhuan* [A critical biography of Kang Sheng]. Beijing: Hongqi chubanshe, 1982.

Zhou Chaojun. *Hongmei ji* [*Story of Red Plums*]. Shanghai: Shanghai guxiang chubanshe, 1985.

Zhou Heping and Xu Ming. "Hu Zhifeng tan *Li Huiniang*" [Hu Zhifeng talks about *Li Huiniang*]. *Dianying pingjie* (November 1981): 36–37.

Zhou Weizhi. "Fazhan aiguozhuyi de renmin xin xiqu—zhu quanguo xiqu gongzuo huiyi" [Developing the patriotism of the people's new opera—celebrating the All-China opera work conference]. *People's Daily*, December 10, 1950.

Archival Documents from the Shanghai Municipal Archives

B172-1-196-23. "Zhonghua renmin gongheguo wenhua bu duiyu Shenyang shi wenhuaju fengfu quyi shangyan jiemu de pifu yijian" [Reply from the Ministry of Culture regarding the Shenyang culture bureau's enrichment of performed operatic arts programs]. October 18, 1956.

B172-1-326. "Shanghai shi wenhuaju guanyu Shanghai shi 1949 nian–1958 nian yanchu jumu de fennian tongji biao, mulu biao" [Shanghai Culture Bureau, regarding repertoire performed in Shanghai from 1949 to 1958—tables of statistics and catalogue, divided by year].

B172-1-527. "Shanghai shi wenhuaju guanyu canjia wenhubu juban de jingju xiandaixi guanmo yanchu de mingdan, zongjie baogao" [Name list and final report of the Shanghai Culture Bureau regarding attending the Ministry of Culture–sponsored festival on contemporary themes in Peking opera]. August 29, 1964.

B172-4-917. "Shanghai shi wenhuaju 1949–1958 nian shangyan jumu tongjibiao" [Shanghai Culture Bureau statistics of repertoire performed, 1949–1958].

B172-5-530. "Shanghai shi wenhuaju yijiusijiu nian dao yijiuliuernian linian shangyan jumu (haoxi, huaixi) bijiaobiao" [Shanghai Culture Bureau comparison table of the performed repertoire (good plays, bad plays) over the years from 1949–1962].

B172-5-664. "Guanyu baihua qifang, tuichen chuxin wenti de xuexi" [Regarding the study of the "let a hundred flowers bloom, pushing out the old to bring in the new" issue].

B172-5-680. "Shanghai shi wenhuaju guanyu jumu gongzuoshi de gongzuo zhidu, fengong yijian ji Shanghai jingju guanzhong qingkuang chubu diaocha" [Shanghai municipal Culture Bureau, regarding the repertoire office work system and separation of work and suggesting a preliminary investigation of the situation concerning Shanghai's Peking opera audiences].

B172-5-682. "Shanghai shi wenhuaju guanyu yijiu e liusan nian quannian shanyan jumu tongji, jingjuyuan jumu paidui, guojia juyuantuan baoliu jumu gelin biao" [Shanghai Culture Bureau statistics on annual performed repertoire for previous years, Peking opera theatre repertoire list, list of every type of national theatre repertoire].

B172-5-934. "Shanghai shi yijiuliuwu nian shangyan jumu tongjibiao" [Statistics of repertoire performed in Shanghai, 1965].

Index

CPSIA information can be obtained
at www.ICGtesting.com
Printed in the USA
FSHW011254280121
78113FS

9 780472 054305